THE SMUGGLING STORY OF TWO FIRTHS

Other titles by the same author, also published by Wyre Forest Press

The Isle of Man in Smuggling History

Scottish Customs & Excise Records

Strathclyde's Smuggling Story

Dumfries & Galloway's Smuggling Story

Family Histories in Scottish Customs Records

THE SMUGGLING STORY OF TWO FIRTHS

[Montrose to Dunbar]

Frances Wilkins BA

Wyre Forest Press

Published by Wyre Forest Press
8 Mill Close, Blakedown, Kidderminster
Worcestershire DY10 3NQ

Printed by The Bath Press
31 Lower Bristol Road
Bath BA2 3BL

ISBN 1 897725 06 X

Contents

Illustrations

Tables

Note: Figures 2, 4, 8, 9, 14 and 15 are from the custom house letter-books, Figure 7 from James Stobie's map of Perthshire and Clackmannanshire (1783) [RHP570], Figues 11, 12, 13 and 16 from John Ainslie's map of the counties of Fife and Kinross and Firths of Forth and Tay (1775) [RHP3801] all Crown copyright reproductions reproduced by permission of the Keeper of the Record of Scotland with the agreement on the controller of HMSO
Figures 3 and 10 are reproduced by kind permission of North Yorkshire County Library
Figure 1 is extracted from the Robert Morden map of Scotland in the 1695 edition of *Camden's Britannica*
Figure 5 is from Fischer, T A *The Scots in Sweden* 1909
Figure 6 is from Vyse, Charles A New Geographical Grammar 1779
The cover is reproduced by kind permission of Imray, Laurie, Norie and Wilson Ltd and of Admiralty Charts and Hydrographic Publications

Tailpieces

PREFACE

This extract from the narrative of James Nimmo, covenanter and sometime customs officer, pre-dates the eighteenth century, which is the main period covered by this book. It is transcribed here, however, in order to set the scene. 'The government being now settled upon King William and the customs to fall in his hand to be managed by the Lords of the Treasury, about July 1690 I was advised thereof and that our dear friend Evan Campbell had got a post ... So near the end of January I went to Edinburgh ... was advised to address myself to the Lords Crawford and Cardross, who were my good friends and two of the Lords of the Treasury, and when I did they told me I was too late for all was filled up. But my Lord Crawford, after second thoughts, thought fit for the present to take out the clerk's name was appointed for the custom house of Prestonpans and cause fill up mine. Evan Campbell being to be surveyor there I judged pressed this. I found the encouragement would be small ... and so refused it, of which honest Lord Crawford hearing sent for me and pressed me to take what they could now give and said he judged there was as many knaves had by moyen got better posts which in a little would make room for me and others. It was what he could do at the time and if I refused he would never more be for me, which with my present strait prevailed though there was such a damp in my mind at the time as the buttons were like to break of my breast'.

In March 1690 Nimmo went to Prestonpans with Samuel Douglas of Heaslside, collector, and his friend Evan Campbell, the surveyor. They seemed to leave him to manage the custom house business on his own, a situation which he found very stressful. 'Meantime came in a ship with French wines which was an addition to my trouble. The merchants told me they used to get some ease of the duty at all ports and I behoved to do the like. I told them I could give nor would give none but that belonged to the collector to act therein as he thought fit. But to please them I told them though it was contrary to my instructions yet I would take a blank report and entry till the collector was sent for, which they were content of. But a few days after, the merchants being absent, George Dundas, surveyor at Leith, hearing our collector and surveyor were absent, procured an order from my Lord Reath, treasurer depute, to come and survey and see the books and managing, which he presented to me at Port Seton, waiting and overseeing the unloading of wines. I told him the order should be obeyed and immediately a waiter he had brought from Leith I ordered aboard with ours. Mr Dundas said he behoved to see the report and entry. I answered, why not. He said would I send for them. I said I trusted them to none but myself. He said then he would go with me. I was in a great strait and feared to be affronted, the books being blank. However spoke privately to the master of the ship, a Dutchman, and told him this Mr Dundas would do harm if the report was not filled up. Therefore desired him on his peril to give me a just account, so he told me but reserved out six tuns. So I thought if Mr Dundas went to a house I could get the books filled up. But when we came near the custom house I said I judged this was his quarters we were going by. He said he would go straight and see the books, which raised a new difficulty. I told him I must then go back to my house and get the key. He said, I will wait at the custom house door till you come. However coming home told my wife the distress I was in ... (blank space in the original mss) and after gone out I remembered there was a back door to the chamber through our landlord's and there undiscerned got in and filled up the books, as the master had given account, and returned out and came to Mr Dundas and opened the for entry and took him in and did let him see the books'. When the merchants returned, they were 'much troubled' that the master had concealed the six tuns. The solution, finally agreed by both sides, was to seize the additional wine as 'short reported' at which point the merchants could claim that this was based on a mistake - 'my not fully understanding the Dutch language'.

There were other problems. 'Mr John Moncrieff, minister there [Prestonpans], had pressed Mr Campbell and me to be elders, the which we could not get freedom to do because as we were stated in our posts we were taken as enemies to most of the parish ... they for the most part traders and many of them endeavouring to run their goods privately ashore, without entering and paying the king's customs'. Nimmo's wife returned to Edinburgh and 'I stayed till the beginning of March and cleared by accounts and got freedom to go. I must say that time was the sweetest to me of all the while I was in that place.'

James Nimmo's son became cashier general of the Excise. In March 1716 Bailie Steuart wrote from Inverness to Commissary Steuart in Edinburgh. In this letter he referred to a bill 'for £50 sterling on James Nimmo'.

It is such links that form the foundation of this book.

ACKNOWLEDGEMENTS

As can be seen from the dedication, the author is very grateful to the Archive and Record Centre, City of Dundee District Council; West Search Room, Scottish Record Office, Edinburgh; the Orkney Library and Archives, Kirkwall; the Perth and Kinross District Archive and Central Regional Council Archives, Stirling. Many thanks are also due to Diane Baptie of 35 Pittville Street, Edinburgh EH15 2BX for her attempts to trace the exchequer case relating to the *Dorothy* and for other research in Edinburgh; David Dobson MPhil of St Andrews for transcribing sections of the St Andrews Coast Guard General Order Book 1831 to 1833 and for providing other references, particularly to Blind Jack of Knaresborough; my mother who took minutes to locate in her notes on industrial archaeology the essential source of information on Blind Jack's smuggling ventures; the Reference Library, North Yorkshire County Library, Harrogate for their speedy response to my request for the relevant sections of Blind Jack's Life and for permission to reproduce their records as illustrations; the States of Guernsey Island Archives Service for information about a debt relating to the master of an Arbroath vessel; the Library (Manx National Heritage), Douglas, Isle of Man for the copy of George Moore's letter-book, used in this context to identify sources of smuggled goods; Frances McDonnell of St Andrews for chasing the 'loose ends' at the Archive and record Centre in Dundee; Sue Mowat of Dunfermline for her reference, plus copies, to the charter party and bond for a voyage of the *Benefactor*; Robert Smart, Keeper of the Muniments, University Library, St Andrews for identifying several of the 'smuggling students'; Simpson Lawrence for providing the 'right' edition of the Imray chart used on the cover; HM Customs & Excise, Edinburgh, for comments on the present situation and last but not least Ainsley Monger, the Blakedown postman who had the unenviable task of delivering all this information. Finally I would like to thank the Social Sciences Section, Mitchell Library, Glasgow for their help over locating James Nimmo's narrative and the Interlibrary Loans Department, Main Library, University of Birmingham for producing the other references that were required.

'The difficult is what takes a little time. The impossible is what takes longer.' Nansen, 1939.

This book is dedicated to all those who made it possible for the necessary research to be completed while the author was housebound in England: to the Archive and Record Centre, City of Dundee District Council; West Search Room, Scottish Record Office, Edinburgh; the Orkney Library and Archives, Kirkwall; the Perth and Kinross District Archive and Central Regional Council Archives, Stirling.

Erratum:
INTRODUCTION
Correct page sequence:
1, 4, 3, 2, 5

INTRODUCTION

'Smuggling and its history never had the appeal on the east coast that it clearly has on the west. I think the reason for this is that by the peak of the smuggling era, prosperity had moved to the west coast of Scotland, and there was no cash around to support the illegal trade'. (Personal communication from Dr Bill Laing, Fairlie)

Everything seemed to militate against the success of a research project into smuggling on the east coast of Scotland. As the student of Scottish history knows, the centre of gravity of the country moved during the eighteenth century from the east to the west with the Clyde becoming supreme. Daniel Defoe on his tour of North Britain in 1724 was critical of several of the east coast ports. He described Burntisland as having 'a very good harbour ... but want of trade renders all this useless; for what is the best harbour in the world without ships? And whence should ships be expected without a commerce to employ them ... so that, indeed, the place is unhappy, and must decay yet farther, unless the trade revive, which, I confess, I do not yet foresee.' In comparison Glasgow 'is a city of business; here is the face of trade, as well foreign as home trade, and, I may say, 'tis the only city in Scotland, at this time, that apparently increases and improves in both'.

Although there were several ports [referred to by the Board of Customs as outports] within the area from Montrose to Dunbar, suggesting that there would be sufficient source material to undertake a detailed review of the smuggling history, the letters from the collector to the Board of Customs in Edinburgh for the most important of these, Leith, are missing until 1834, beyond the main period of smuggling. Other workers have looked at some of the smaller outports: T C Smout has studied the Dunbar letter-books for 1765; Duncan Fraser used the Montrose letter-books to produce his book *The Smugglers* while the meaning of a word is not clear, and that word cannot be found in the modern dictionary, a brief explanation has been included in the text. Bracketed comments do exist in the original documents. Any comments added by the author have been put in [square brackets].

The Ordnance Survey gazetteer has been used to identify the places named, where possible, and once again the modern spelling has been used to aid identification. The problem with this as a method of identifying the exact location of a particular event is the popularity of certain place names - there are fifteen places called Newbigging in Tayside, out of the total of forty-eight in the whole British Isles, and two Pathheads in Lothian.

A format first adopted in *Family Histories in Scottish Customs Records* has been used here to include some of the 'classic' pieces of information discovered. In each case it was thought that these justified highlighting whereas they might have tended to clog the general text. At this point it can be stressed that the material in this book is by no means the sum total of the information available in the letter-books alone. One of the main problems has been selecting not only the best but also typical stories from the various outports yet at the same time not drowning the reader in too many examples.

As always illustrations have posed a problem. The general aim, in line with the 'they saw it happen' ethos, has been to include contemporary maps. But here Morden has let us down. The whole of Scotland is portrayed on one A3-sized sheet so that reproduction of smaller areas are not advisable [as we have discovered elsewhere to our cost]. However, here we have been fortunate in the availability of contemporary maps, appropriate sections of which were selected and photographed by the West Search Room of the Scottish Record Office. A different format has been used to explain the significance of the illustration selected to the text by including a page of commentary on each.

At the request of several genealogists, an index has been produced of the individuals mentioned in the text. Here there is a further problem. One individual may be referred to by several different names, sometimes include the 'Smuggling Act' [the author's title] following the behaviour of some of their students; the minutes of the Board of Customs in Edinburgh, supplementing some of the missing custom house letter-books; a coast guard letter-book and last but not least the Gentleman's Magazine with its blow by blow account of the events following the Porteous riot in Edinburgh.

It is always difficult to define smuggling exactly - in other words when is a fraud against the revenue a fraud and when is it a smuggle? The collectors of the eighteenth century had the same problem referring in turn to notorious practices, frauds against the revenue and smuggling often in the context of one particular case. In this book a variety of events have been included all of which involved attempts, successful or otherwise, at running goods that were uncustomed (i.e. had not paid duty) or prohibited (i.e. there was an Act against their importation). One interesting point here is that both men and women were prepared to risk life and limb not only in smuggling the traditional brandy, tea, lace and tobacco but also the more basic commodities of grain and coal.

The area embraced by this book - Montrose in the north to Dunbar in the south, including the modern regions of Tayside, Fife and Lothian - is partly defined by the location of the outports. But there is a stronger link between this group. Whenever there was the chance of a smuggle, warnings were sent to Dunbar, Leith, Alloa, Anstruther, Dundee and Montrose. In other words they tended to form a cohesive unit.

In his introduction to James Nimmo's narrative quoted in the Preface, Scott-Moncrieff writes 'The acts of any particular age cannot be properly studied apart from some knowledge of the beliefs and the mental condition of those who performed them'. In the present context it is believed that the best way to achieve this is to produce a smuggling story based on contemporary writings i.e. a 'they saw it happen' approach. However, the spelling and punctuation used in the contemporary documents have been modified in an attempt to clarify the extracts and make them more easily read. At the same time the words 'And' and 'That' at the beginning of a sentence have been deleted, except where this resulted in a change in meaning. Also the word 'said' has not been transcribed, except where this altered the sense of the quotation. Where

Rosemary Goring compared the records for Montrose and Dumfries. Was there anything worthwhile to be learned about the area?

Two days in a flood-marooned Stirling in January 1993 showed that the Alloa custom house letter-books justified a more than casual study. The shipping information that could be abstracted from these emphasised the port's trading links with the 'notorious' supply centres of contraband goods. Was it really surprising that, as both the Board of Customs in Edinburgh and the local collector constantly predicted, several of these vessels 'ran' part of their cargoes on their return to the Forth? The Alloa letter-books also included a remarkable density of smuggling letters. Inspired by this the other outport records were sampled and these produced yet more interesting material, some of an unexpected nature - particularly the high level of smuggling at Newburgh and Perth.

There were two major differences when compared with the west coast ports already studied. On the east, with the absence of offshore islands such as the Isle of Man, Rathline and Sanda to act as contraband warehouses, a different style of smuggling dominated. This was the pretended voyage, which meant that a vessel had papers to prove that she was actually going to Bergen in Norway but had been forced to come to the Scottish coast because of stress of weather, the need for repairs or want of supplies. Also the very size of the ports, so heavily criticised by Defoe, means that the records can be analysed in sufficient detail for it to be comparatively easy to trace the fortunes of a particular smuggling vessel and the success of a revenue cruiser not only throughout one year but from year to year and from one port to another. The careers of customs officers who transferred between the local ports can also be studied in detail.

Another unexpected bonus is the variety of alternative source material in the form of contemporary records not only from the eighteenth but also the seventeenth and nineteenth centuries: the autobiographies of a sometime customs officer and a sometime smuggler; the correspondence of a merchant house based in Orkney, one of whose vessels was seized and taken first into Montrose and then Leith; the minutes of St Andrews University, which changed their statutes to in the same paragraph of a letter. As a result reference has been made to the modern telephone directories in an attempt to clarify the exact name. Inconsistencies may still exist. When the index was completed, it was surprising to discover that it included some 650 names - this was not intended to be a book emphasising the value of the custom house letter-books in the study of family history.

Finally there was the problem of a title. The original idea of producing two separate books: Tayside's Smuggling Story and Lothian and Fife's Smuggling Story was shelved at an early stage - it was impossible to separate the stories sufficiently without unwarranted repetition, especially as the Dundee outport stretched across Fife as far as the north shore of the Eden estuary. The combined title 'Fife, Lothian and Tayside's Smuggling Story', whatever the order of the Regions, was cumbersome. Yet it is not the story of the whole of Scotland's east coast smuggling history - only of a fraction of it. As a result a decision about the final title was postponed until the book was written - then it became obvious: *The Smuggling Story of Two Firths.*

We hope that the resultant book will give you half the pleasure in reading that it has given us in the production. If so, we will have proved the irrefutable point: there is a smuggling story to be told about the east, as well as the west of Scotland.

Figure 1: The Two Firths - Montrose to Dunbar

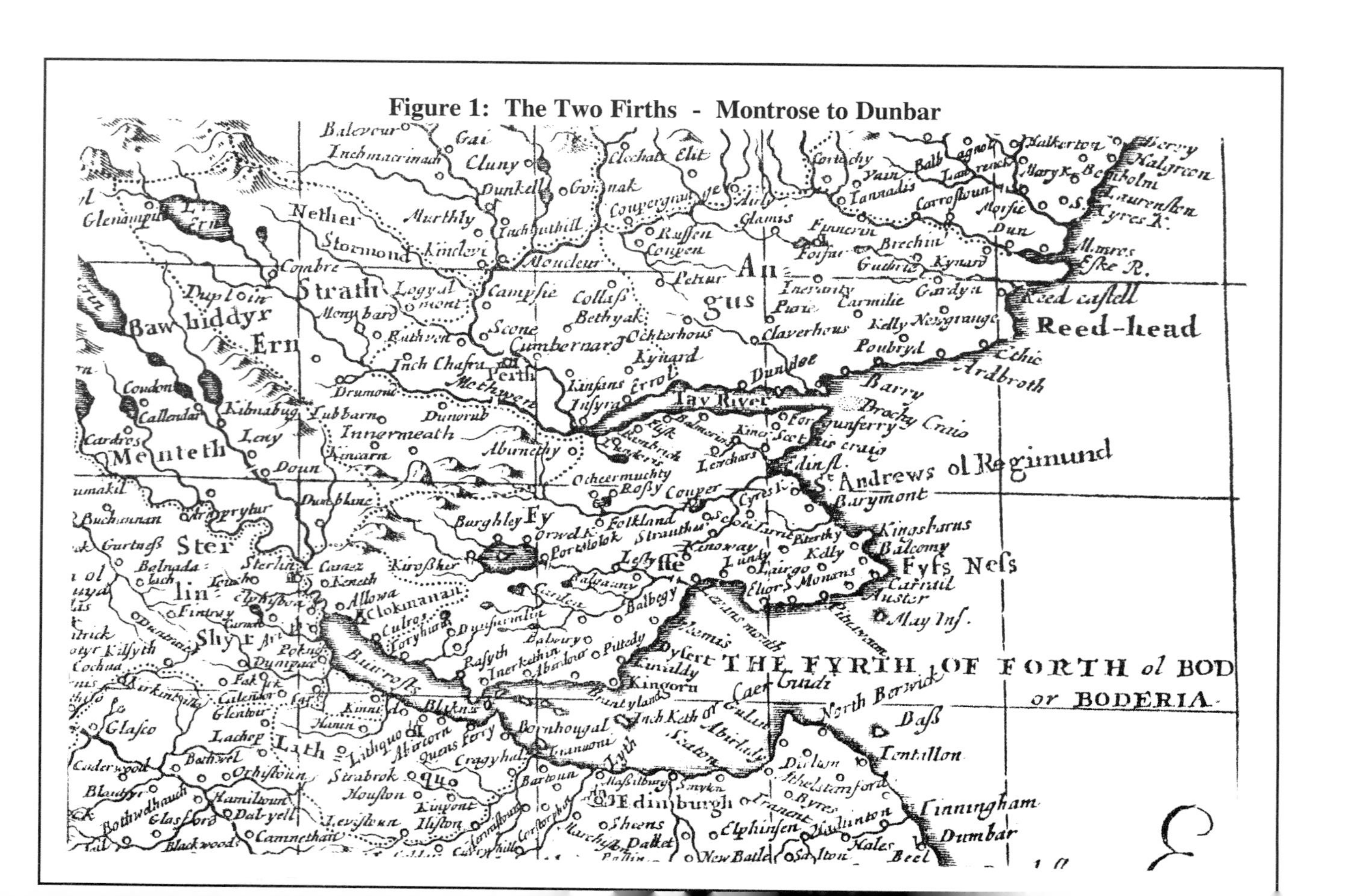

CHAPTER ONE: SOURCES OF INFORMATION

'The student of the eighteenth century has ... a series of great quarries from which he may extract virtually unlimited amounts of information.' [M S Anderson: *Europe in the Eighteenth Century*]

The area between Montrose and Dunbar is rich in supposed evidence of the former smuggling days - numerous caves, tunnels in the cliffs, large cellars under houses near the shore and old hostelries, often **now** named the Smugglers Inn. This book is <u>not</u> a collation of such folklore.

The problem of a real story about which some of the contemporary evidence is missing can be illustrated by the slightly different versions told by more modern writers of the theft of money from the Kirkcaldy collector in 1736. Andrew Wilson, a baker from Pathhead [near Kirkcaldy], was well-known to be a smuggler so that he became a target for the revenue officers and his contraband goods were seized frequently. When he heard that the Kirkcaldy collector, James Stark, had stopped at Pittenweem for the night on his return from Anstruther with £200, the proceeds of a sale of seized goods, in company with Robertson and a couple of other local smugglers he broke into the lodging house and stole the collector's saddle-bags.

These were found, empty, on the highway and with the help of the military, plus an informer, Wilson and Robertson were arrested. They were subsequently tried in Edinburgh and, having been found guilty, were sentenced to be hanged. Aided by Wilson, Robertson escaped from his guards during their traditional pre-execution attendance at the Sunday service in the Tolbooth church. Wilson was led to the gibbet in the Grassmarket on 14 April 1736. The magistrates, 'apprehending a rescue', ordered the city guard under the command of Captain Lieutenant

John Porteous to be present 'to support the execution of Wilson and to repel force with force'.

The rest of the story can be found in the Gentleman's Magazine for September 1736. There is a six page summary of the trial of John Porteous, including details of those who were killed and wounded when he and his men opened fire on the crowd, the evidences of twenty-eight witnesses for the prosecution and sixteen witnesses for the defence, the names of the jury [including Thomas Dundas of Letham, who appears in Chapter Seven], the verdict and sentence. This is followed by the transcript of Porteous's petition to 'her most excellent Majesty, Queen Caroline, guardian of these realms'. The section concludes 'Great application having been made to Her Majesty for changing the sentence passed on Captain Porteous from death to transportation, there was a reprieve granted for six weeks, which arrived at Edinburgh on [the] Thursday before the execution was to have been, which was appointed for [Wednesday] the 8th of September; but the populace hearing of it, their leaders laid a scheme to render it ineffectual and executed it with surprising conduct'. At this point the reader of the magazine is referred to the Historical Chronicle for September and the reader of this book to the tailpiece of this chapter.

According to the Gentleman's Magazine, Wilson had been convicted 'for a robbery of the public money, committed on the highway'. In his 'so much talked of speech' in Parliament on 16 May 1737 Patrick Lindsay, late Lord Provost and now member for Edinburgh stated 'Every gentleman has heard of the execution of that noted smuggler, Andrew Wilson, whence all this mischief has flowed. That deluded man maintained to the hour of his death that he was unjustly condemned. He maintained this in a debate with one of the reverend ministers of Edinburgh ... [when the minister was] endeavouring to ... bring him to a sense of his guilt of the crime, he admitted that he had taken money from a collector of the revenue by violence; that he did it because he knew no other way of coming at it; that the officers of the revenue had by their practice taught him this was lawful, for they had often seized and carried off his goods by violence, and so long as they had goods of his of greater value in their hands than all the money he took from them, they were still in his debt, and he had done no wrong'.

The records of the Board of Customs in Edinburgh refer to the theft of £96 12s 7d by a different method. Their minute dated Thursday, 22 January 1736 states 'from the examination of the several persons who were guilty or accessory to the breaking open and stealing of a sum of money out of the custom house at Kirkcaldy, and particularly one **Wilson**, there is good ground to believe John William Cosens, tidesman, has been in the knowledge of the robbery, and discovered the place where the money was lodged, but that there is not sufficient evidence for prosecuting him criminally ... the Board agreed to his being dismissed the service'. One wonders if there were two robberies in which one or two Wilsons were involved or if the time-honoured story of the robbery at Pittenweem is incorrect.

This book does not aim to challenge or correct such stories. Nor does it regurgitate the other information available in more modern sources. Instead, having started with a clean sheet of paper, an attempt has been made to re-create the smuggling story of the area from contemporary eighteenth century material - the custom house letter-books, other official/semi-official commentaries on events and the personal records of individuals.

Custom House Letter-books

By the Act of Union in 1707 'All parts of the United Kingdom were for ever ... to be liable to the same customs and duties on import and export and to be under the same restrictions and regulations of trade'. From the viewpoint of the modern researcher into smuggling history the great advantage of this is that shortly afterwards the Scottish ports were redefined [see Table I] and a standard reporting system was established whereby all correspondence to and from the Board in Edinburgh [now defined as Class 1 and Class 2 respectively] had to be transcribed in books which were held at the local custom house, as well as at head office. These letter-books form the foundation upon which the research for this book has been built.

Table I lists the ports, members and creeks from Montrose to Dunbar at the beginning of the eighteenth century - there were subsequently several changes and modifications. Sadly, as can be seen from the bracketed dates in this Table, not all the records have survived.

TABLE I: Ports, Members and Creeks from Montrose to Dunbar, as constituted shortly after the Union of 1707

Montrose (Class 1 1714; Class 2 1707)
Creeks: Arbroath, Auchmithie, Lunan Water, Usan, Ferryden, *Mathers, Johnshaven, Gourdon, Bervie, Tod Head*

Perth (Class 1 1721; Class 2 1752)
Creeks: Earn Mouth, Inchture, Pow of Errol

Dundee (Class 1 1724; Class 2 1708)
Creeks: Ferryport-on-Craig, Balmerino, Monifieth, Buddon Ness

Kirkcaldy (Class 2 1789)
Member: **Anstruther** (Class 1 1801)
Creeks: Aberdour, Burntisland, Kinghorn, Dysart, West Wemyss, East Wemyss, Buckhaven, Methil, Leven, Largo, Elie, St Monance, Pittenweem, Crail, Fife Ness, St Andrews, Eden Mouth

Bo'ness (Class 1 1868; Class 2 1780)
Member: **Alloa** (Class 1 1718; Class 2 1755)
Creeks: Queensferry, Blackness, Avon Water, Carron Mouth, Airth, Stirling, Clackmannan, Kincardine, Culross, Torryburn, Limekilns, Inverkeithing (in the port of Bo'ness)

Leith (Class 1 1834; Class 2 1780)
Creeks: Newhaven, Muirhouse Haven, Crammond

Prestonpans (No records extant)
Creeks: North Berwick, Aberlady, Port Seton, Musselburgh

Dunbar (Class 2 1754)
Creeks: *Eyemouth, Coldingham, Cocksburnpath*, Skateraw, Tynninghame

Notes: (i) There were frequent changes in this list - Kirkcaldy and Anstruther separated in 1710 and Alloa and Bo'ness in 1713; Grangemouth became an outport in 1810 and Arbroath in the 1820s. (ii) The figures in brackets after the name of each port or member port indicate the earliest letters in Classes 1 and 2 identified so far. (iii) The Dunbar and Montrose creeks in italics are not included within the present book.

The earliest extant Bo'ness letter from a collector is dated 30 January 1868 and reads 'My telegram of an early hour this morning would inform your Honours of the total destruction by fire of the custom house at this port - so sudden was it that the housekeeper with her son and the other inmates of the building had a narrow escape of their lives ... A few minutes after twelve this morning, just before retiring to bed, I went into the kitchen of my own dwelling to see that the gas was safely put out (as is my usual wont). The house being built on land considerably above the town, of which we have a full view through the window, I observed a dull red glare accompanied with smoke and just opposite the illuminated dial of the clock of the town hall. This struck me as being something unusual. I continued looking for a few moments, when I heard the faint tolling of a bell, which I presumed was an alarm ... I said to my wife 'There is a fire somewhere in the town and from the situation it cannot be far from the custom house'. I instantly put on my boots and coat and was in the act of leaving the house when the doorbell rang violently. It was Bryce, the outdoor officer, informing me that the custom house was on fire. I hurried down and found that any attempt to save anything would be not only fruitless but dangerous ... I trust under the circumstances your Honours will excuse this rambling statement '.

He wrote again the following day 'I am afraid that nothing will be saved. There is not the slightest appearance at present of the smallest scrap of paper, the fire being left to burn itself out. The loss to myself pecuniarily will be trifling but all my private papers - examples, references etc., which I had collected together during the time I have been in the service, will be a loss I am afraid I shall never get over. The examining officer informs me that all his private documents etc. are gone - also three one pound notes and ten shillings in gold which he had in his desk. The poor woman who lived in the spare room of the custom house has lost her all'.

On 6 February the collector described his attempts to reconstruct the records, including all the transactions since the beginning of the year and the list of goods in warehouse. 'I am in the hopes of being able to trace each separate importation but the class of individuals [involved] ... is such that I may have difficulty in arriving at this ... The general and local orders for the past year and also the orders for the year '62 or '63 are saved - these having been in the hands of the bookbinder at the time the fire took place'.

Today the Class 1 records begin with this correspondence in 1868. In Class 2 there are a few earlier records - the single letter dated 1780 reproduced in Figure 2, and the books for 1862 and 1867, which the collector had reported were with the bookbinder. The loss of these records is a major tragedy because, according to Daniel Defoe writing in 1724, Bo'ness had been 'a town of the greatest trade to Holland and France, before the Union, of any in Scotland, except Edinburgh; and, for shipping, it has more ships belong to it than to Edinburgh and Leith put together'. [see also Tucker's comments in the Appendix]

Despite this one must remember that rather than being frustrated by the missing records the researcher should be aware of the miracle that so much material has survived, in certain cases for nearly three hundred years. On 17 February 1746 the collector at Montrose sent a letter to the Board stating 'Upon the 17th of September last we wrote your Honours per express acquainting you that upon the 14th of said month a party of the rebel army came into this place, broke all the doors and desks in the custom house, burnt, destroyed and carried away many of the papers ... therefore we had stopped doing any manner of business at the custom house until we should receive your Honours directions. Upon the express returning and acquainting us that he had delivered our letter to the doorkeeper but that no answer could be procured at that time, our custom house has been ever since shut. This place being now possessed by a party of His Majesty's forces sent us by Admiral Byng ... we humbly beg your Honours orders for opening the custom house and carrying on the business as formerly, which we humbly judge we ought not to do without your directions'. The next letter is dated 27 February 1746. Before getting back to normal work, the collector had to report on 'the conduct and behaviour of all the officers in this precinct during the unnatural rebellion' [see Figure 14 in Chapter Nine]. Despite this dramatic event, some of the Montrose letters have survived from 1707 and form one of the more valuable information sources for the area under study.

The Scottish Record Office have divided the custom house records into five separate classes:

Class 1: Letters from the collectors and comptrollers at the outports to the Board of Customs in Edinburgh or London
Class 2: Letters and Orders from the Board to the collectors
Class 3: General Letter-books
Class 4: Miscellaneous Customs Records
Class 5: Material originating in subordinate Ports or Creeks

Not all these Classes are as clear-cut as this suggests. For example, Perth Class 1 volume 3 includes letters from the Board to the Collector between 1739 and 1749. The earliest Class 1 letter for Montrose, dated 26 April 1714, is at the back of the first Class 2 letter-book. This was not a case of the collector's clerk making a mistake but the fact that the outports were under constant pressure from Edinburgh to save paper and so every available page in a letter-book was used. According to a letter from the collector at Perth dated 17 August 1795 'in order to save as much [paper] as possible we cut up a number of old blue books [the books used to record a ship's cargo on entry]'.

Records from these classes exist for some if not all of the 'outports' in the area but usually only Classes 1, 2 and 4 have been consulted. Class 11 includes Shipping Registers and those for Alloa have been studied, originally to identify the owners of vessels seized and condemned for smuggling but later for more general information. These shipping registers are of importance as they are one of the few sets that date from the eighteenth century - the only other Scottish ones that have survived are for Greenock and Port Glasgow.

The Class 1 letters were addressed to 'Honourables' or 'Honourable Sirs' and tended to be signed 'We are etc'. The Board wrote to 'Gentlemen', and often signed themselves, as is the case in Figure 2, as 'Your loving friends'.

Not every event was recorded. The Perth collector wrote on 20 July 1725, 'Nothing remarkable has happened here since our last but that the *Blessing* of Perth, Charles Greig master, has laden here ... William May, tidesman at Newburgh, has broken his leg'. His previous letter was a brief note dated 13 July, also about the *Blessing*. Such references to the arrivals and sailing of vessels are used in Chapter Two.

Gentlemen

We have received and considered your Letter of the 12th instant, with the answers of Mr. Dick Tidesurveyor and William Gray Boatman belonging to the Kings Boat stationed at North Ferry, to a Complaint of the Tidesmen at your Port against the said Gray for Collecting Money with the privity of the Tidesurveyor, in the name of John Bayne Tidesm without his knowledge, from the Merchants concerned in the Cargo of the Ship Jane from Riga; And it appearing that it has been the practice of the Tidesm when boarded on vessels from foreign ports to receive Fees from Merchants ;- We disapprove thereof, and You are to signify to them and the Boatmen in your district that we forbid the same in future on any pretence whatever.. We are

Your Loving Friends

George Clerk Maxwell

Basil Cochrane

Adam Smith

...m ho. Edinburgh
...tober 1780. J.m

Figure 2: Example of Class 2 Custom House Letter

This is the only letter in the first Bo'ness Class 2 Letter-book and is an original, dated 17 October 1780, rather than the more typical transcriptions.

In the context of smuggling history the members of the Board tend to be shadowy individuals. These signatories are of interest as they include Adam Smith and Basil Cochrane, previously a governor of the Isle of Man, whose resultant feelings towards the Manx people possibly strengthened the Scottish viewpoint over the necessity of the crown purchasing the fiscal rights of that Island in 1765 [see tailpiece to Chapter Two].

Adam Smith was born on 5 June 1723, the posthumous son of the customs comptroller at Kirkcaldy. This was a common name among local customs staff in the first half of the eighteenth century. Adam Smith was appointed collector at Alloa in 1747. According to a letter dated 8 July 'I have some private affairs to settle at Edinburgh and likewise to remove my family to this place and therefore entreat you will be pleased to grant me fourteen days leave of absence from the port for that purpose'. On 1 December 1762 he applied to the Board for a prolongation of his current leave of absence for another twenty days for the recovery of his health. He died on 28 March 1763 and John West, Inspector General, was appointed to act in his place.

In the meantime on 12 January 1763 Adam Smith, clerk to the collector, and possibly his son, was appointed as surveyor at Alloa 'in room of David Mather diseased'. However, this was only a temporary appointment, as John Orrok was appointed surveyor on 9 March 1763 and on 7 June that year Adam Smith is referred to as 'the clerk in the new collector's room', the new collector being James Pattullo.

The Adam Smith, having attended both Glasgow University and Balliol College, Oxford for ten years, between the ages of fourteen and twenty-four, returned to Kirkcaldy in 1748. This is not the place for a detailed biography but he became a Commissioner of the Scottish Customs in 1778 with a salary of at least £500 and an annuity of £300 so that he was 'in a favourable position'. It has been suggested that this appointment 'arrested his literary labours' because 'the performance of petty routine duties engrossed the greater part of his time'. In 1787 he became Lord Rector of Glasgow University.

In cases, such as that of Dunbar, where only the Class 2 letters exist, it is still possible to reconstruct the story because the respondent tended to start by repeating the main points in the letter to which they were replying. This letter was sent by the Board to the collector on 3 October 1769. 'Having received your letter of the 29th of last month, acquainting us that the character given by you ... of Alexander Thomson being incapable and crazy in his judgement is unjust and proceeded from your being misinformed by the late surveyor and certifying that Alexander Thomson, who was placed upon the superannuation fund on account of the character above-mentioned, is still fit for the execution of his duty, we fine the collector who is most to blame, the comptroller being a young officer, £5 which he is to remit ... and reprimand you both for your rashness in representing a person as unfit for duty, by which he was deprived of his office, before you were properly informed of the fact. You are to continue Alexander Thomson in his employment till further orders'.

On other occasions vital letters are not transcribed. The collector at Anstruther wrote to the Board on 15 April 1805 'As to S Coulter's information ... being rather of a singular nature, we think it better to transmit the letter itself rather than an extract ... we pray leave to report that the writer thereof is a man of credit and character and from his situation has a good opportunity of knowing all the plans of the smugglers'. Would it have been less frustrating not to know that Coulter's letter ever existed?

It would be an impossible task to read the letters in every letter-book [the Leith records include some 27 letter-books in Class 1, 341 in Class 2, 140 in Class 4 and 14 in Class 5]. Instead the letter-books have been sampled, all the letters for each fifth year have been read from the earliest possible date to 1805. Where necessary, reference has been made to letters for other years to complete a story or to include the correspondence on a particular date, for example the port's response in 1786 to an enquiry from the Board about spirits smuggling.

The outports of Montrose, Perth, Dundee and Alloa are of particular interest because they form a cohesive group. Problems experienced by one tended to be shared by all. On 20 June 1749 the collector at Alloa forewarned the collectors at other outports, including Kirkcaldy, Prestonpans, Dunbar, Anstruther, Dundee and Montrose, as well as Aberdeen and Inverness 'A square-sterned sloop of about 50 tons burthen with a batten on her topmast, called the *Christian & Magdalene* of Kincardine, William Norris master, from Holland pretending to be bound for Norway sailed from Kincardine Road this morning'. [This vessel is discussed further in Chapters Two and Three]

In 1805 'certain noblemen and gentlemen of the county of Fife' sent a petition to the Board praying that the quay at Guardbridge on the river Eden might be made a legal place for the landing and shipping of goods to and from foreign parts. Both Perth and Dundee listed the quantities of foreign goods imported into their precincts for merchants, manufacturers and others residing at Cupar or in its neighbourhood - these consisted of linseed, cloverseed, undressed flax, tallow and linen yarn. Anstruther, which appeared to have a better view of the type of trade in the Eden estuary, responded 'if an active, intelligent tidesman were stationed at or near Guardbridge, he might prove a great service to the revenue in the suppression of smuggling, independent altogether of this landing place being made a legal quay, and, were it made so, his salary would be the only additional expense'.

Despite this commonality, each outport had its particular problems. Alloa included Stirling, where the customs staff came under the Glasgow collection [see Chapters and Six and Nine]. The Board were informed in November 1742 that Alexander Dalmahoy, surveyor of landcarriage staff, had been 'ailing' while he was in prison at Stirling for debt yet the Alloa collector had certified that Dalmahoy had served all the Michaelmas quarter. As the collector explained 'when found off their duty they [the Glasgow staff] pretend to be absent either by liberty from that port or your Honours' so that it was difficult to know what they were doing. In fact Dalmahoy had not been imprisoned until 10 November so that the collector's return was correct.

Newburgh, although not listed in Table I, was a 'remote creek' within the Perth outport. Once again the collector found it difficult to 'watch the proceedings of staff there'. The story of John Petrie, extraordinary tidesman at Newburgh, is told in Chapter Nine.

In April 1765 Ambrose Starks, tidesurveyor at Dundee, complained of bad usage from John Young, master of the *Unity* from Rotterdam. The collector explained 'As this affair happened in the river Tay ... betwixt Fife and Perthshires, we are at a loss what court to commence this prosecution [in] ... John Young, the person complained of, sails a ship from Perth and his residence is in Ferry Pantoncraigs in Fifeshire'. Starks's witnesses included George Davidson, Thomas Miln, William Key and David Young from Fife and David Baxter, James McDonald and George Adam from Dundee. As the sheriff depute lived at Forfar, the local witnesses were summoned before the Dundee magistrates 'as a judge equally competent in this case, and attended with less charge'. The collector thought that Starks did not have a strong case so that the Fife witnesses had not been examined 'not liking to put the revenue to any unsuccessful charge'.

Both Montrose and Dunbar can be classed as border ports, only part of their 'precincts' covering the present area and their borders extending to include places to be discussed in two future books (as indicated in Table I). They are ports in the real meaning of the term i.e. they are on the exposed sea coast. The records for Kirkcaldy include some letters from the collector at Anstruther, which give a vivid picture of what was happening on the coast when smuggling along the Forth and Tay had declined to a low ebb. All this local information has been supplemented by an occasional letter from other ports, from Aberdeen and Dumfries in Scotland and Whitby and Whitehaven in England.

Other writers are known to have studied the letter-books. Duncan Fraser in *The Smugglers* used the Montrose records together with other source material to describe the history of the port. In *Eighteenth-century Scottish Smugglers: The Evidence from Montrose & Dumfries* Rosemary Goring compared the two outports in the periods 1725-35 and 1782-85. Richard Platt in *Smugglers' Britain* described stories found in the Montrose, Perth and Dundee letter-books. Stephanie Stevenson quoted from the Anstruther letter-books in *Anstruther A History* and the reader is recommended to this publication for the story of the *Barbara & Mary*. Finally sections from the Dunbar letter-books were transcribed by T C Smout in his article *Customhouse Letters to the Officers at Dunbar, 1765*. His Appendix includes 1765 Departures and Arrivals taken from the

Port-books of Dunbar, an information source not used by the present author. Details of these publications and all the custom house letter-books consulted for the present book are given in the Bibliography.

Other Contemporary Records

Other seventeenth and eighteenth century records add the finishing touches and a degree of authenticity to the information that can be gleaned from the custom house letter-books - in effect a double check. These can be divided into two broad categories. First there are the official/semi-official commentaries on events. In 1656 Thomas Tucker was sent by the English Government 'for the purpose of introducing order into the collection of the revenues of the Excise and Customs' and appointed as one of the Commissioners of the Scottish Board. His subsequent report was published for the Bannatyne Club, of which Sir Walter Scott was president, in 1825. The section relating to the two Firths has been reproduced in the Appendix to give those not familiar with the area an appropriate introduction. Another traveller, quoted already, was Daniel Defoe, who included the east coast in his 1724 tour of Scotland.

The Coast Guard letter-book for St Andrews has survived for the 1830s and gives a slightly different viewpoint of the level of smuggling in the area at that time. A hundred years earlier the minutes of the University of St Andrews include the problems faced when students became involved in a smuggling venture. Their reaction is familiar to those at universities today - they set up a working party to investigate the facts and make a recommendation for further action. A case involving Pierre Goguet, master of the *Nancy*, and a Mr Jonas of Arbroath ['Ahbroth'] was heard at a Guernsey court in 1765. It has not been possible to link the event with anything happening in Arbroath, as yet. But if nothing were put in print until the last loose end had been tied up then this type of research would never be published.

The Gentleman's Magazine has been mentioned in the context of the Porteous riots. In 1737 the editor commented 'Our readers press us to give them the speeches in Parliament single and entire ... not considering that inserting them in that manner would take up a whole year's magazines; however we shall give some of the most remarkable'. As a

THE

LIFE

OF

JOHN METCALF,

COMMONLY CALLED

Blind Jack of Knaresborough.

WITH

Many Entertaining ANECDOTES of his EXPLOITS in

Hunting, Card-Playing, &c.

Some PARTICULARS relative to the

Expedition against the REBELS in 1745,

IN WHICH HE BORE A PERSONAL SHARE;

AND ALSO

A Succinct ACCOUNT of his various CONTRACTS for

Making ROADS, Erecting BRIDGES,

AND OTHER UNDERTAKINGS,

IN

Yorkshire, Lancashire, Derbyshire, and Cheshire;

Which, for a Series of Years, have brought him into PUBLIC NOTICE, as a most

EXTRAORDINARY CHARACTER.

EMBELLISHED WITH

A STRIKING HALF-LENGTH PORTRAIT.

YORK:

PRINTED BY E. AND R. PECK, LOW-OUSEGATE.

1795.

Figure 3. Frontispiece of The Life of John Metcalf, commonly called Blind Jack of Knaresborough 1795

John Metcalf was born in 1717 and blinded by smallpox in 1723. Over six feet in height, he learned to play the fiddle and at the age of fifteen was playing at dances in the Long Room at the Queen's Head Inn in Harrogate. Having eloped with Dolly Benson of the Royal Oak Inn also in Harrogate, he set up a fish business. As this used pack animals, he also bred and sold horses.

In 1745 Squire Thornton of Thornville Royal near Knaresborough raised a company of volunteers who marched to Newcastle to join General Wade. In the context of Blind Jack's future career, it is significant that Wade supervised the construction of approximately 250 miles of military roads and numerous bridges in Scotland, including the now disused road from Fort Augustus over the Corrieyairach pass. 'Ironically the Jacobites were to use them [these roads] to good effect in 1745, by which date Wade ... was commander-in-chief in England'. The volunteers took part in the battle at Falkirk, which was a victory for the rebel army. Because of his failure to defeat the Highlanders, Wade was replaced by the Duke of Cumberland. On one occasion Jack was asked to play the fiddle before the Duke. Shortly after this, and before the battle of Culloden in 1746, the volunteer army disbanded. Cumberland continued in Scotland and followed Byng in the relief of Montrose.

Back home, Jack continued to play the fiddle and ran a stage wagon between Harrogate and York, often driving the vehicle himself. He also traded in Aberdeen woollen stockings, selling them to the local gentry. When the Turnpike Act was passed for a road between Harrogate and Boroughbridge, Jack was given the job of making a stretch of the road, so beginning his road building career. In this present publication it is Jack's smuggling adventures that are of particular interest. Details of these have survived only because in his old age he was encouraged to dictate his memoirs.

The Narrative of James Nimmo has survived because it was 'printed from a copy very faithfully made by Mr Mill of the Signet Library of an old manuscript in the possession of Mr Pringle of Torwoodlee. It was doubtless in the handwriting of the author, and was probably written shortly before his death in 1709'. This was checked against a copy made by William Hogg, the author's son-in-law, and 'now [1889] in the possession of Archibald Gibson Esq, Huntly Gardens, Glasgow'.

result from the issues of the magazine for June, July and August that year it is possible to reconstruct much of the debate associated with the bill 'to disable Alexander Wilson Esq from taking, holding, or enjoying any office or place of magistracy in the city of Edinburgh, or elsewhere in Great Britain, and for imprisoning Alexander Wilson; and for abolishing the guard kept on the city, commonly called the town guard; and for taking away the gates of the Nether Bow port of the city and keeping open the same' - the Scottish Riot Act. This style of reporting pre-dates Hansard by some forty years. The reader is referred in particular to the 'Letter to a Gentleman, containing a summary account of the proceeding on the above Bill' on pages 348 to 353 of the June issue.

The Gentleman's Magazine includes other items of interest. According to the Historical Chronicle for Wednesday, 12 July 1732 'The Commissioners of Customs at Edinburgh received a bank note for £50 in a letter from an unknown person, who intimated that he had wronged the King in duties to that sum and could not be easy, though some years since, till he made restitution'. Inflation since that date is approximately fifty times so that the payment was worth £2,500 in modern terms.

Secondly there are the sources which add a more personal touch to the story. To quote Scott-Moncrieff in his introduction to the Narrative of James Nimmo 'The acts of any particular age cannot be properly studied apart from some knowledge of the beliefs and the mental condition of those who performed them'. It is the narratives, memoirs and letter-books of individuals that provide this insight.

From the letter-books of three merchants in Inverness, Ayr and on the Isle of Man it has been possible to draw up a list of the names of their contacts based at the main places in Europe visited by vessels sailing to and from the ports discussed in this book [see Chapter Two]. Several of the letters from Bailie John Steuart of Inverness refer to people or vessels belonging to the two Firths area. For example, he gives instructions to the master of the *Catherine* of Leith about what to say if stopped by the revenue cruisers [see Chapter Three]. The manuscript of a charter party between Edinburgh merchants and the master of the *Benefactor* of Bo'ness, sets up contingency arrangements should a cargo of brandy be seized [see the tailpiece to Chapter Three].

Other letters from people living outside the area help to complete the picture. William Watt junior & Co of Kirkwall owned the *Peggy* of Stromness, which was seized in 1780. The event has been described by W S Hewison in his paper *Smuggling in Eighteenth Century Orkney*. The story is included here because of its significance as a pretended voyage and the parallel references to the case in the custom house letter-books [see Chapter Three].

Better known as a road builder, Blind Jack of Knaresborough dictated his memoirs in 1795. These were the source of the quotation in the chapter on *Magistrates and Smuggling* in George Hay's book about Arbroath, published in 1876, which gave this author the first hint of Blind Jack's smuggling activities. The frontispiece of the memoirs is reproduced in Figure 3 and more details of Jack's smuggling adventures together with a picture of him in his old age are found in Chapter Seven. James Nimmo's narrative was quoted in the Preface.

Where necessary, modern reference books have been used to complete the picture.

The Story of Captain John Porteous, as told in the Gentleman's Magazine, September 1736

Tuesday, 7: 'Betwixt nine and ten at night a body of men entered the West Port of Edinburgh, seized the drum, beat to arms and calling out 'Here! All those who dare avenge innocent blood!' were instantly attended by a numerous crowd. Then they seized and shut up the city gates and posted guards at each, to prevent surprise by the king's forces, while another detachment disarmed the city guards, and advanced immediately to the tolbooth or prison, where not being able to break the door with hammers etc., they set it on fire, but at the same time provided water to keep the flames within bounds. Before the outer door was near burnt down several rushed through the flames and obliged the keeper to open the inner door and going into Captain Porteous's apartment called 'Where is the *buggar* Porteous?' who said 'I'm here, what is it you are to do with me?' To which he was answered 'We are to carry you to the place where you shed so much innocent blood and hang you'. He made some resistance, but was soon overcome, for while some set the whole prisoners at liberty, others caught him by the legs and dragged him downstairs and then led him to the Grassmarket, where they agreed to hang him without further ceremony; accordingly, taking a coil of rope from a shop, they put one end of it about his neck and flung the other over a dyer's cross, post or gallows and drew him up; but having got his hands to the rope, they let him down and tied them, and drawed him up again. But observing what an indecent sight he was without any covering over his face, they let him down a second time and pulled off one of the two shirts he had on and wrapped it about his head, and hauled him up a third time with loud huzza and a ruff of the drum. After he had hung till supposed to be dead, they nailed the rope to the post, then formally saluting one another, grounded their arms and on t'other ruff of the drum, retired out of town.

'Nothing of this kind was ever so boldly attempted or so successfully executed, all in the space of two hours, after which everything was quiet. The magistrates endeavoured to prevent their design, but were attacked and driven away. Next morning at four when the Captain was taken down, his neck was broke, his arm wounded and his back and head bruised ... About fourteen persons were taken into custody the next day on account of this riot but, no evidence appearing against them, eleven were soon discharged and the others not long after'.

CHAPTER TWO: THE FAIR AND UNFAIR TRADE

'As to the bankruptcy of Braid, although he became bankrupt more than two years since ... and his funds collected into cash in the hands of Mr Meldrum, banker in St Andrews, yet no dividend or settlement has ever taken place and Braid carries on his business in St Andrews both as a fair trader and unfair trader the same as formerly'. [Letter from the collector at Anstruther to the Board dated 23 September 1805]

A picture of the overseas trade to and from the east coast of Scotland can be re-constructed from the custom house letter-books. For example, Perth tended to report the arrivals and sailings of every vessel [see Chapter One] while the letter-book for Dundee from 19 December 1724 to 22 December 1725 has been used to produce the following list of imports:

From Holland: flax, linseed, madder, old iron, earthenware, paper, rope, soap and toys (7 vessels); **from Sweden**: deals and other species of timber, iron bars and hanks of wire (5 vessels); **from Germany**: barrel staves, clapboards, oak knees, lampblack, cut glass and iron (1 vessel); **from Norway**: balks, both small and middle, barrel staves, cart spokes, deals, harrow bills, hazel cuts, iron, oak board, trenails, pitch, tar, other species of timber, brandy and salt (11 vessels); **from Spain**: almonds, raisins, prunes, wine, cork, paper and salt (3 vessels); **from Poland**: barrel staves, clapboard, deals, oak board, flax (1 vessel) and **from Livonia**: flax (1 vessel).

Further details about this port can be found in *The Trade and Shipping of Dundee 1780-1850*, which is recommended to the reader.

Overseas trade was also discussed by Tucker [see Appendix] and Daniel Defoe during his tour of Scotland in 1724, when he listed the main exports from the Forth as white fish and salt. Oysters were shipped

8) I John Mackenzie Master of the Fortrose of Leith a British built Ship property all British about Sixty Tons burthen, navigate with 3 women, & two boys besides my Self all British men, Enters to load Coals for Rotterdam promising before departure to make a true Report of all the Goods I shall take on board
Jo: McKenzie

I Alex.r Boyter Ma.r of the Catharine of Leith British Built property all British about Thirty five Tons burthen Navigate with three men & Two Boys & myself all British men & boys Enters to Load for Rotterdam promising before Departure to make a true Report of all the Goods I shall take on Board
Alex.r Boyter

D.o 10

I James Duncanson Ma.r of the Mary of Stirling a British Built Ship property all British about Thirty five Tons Burthen navigate with Three men & two Boys besides myself all British Men Enters to Load for Campvere promising before Departure to make a true Report of All the Goods I shall take on Board
Jam.s Duncanson

Figure 4. Extracts from the Shipmasters' Entries to Foreign Parts at Alloa September 1746 to February 1748

Rotterdam: *Catherine* of Leith, Alexander Boyter; *Providence* of North Berwick, David Sharp; *John David* of Arbroath, Charles Kenney; *Margaret & Euphan* of Inverkeithing, Thomas Henderson; *Jean* of Alloa, Alexander Nicol; *Margaret* of Dundee, Robert Wardropper; *Forster* of Sunderland, Thomas Teasdale; *Pretty Jean* of Dundee, Alexander Ramsay; *Fortrose* of Leith, John Mackenzie; *Margaret* of St Andrews, James Birrell; *Success* of Leith, Thomas Duff; *Primrose* of Elphinstone, John Dick and *Charming Susan* of Dundee, John Henderson
Campvere: *Mary* of Stirling, James Duncanson; *Daily Hope* of Leith, John Short; *Fortrose* of Leith, John Mackenzie; *Margaret* of Queensferry, Robert Buncle; *Helen* of Elphinstone, James Garriock; *Christian* of Alloa, Thomas Younger; *Margaret* of Leith, Richard Scougall; *Janet* of Alloa, Joseph Robertson; *John & Alexander* of Edinburgh, John Gogan; *Betty* of Bo'ness, David Stevenson and *Joseph & Amity* of Inverkeithing, James Greig
Middleburgh: *Margaret* of Dundee, James Hay; *Stirling* of Ipswich, Robert Goodrich; *Friends Good Will* of Anstruther, Henry Thomson; *Forster* of Sunderland, Thomas Teasdale; *Thomas & Dorothy* of Sunderland, Thomas Forster [two voyages] and *Four Brothers* of Mandale, Anders Hemmeson
Gothenburg: *Greenock* of Inverkeithing, William Hodge; *Primrose* of Elphinstone, John Dick; *Princess Carolina* of Dysart, John White and *Friendship* of Anstruther, Alexander Reid
Mandale: *Patience* of Mandale, Boh Peterson; *Anna Catharina* of Mandale, Biorn Salvison and *Providence* of Mandale, Toms Christianson
Bremen: *Christiana*, Henrich Wessells and *Helena* of Bremen, Abraham Wishausen
Christiansands: *Margaret* of Bo'ness, Duncan Glasford and James Glasford
Amsterdam: *Four Brothers* of Mandale, Anders Carstenson; **Dram**: *Elizabeth* of Dram, Peter Neilson; **Hamburg**: *Seaflower* of Dunbar, Thomas Gullan; **Stockholm**: *Jean's Adventure* of Lynn, William Vincent and **South Carolina**: *Betty* of Airth, John Connochie

The most interesting point about these entries is that they include the shipmasters' **actual** signatures.

coastwise to Newcastle. According to the Montrose letter-books, there was a good market for Scotch salmon in Campvere, the *Hazard*, the *Union* and the *Charming Nelly* carrying 384 barrels and 36 half barrels there in November 1760 alone.

Preserved in the Alloa letter-books are the shipmasters' entries to foreign parts between September 1746 and February 1748 [see Figure 4]. These have been summarised in terms of destination, vessel and master. Where a particular vessel is mentioned elsewhere in this book, reference is made to the Figure. The most significant part of these entries is that they include the actual signatures of the masters.

Table II lists ports mentioned in the customs records where it has been possible to identify eighteenth century merchants through the letter-books of Bailie John Steuart of Inverness, Alexander Oliphant & Co, wine merchants in Ayr and George Moore from Peel in the Isle of Man. Those who were definitely involved in smuggling have been highlighted in bold. Although he was based in Inverness, Steuart clearly had links with the area to the south - he wrote to Alexander Arbuthnot senior, Thomas Brown, James Cumming, Alexander Falconer and Charles Gordon in Edinburgh. Gordon's brothers Alexander and Robert were based in St Martins and Bordeaux respectively. In May 1718 Steuart wrote to Robert Gordon about a cargo of wine shipped on the *Joseph* of Pittenweem. His other contact in St Martins was John Souper from whom he ordered 'best wine the growth of St Martins Island'. His instructions to Alexander Todd, master of the *Catherine* of Leith are discussed in Chapter Three. Other vessels from the Montrose to Dunbar area mentioned in his letters include the *Agnes* of Alloa, James Jarvie master, *Jean* of Alloa, Thomas Arthur master [see Figure 4], *Unicorn* of Dundee, John Cleatton master, *Jean* of Kinghorn, James Leighton master, *Lamb* of Kinghorn [master unspecified], *Good Fortune* of Montrose, Thomas Greig master and *William & James* of Prestonpans, John Gilles master.

A more comprehensive list of ports is given in Chapter Three, Figure 6: Europe during the eighteenth century. Several of these ports were involved in the East India trade. The East India company in London held a monopoly. This meant that the prices of tea, spices, porcelain and cotton, silk and fine Indian textiles were high even before the

TABLE II: Ports mentioned in the custom house letter-books together with the names of eighteenth century merchants resident there

Country/Port	Merchants
France	
Bordeaux	**George Ainslie, John Black & Co, Alexander and Robert Gordon**, George McLeod
Boulogne	Charles Smith
Cette	**Peter Berail**
St Martins	**F Baudin, Alexander Gordon, John Souper**
Germany	
Hamburg	David & Robert Barclay, **Bartholomew Bloodworth, Bertram van Heihuysen**
Holland	
Amsterdam	Jackson & Bradley, James Morrison, Alexander Steuart
Campvere	**David & John Gregory, John Mowat**
Rotterdam	**Alexander Andrew, Martin van Banken, James Crawford & Francis Twiss**, William & John Davidsons, Theo Dillon, **Marcus Ezechiel**, Robert Gerard, John Gordon, **Isaac & Zacherie Hope, Livingston & Symson, John Stedman, Andrew Stuckey & Co**
Livonia	
Riga	Alexander Ross, Windar & Aikman
Poland	
Dantzig	Alexander & James Coutts, Andrew Marjoribanks
Portugal	
Lisbon	**Cunningham & Gordon, Mayne & Co**
Oporto	**George Wye & Co**
Norway	
Bergen	**Wallace & Co**
Spain	
Bilbao	**Ivan van Duffle**
Cadiz	**James Duff**
Sweden	
Gothenburg	**Messrs Bagge, Wilson & Hall**
Stockholm	Campbell, Gerard & Dobson, Nelletoun & Campbell, Mountgomerie, Mould & Fenick

Note: Those highlighted in bold had **definite** smuggling connections.

government-controlled duties were added. Unless they were purchased through the East India Company's sales in London these were in effect prohibited goods. There were other East Indian companies in Europe, including the Ostend company, the French Compagnie des Indies Orientales, the Danish Asiatic Company and the Swedish East India company [see the section on Gothenburg]. These provided the British smugglers with East Indian goods - according to contemporary calculations at least two thirds of the tea drunk in Scotland, England and Ireland had been smuggled.

In 1760 the Board forewarned the outports to be on their guard because they had received information 'that great quantities of tea and other East India goods are come in ships lately arrived in the ports of Denmark, Sweden and Holland' and they had 'reason to believe attempts will be made to run part of the same into this kingdom'. The problem continued as the Board wrote in 1783 'a great quantity of tea and other goods lately imported at Copenhagen will be sent to the British dominions'.

Forewarnings included information varying from details of actual vessels and their masters, the goods that they were lading at some foreign port and their intended destination to more general comments like those quoted above. In each case the collector was directed 'to put the officers in your district on their guard in order that they may prevent or detect this fraud, if the same be attempted'. These forewarnings were not always correct. In September 1735 the *St Johnstown* arrived at Dundee and the collector was concerned because he had been told that the vessel was intending to run 1,000 bushels of the salt at Newburgh 'which I doubt is too true'. However, the tidesurveyor from South Ferry visited the vessel at Perth, where she entered 500 bushels legally 'and it does not appear to him by the situation of her hold there's any more [run] out . By which it would appear the report must have been groundless, though it came to me from Lord Sinclair, as currently talked [about] in Fife'.

The following sections on selected countries are based on forewarnings together with other information about actual smuggles. They do not include a complete gazetteer of all the places involved but give some idea of the general pattern.

Denmark

A second forewarning from the Board about two vessels loading at Copenhagen in October 1785 described one as 'a smack-rigged Scottish sloop of 30 tons burthen; is all over black and will go to some place near the river Tay [the other was bound for the east coast of Ireland]. Both these ships are unarmed and their cargoes in teas and East India goods will be worth £10,000'.

France

In April 1735 the collector at Dundee was informed that two ships from France had been running their cargoes in St Andrews Bay and about the mouth of this river. 'But the wind has blown so hard easterly that though we have two sloops here neither vessels or boats were able to put to sea, though they have been constantly on the watch night and day within the river to prevent any goods from being brought up to this place. One of our tidesman stationed at Panbride has seized about twenty ankers of brandy, which are lodged in the warehouse, and I hear that much about the same quantity was brought to town last night late by the officers of excise'. The rest of the goods were supposed to have been lodged round Cupar and other places in Fife. The following November one Greig [see tailpiece to Chapter Five] had run his whole cargo from France near St Andrews. Once more 'the goods are all carried into the middle of the country'.

Germany

Both these stories relate to Emden. In October 1805 the collector at Anstruther was informed that 'a considerable quantity of gin and brandy' from Emden had been smuggled at Aberlady Bay by a sloop from Emden. This was believed to be the *Farmer*, [from Alloa] 'an old vessel about 70 tons' and she was expected to return within a few weeks. The only *Farmer* of the right age traced so far in the Alloa shipping registers was sold to Aberdeen in 1791.

The following August, Alexander Hodge, commander of the king's boat at Crail, received information about a schooner-rigged vessel lading prohibited goods at Emden for the Firth of Forth or the coast of Angus. This was chased by the *Henry Dundas* excise cruiser off Red Head [to the north of Arbroath]. She had thrown most of her cargo overboard during the chase but a hundred ankers of gin, landed by her boat, were seized.

Holland

Holland was one of the more common sources of smuggled goods. On 12 May 1715 the Board informed the outports that 'the *Success* of Montrose, William Thompson master, sailed from Leith about the 22nd April last for Holland with three or four of the greatest runners [smugglers] aboard and is to run her cargo at Montrose and Peterhead. She is a square-sterned vessel of three masts and about 60 tons'. In March 1755 the collector at Dunbar was warned about two vessels 'laden with high duty and prohibited goods' ready to sail from **Rotterdam**. One was a 'pretty large square-sterned sloop belonging to Kinghorn, John Arthur master' and the other 'also a square-sterned sloop, belonging to Dundee, Thomas Ross master'.

On the south bank of the river Tay, between Dundee and Perth, Newburgh, which was mentioned in Chapter One, features in many of the stories about smuggling of Dutch goods. In April 1735 the collector at Dundee noted that a large ship from **Rotterdam** had sailed up the Tay, full laden and bound to Newburgh. 'There being great reason to believe some part of that cargo was intended to be run and there being only one tidesman there, the collector directed the tidesurveyor with his boat's crew to attend the ship until such time as she should either be reported or guarded by a proper number of officers'. Four days later he wrote that the tidesurveyor had seized 'some trifles of prohibited goods on board the ship ... and he had secured a very considerable quantity of high duty goods to be brought to an entry, which would infallibly have been run. Indeed it is too great an indulgence to allow any ship from foreign parts to unload at such a creek, where there is no guard to prevent them from doing what they please'.

In September 1739 Francis Blakie, merchant in Perth, took out a protest against the collector, who had refused to deliver six casks of ashes [potash to be used as fertiliser] to him 'unless he produced a bill of loading or receipt ... proving the property, as they were not reported by the master'. The situation worsened rapidly. 'He has since summoned me before the town court ... it is an unheard of thing to sue an officer of the customs before a burgh bailie for anything done in the execution of his office. The design of making this illegal attempt is obvious ... I must beg leave to observe that all the malice and resentment of the smugglers is pointed at me. When this ship came from **Rotterdam**, the surveyor and I, who were both present at Newburgh at rummaging her, were sensible there were goods run out of her for we found under the steerage a void place as large as a room', where the ashes and other goods, including spices and calicoes, were found. [see Concealments in Chapter Five]

On 11 March 1740 the Board warned the collector at Dundee about three ships belonging to Perth 'soon expected from Holland having on board goods which are designed to be run in the River Tay. You are to order the tidesurveyor upon their arrival to see these ships up the river to Newburgh and there to deliver them over to the care of the officers at Perth and this he is to do with diligence and secrecy'. These can be identified from the Perth letter-books as the *Joseph & Ann*, the *Elizabeth & Ann*, John Westwater master, and the *Thomas & Elizabeth*, John Watson master [the name combinations suggest a possible link between these three vessels]. They all had contraband goods on board. The *Joseph & Ann* appears to have arrived first and was searched on 7 April 1740 when soap and grocery ware and spectacles 'under a concealed scuttle' were seized. The *Elizabeth & Ann* arrived a week later. Geneva, soap and 'one bundle of senna leaves ... being drugs not the growth of Europe therefore prohibited' were seized. This vessel is mentioned again in Chapters Five and Nine. Finally the *Thomas & Elizabeth* arrived in May with a cargo including prohibited wire and aniseed not entrable from the Netherlands.

The *Christian & Magdalene*, William Norris master, was a regular trader with Holland [see Chapter One]. This vessel arrived at Kincardine on 26 October 1748 and, because he knew of her reputation, John Paterson, the salt watchman, informed the collector, who had been told by the tidesman already. 'It appears that Paterson's information had taken air for that night he was attacked ... by three sailors or persons disguised in sailors' habit, beat, bruised and wounded to the degree that he was rendered incapable of doing duty ... the collector has caused a surgeon dress Paterson's wounds and ordered him to attend him till his cure is complete'.

Figure 5. Campvere during the Eighteenth Century

Traditionally the Scottish staple was established at Campvere when Mary, sister of James II, married Wolphaert van Borselen, son of the Lord of Campvere. In fact there was rivalry between Campvere, Middleburgh and Antwerp for the staple until it was fixed at 'the Veere' in 1541. From then 'with the exception of a short period during the revolt of the Netherlands, when trade went back to Bruges, and a few years in the seventeenth century, when the conservator resided at Dordrecht, the Scottish staple remained at Campvere until the institution perished in the convulsions which shook Europe during the Napoleonic Wars'. The formal contract between the two countries was cancelled on 1 October 1799.

An anonymous Dutch pamphlet described the natural advantages of Campvere. It was close to the sea and 'so easy of entrance that a skilful seaman who had already been there once or twice could safely undertake to unload his vessel in the harbour'. The Campvere Road was safe in stormy weather and was 'so situated that a vessel sailing from Campvere could in an hour or two be in the open sea free from all banks and rocks. Moreover, the Veersche Gat (the passage between Walcheren and North Beveland) was hardly ever blocked with ice, and even in such a severe winter as 1740 ships could at almost any time sail out and in'. The final advantage was that owing to its high quay, the cellars of the town were not liable to be flooded

In 1814 Mr Laing, who had frequently acted on behalf of the conservator, wrote this description of how the staple had operated. 'In point of practice for forty or fifty years previous to the revolution in France and Holland the privileges, I understand were these. Salt, grain, coals, lead, woollen stockings and other woollen goods, salted fish and provisions, and generally all raw products, and certain, if not all, manufactures from products in Scotland could be exported by a Scotch burgher from a royal burgh and landed at Campvere free of any import duty of any kind. Goods of this description, lead for example, was accordingly always landed at Campvere, although the merchant to whom such goods were consigned lived at Amsterdam or Rotterdam. The subsequent reshipment of the goods to the consumer or the market for them was in that country, and in those days a trifling expense compared to the duty saved, and this reshipment and transiter trade was exactly the kind of trade suitable to the capital of the place and which the Dutch Government wished to secure to that Province'.

Spain

Again both the stories relate to the same port, Bilbao. Hercules Smith, the collector at Montrose, seized the *St John Baptist* of Leith, Robert Allen master, in February 1710 with wine from Bilbao but suspected to be French. [see also the wine section in Chapter Four] The collector was to allow her to proceed to her home port 'taking care to secure the hatches and that you put such a number of waiters aboard as may be sufficient to secure the cargo from embezzlement'. A second letter of the same date reported 'we have received information ... [she] has been hovering on your coast for about a fortnight and that part of her cargo has been run before she came into your port. You are therefore to make diligent search and report to us if you have any suspicion of bulk being broken either since or before she came into port and be careful to secure the main hatch and scuttles and see if there be no scuttle under the hearth of the cook room etc.' On 1 March 1710 four waiters attended her to Leith.

In December 1724 the collector at Dundee wrote to the Board about the *Gloucester*, James McKellen master, from Bilbao. Her owners, George Yeaman of Therrie [see also Chapter Six], Henry Guthrie of Clephanton, Henry Smith of Saddlestown and Alexander Watson of Wallace Craigie had been trading in Scots linen for the last two years. The *Gloucester* sailed for London with a cargo of linen in July 1724, was freighted by merchants there with wheat for Bilbao and had now sailed back to Dundee, where it was suspected that much of her cargo of wine and other goods 'on the master's account' had been smuggled.

Sweden

According to Thomas Fischer the Swedish west coast ports were the most attractive to the merchants, because of the comparatively short journeys from the east coast of Scotland. He describes Gothenburg as lying 'in a wild, picturesque surrounding of rock and water at the mouth of the Gota Elf (river). The distance between it and the nearest Scotch harbour of Leith would only be a few hundred miles. Originally the town had been founded on the neighbouring island of Hisingen in 1603 but it was destroyed by the Norwegians in 1612, and rebuilt only seven years later by King Gustavus Adolphus in its present situation. The hope of its rapid development largely depended on the possibility of attracting strangers of means and energy, and of persuading them to settle in the new borough. With this end in view, letters were written to Germany, France, Holland, England, and Scotland, inviting immigration and promising at the same time great advantages and privileges. Gothenburg's hope was not disappointed. The foreign element so largely increased that, during the first half of the seventeenth century, of twenty-five town councillors only thirteen were Swedes, the rest Dutchmen, Germans or Scots.'

One of the more successful Scottish merchants to settle in Gothenburg was Colin Campbell, who became a Director of the 'Svenska-Ostindiska' Company. Thomas Erskine, His Majesty's consul for the protection of trade at Gothenburg, was co-owner of two vessels registered at Alloa in 1786. These were the *Christina,* 148 tons, originally built in Sweden and now owned by Erskine with his partners in trade John Higgins, merchant of Newch, and Andrew Scott, shipmaster of Airth, and the *Villa Nova*, 312¾ tons, originally built in the Gulf of Finland and now co-owned with James Spittal, shipmaster, with whom Erskine was also involved in trade. Both these vessels were re-registered in 1787 at which stage Erskine was no longer a co-owner.

The smuggling was carried on in both directions because on 22 June 1636 a resolution was passed in the Riks-Rad that the goods 'for which certain 'Skottars' had not paid duty should be confiscated, and the would-be smugglers moreover mulcted in the sum of 200 thaler, payable to the Church of St Jacob'.

On the southern shores of the Baltic, in Lithuania, Memel was a Swedish possession in the eighteenth century. In August 1790 Oliphant, the tidesurveyor from Bo'ness, seized out of the ship *Rebecca*, Robert Paterson master, from Memel goods, including spirits, tea and china, valued at £22 13s 9d. The Board instructed the collector at Alloa to forewarn the merchants involved that if this happened again 'we will order the vessel to be prosecuted to condemnation and the owners and master are to be informed that if the like transgression shall be again committed they will not to expect any levity'. According to the Alloa shipping registers the sole owner of the *Rebecca* was Charles Virtue, merchant of Alloa - she was captured by the French on 22 May 1796.

The Story of Vessels Pretended Bound to the Isle of Man

(i) From: The Representation and Memorial of the Commissioners of His Majesty's Customs & Excise in Scotland to the Right Honourable the Lords Commissioners of His Majesty's Treasury dated 24 December 1764. [see comment in Figure 2 about Basil Cochrane]

'However convenient this Island may be for exporting and running goods to the coasts of Great Britain and Ireland, yet there is another advantage the smugglers draw from its situation. For at present the greatest part of the vessels loaded from Holland, Gothenburg etc. with uncustomed and high-dutied goods, intended for the east and northern ports of Britain, take out clearances and bills of lading for the Isle of Man, then run for the east coast, and if not discovered, unload their cargoes; but if they are found hovering, and are boarded by any of His Majesty's ships, they produce fictitious bills of lading, and consignments; and as they are really and truly but little out of their thus pretended course, they often save themselves under the pretence of being bound to the Isle of Man.

'Formerly vessels loaded in Holland etc and intending to run their cargoes on the east side of Great Britain, took up clearances for some port in Norway. But as nothing but contrary winds, stress of weather or want of provisions could be pleaded in excuse of their being found within the limits of a port, or the forbidden distance of the shore, they have changed their practice, and pretend they are bound for the Isle of Man; which is found by experience to be fatal to the revenue, and more safe and convenient for the illicit practices of the smugglers'.

(ii) From a letter from the collector at Perth to the collector at Dundee dated 2 October 1760.

'Thomas Young, master of the ship *Catherine* of Dundee, from Gothenburg, having reported seven hogsheads of brandy for the Isle of Man, the Commissioners ... directed us to allow the master to sail on his pretended voyage, unless he shall make a longer stay in port than necessary, in which case they order the brandy to be carried to the warehouse for security of the duties. The above-mentioned ship sailed from this place this morning and, as it is not impossible but the master may make a longer stay at your port than necessary, we thought it our duty to let you know what the Commissioners pleasure is, if that case shall happen'.

CHAPTER THREE: PRETENDED VOYAGES

'The surveyor having represented to us that sometimes ships from foreign parts put into this port (by stress of weather or want of provisions, as is alleged by the masters) with all their hatches chalked, pretending to be bound for Norway and other foreign parts, that the masters refuse to allow him to make open their hatches that he may survey their holds, he prays to be informed if he may legally make open the hatches of such ships and take an account of what's in their holds'. [Collector at Montrose to the Board 29 July 1735]

There is evidence of the concept of the 'pretended' voyage from both sides. On 22 June 1726 Bailie John Steuart, merchant in Inverness, wrote to Alexander Todd, master of the *Catherine* of Leith, 'You are to proceed without loss of time to St Martins, and you are there to address yourself to Mr Alexander Gordon, merchant there, and deliver him the letter herewith given you, who will furnish you with what quantity of salt your ship can take in, with the liquor which Mr Robert Gordon of Bordeaux is to ship for our account, which will be about 12 tuns. Mr Gordon is to provide you in foreign clearances. You'll endeavour to get as much [liquor] as possible. Notice that when, please God, you return, in case you meet or is taken up to any custom house yachts, to declare yourself <u>bound for Riga in the Baltic</u>; and be sure you be well furnished with clearances accordingly'. [see Chapter Two, Figure 4 and Table II]

In 1770 William Rutherford, mate on board the *Princess Caroline* revenue cruiser commanded by Captain John Read, took into Montrose the *Peggy* of Stromness, Jerom Setter master. According to a letter from the collector dated 30 June the master 'appeared in this office this day about eleven o'clock and gave in the enclosed intimation, narrating that he had sailed from Rotterdam upon the 23rd inst with a cargo of tea, spirits and other merchandise [including tobacco, playing cards and cotton handkerchiefs] with which he pretended to be bound for the port of Bergen in Norway. That by contrary winds, since the morning of the 26th he was forced upon the coast of Scotland and that on Monday the

28th about two o'clock afternoon, being off the Tod Head [north of Montrose], 10 leagues distant from land, he was boarded by William Rutherford'. On 7 July it was reported that the *Princess Caroline*, 'together with her prize the *Peggy*', had sailed for Leith.

The next part of the story comes from the Skaill papers in Orkney. The vessel's owners, William Watt junior & Co, merchants, employed Walter Ferguson, writer in Edinburgh, to defend their case in the court of exchequer. Their letter dated 29 September 1770, replying to his list of eight queries about the *Peggy*, is particularly interesting.

'1st. The Charter Party [see tailpiece] to Bergen must be insisted upon, and all the weight given to it, it can bear. 2nd. There is little doubt that the winds which carried the *Peggy* from Holland to the coast of Scotland (viz. from east to south-south-east) might have carried the vessel much nearer to the coast of Norway than where she was found, so that this point is certainly unfavourable'. The captain had reckoned he was 25 leagues further east 'whether this was owing to his inattention in not giving proper allowances for the tides or for the swell or surf of the sea, which falls strongly from the eastward, the winds having been long from that quarter, or was his mistake occasioned by fog, it is not easy to say. On Saturday the 23rd of June the sloop came from Rotterdam to sea. On the 24th they left sight of the coast of Holland, the little wind they had easterly. On the 25th in the afternoon the fog came on and continued as thick as perhaps ever was known and without any intermission until [the] Friday morning that they were carried in to Montrose. During all this period they had not the least assistance from sun or stars ...

'5th. There was no agreement with the crew for wages to Bergen nor indeed was there any agreement for wages on the commencement of the voyage. The master told the crew before they sailed from Orkney that the sloop was first to go to Leith to discharge yarn etc. and from thence to Newcastle to discharge the remaining part of her cargo and from thence to Rotterdam with coals, where they were to seek a freight. This was made no secret in Orkney. It is very common in this country to leave the men's wages to be settled when the voyage is finished, the more so when the respective ports of delivery cannot previously be condescended upon. The men were indeed told both by Mr Murdoch and Captain Setter, the master, that they were to go to Bergen and from thence to Orkney. Whatever might have been their own opinion with respect to the destination of the voyage they never heard any thing suggested to the contrary ...

'7th. The papers given [to] or taken by Rutherford were the charter party and bill of lading. Nor was there any other letters or papers on board except Mr Murdoch's letter to **Mr Wallace of Bergen** [see the *Mary* of Montrose in the section on Supply of Hands]... His orders were to apply to Mr Murdoch to get a freight and it may be easily guessed what passed between them on the subject. Indeed the captain had a letter from one of the concerneds, advising that if he got a freight at Rotterdam for any foreign place he should call at the island of Westray, being the northernmost island in the country, for letters to carry to his friends abroad. But this letter Setter declares nobody ever saw besides himself and that he burned it the morning he was carried into Montrose'.

The trial was to have taken place on 27 June 1771 but was withdrawn that very morning because of the conflicting evidence about the exact position of the vessel when she was seized.

The bulk of the information on pretended voyages comes from the custom house letter-books. In March 1735 the collector at Dundee reported to the Board that the *Isobel*, James Abercrombie master [see tailpiece to Chapter Five], the *Alison*, Patrick Williamson master and the *David*, Robert Maver master, were all ready to sail 'the first fair wind' and 'as it's very reasonable to believe these cargoes are intended to be landed on this coast either about St Andrews or the Red Head' he had forewarned the collectors at Montrose and Anstruther of their 'pretending to be bound to Norway'. The cargoes included white wine, black soap and 'uncustomed or high duty goods'. The ships were still in port on 28 March and the *Princess Caroline* revenue cruiser was lying at South Ferry and 'her boat every day at sea when the weather will permit'.

The *David*, Robert Maver master, was back on 1 October from Campvere, laden with tobacco, brandy and soap, again pretending bound for Norway. 'I'm informed that her cargo belongs to St Andrews and is intended to be run thereabouts. The ship being under burthen, I shall take care the master gives a hovering bond [which was basically an undertaking not to hover off the coast]'. On 7 October the Board directed the collector to 'order the tidesurveyor with his boat and crew to go and station himself at or near St Andrews the better to watch the motions of this vessel'. Whatever happened on this voyage, Maver was expected from Norway in December 'with a cargo of brandy belonging to Arbroath and Montrose'.

Apart from stress of weather, vessels 'pretended bound' had other excuses why they should need to call into a British port or come close on shore while in theory on an overseas journey. The main reasons were repairs, including torn sails and leaks, want of provisions and crew or to obtain instructions from their merchants as to where the cargo was to be unloaded, or a combination of these.

Stress of weather and provisions

On 30 January 1730 the *Eagle* of Montrose, Robert Beattie master, a sloop about 30 tons burden, laden with wine, brandy, one case of white powder and two pieces of cambrics from Bordeaux 'pretending to be bound for Bergen' came into harbour 'being disabled at sea by bad weather and want of provisions, as is alleged. The master this day entered into bond to discharge his cargo at Bergen aforesaid under penalty of £3,500 sterling'.

Five years later, on 17 March 1735 Captain Bowen, commander of one of the English revenue cruisers, took the *Eagle*, William Beattie master, from Rotterdam into Holy Island with two hundred and seven ankers, twenty-one barrels, twenty-one boxes, twenty-six paper parcels, thirty-three hogsheads, twenty-five bundles, twenty dry ware casks eight bags and fourteen matts of goods on board, all or part of which he suspected she intended to run. Captain Starks of the *Princess Caroline* revenue cruiser and the tidesurveyor at Dundee had sailed upon a cruise with their boats 'in order to interrupt that vessel and they have directions (so long as wind and weather will permit) to keep backward and forward betwixt Montrose and the mouth of the river [Tay]'. In the meantime she had run the whole of her cargo except for thirty-three hogsheads of linseed, a few matts of flax and a some young trees, which she reported when she arrived at Montrose.

According to the collector 'We have interrogate the master if he was in Holy Island and what was become of the rest of the goods Captain Bowen found aboard him there. He acknowledges ... that one of Captain Bowen's men came aboard his sloop but that he did not go down to his hold ... and in short refuses that he [Beattie] had any more goods aboard than what he brought in here. James Duncan, one of our tidesmen, being toward Lunan Bay looking for ships informed us that he saw a sloop that day lying off the bay with some boats about her, which he took to be Mr Beattie's sloop, upon which we put all our officers on their guard and watched the town and river all that night. About midnight two officers went out with a party of soldiers to prevent as much as possible the boats landing the goods and to search the country but are not yet returned'.

The *Eagle* was back in Montrose in April 1735, Patrick Ogilvie master, from Cadiz with '800 bushels Spanish salt, six chests oranges and lemons and a parcel of cork for this country and seventeen half hogsheads of wine for Bergen in Norway. The fruit and cork were landed here and the vessel proceeded to Aberdeen (having two of our tidesmen on board) where she discharged her salt and on the 15th instant sailed from thence with the wine on her pretended voyage to Norway. Last night, being the 19th inst, came into the port in ballast. We have interrogate Mr Ogilvie, the master, what was become of the wine. He told us he discharged it at Norway. We then required him to report his ship from thence but he said he was only in part master for that voyage and that he had nothing to do with the ship after she had discharged her wine at Norway. William Beattie, the sole owner of the vessel, was with him at Norway and took the charge of her home. Upon which we sent for Mr Beattie who has reported his ship from Norway in ballast. But as this expeditious trip is a little surprising to us we thought proper to lay the same before your Honours'.

On 19 June 1749 the *Christian & Magdalene*, William Norris master [see Chapter Two] , was forced up the Forth 'by stress of weather and want of provisions but has offered no proof of his distress'. Two days later the collector reported 'We understand he had lost his boat and spent a sail and yesterday morning. Having got a boat and his sail repaired he proceeded down the Firth with only one officer on board, having no more off duty at the time.'

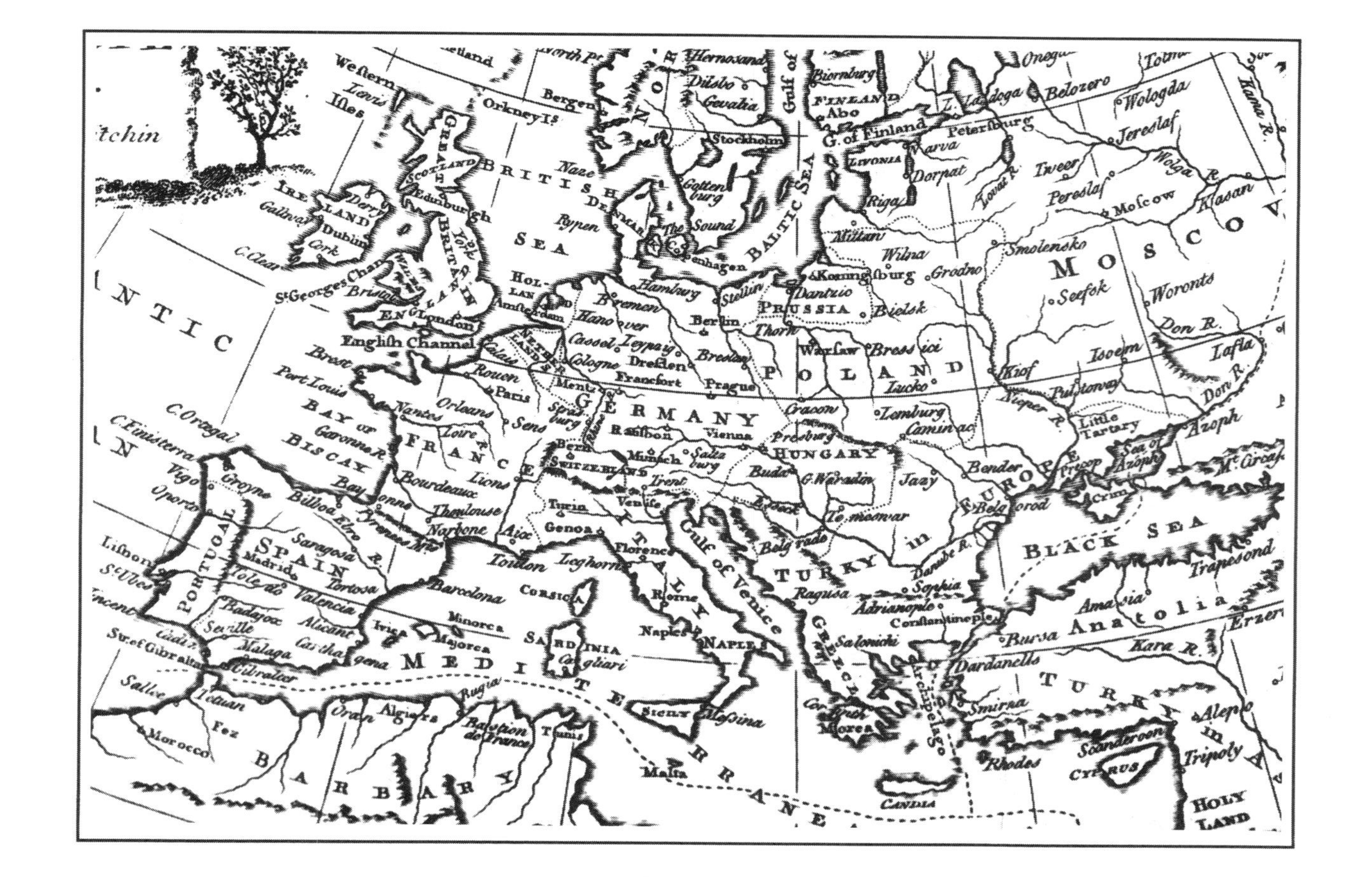

Western Isles
Orkney Is.
Bergen
Hernosand
Dilsbo
Gevalia
Stockholm
Gulf of
Biornburg
FINLAND
Abo
G. of Finland
L. Ladoga
Belozero
Onega
Wologda
Petersburg
Jereslaf
Narva
LIVONIA
Dorpat
Riga
Tweer
Wolga R.
Klasan
Pereslaf
Moscow
IRELAND
Derry
Gallway
Dublin
Cork
C. Clear
SCOTLAND
Edinburgh
GREAT BRITAIN
York
BRITISH SEA
Naze
DENMARK
Rypen
Gottenburg
The Sound
Copenhagen
BALTIC SEA
Mittau
Wilna
Grodno
Smolensko
MOSCOV
Seefok
Woronts
Don R.
St. Georges Chan.
Bristol
ENGLAND
London
HOLLAND
Amsterdam
Hamburg
Bremen
Hanover
Stettin
Koningsburg
Dantzic
PRUSSIA
Bielsk
Berlin
Thorn
English Channel
NETHERLANDS
Cassel
Leipsig
Cologne
Dresden
Breslaw
Warsaw
Bressici
POLAND
Kiof
Isoem
Lafla
Brest
Port Louis
BAY of BISCAY
Garonne R.
Rouen
Paris
Mentz
Francfort
Prague
Lucko
Pultowa
Nieper R.
Don R.
C. Ortegal
C. Finisterra
Nantes
Orleans
Loire R.
Sens
Strasburg
GERMANY
Ratisbon
Vienna
Cracow
Lemburg
Caminiec
Little Tartary
Azoph
FRANCE
Bern
SWITZERLAND
Munich
Saltzburg
Presburg
HUNGARY
Bender
Precop
Sea of Azoph
Vigo
Oporto
Groyne
Billboa
Ebro R.
Bayonne
Pyrenees M.
Bourdeaux
Lions
Trent
Buda
G. Waradin
Jassy
EUROPE
Belgorod
Crim
Thoulouse
Narbone
Turin
Venice
Temeswar
BLACK SEA
PORTUGAL
Lisbon
St. Ubes
SPAIN
Madrid
Saragosa
Toledo
Tortosa
Valencia
Aix
Genoa
Toulon
Leghorn
Florence
Gulf of Venice
Belgrade
TURKY in
Danube R.
Sophia
Trapesond
Barcelona
CORSICA
Rome
ITALY
Ragusa
Adrianople
Constantinople
Amasia
Anatolia
Badajox
Seville
Alicant
Carthagena
Ivica
Minorca
Majorca
SARDINIA
Cagliari
Naples
NAPLES
GREECE
Salonichi
Bursa
Kara R.
Erzerum
Cadiz
Str. of Gibraltar
Malaga
Gibraltar
MEDITERRANEAN
Dardanells
TURKY
Sallee
Tetuan
Oran
Algiers
Bugia
Bastion de France
Tunis
SICILY
Messina
Corinth
Morea
Archipelago
Smirna
Aleppo
Morocco
Fez
BARBARY
Malta
Rhodes
Scanderoon
CYPRUS
Tripoly
CANDIA
HOLY LAND

Figure 6. Europe in the Eighteenth Century

The following is a list of the European countries, islands and ports mentioned most frequently in the custom house letter-books for the Montrose to Dunbar area:

France: Bordeaux, Cette, Crosweck, Hlena, St Martins
Germany: Bremen, Emden, Hamburgh
Gibraltar
Holland: Amsterdam, Campvere, Flushing, Middleburgh, Ostend, Rotterdam
Livorno: Riga
Madeira
Norway: Bergen, Christiansands, Dram, Drunton, Fleenflower, Mandale, Moss
Poland: Dantzick, Pillau
Portugal: Lisbon, Oporto
Russia: Archangel, St Petersburg
Spain: Bilbao, Cadiz, Malaga, St Lucas, St Sebastian
Sweden: Gothenburg, Memel, Redmen, Stockholm

Research for this chapter included the analysis of nearly 50 pretended voyages described in the letter-books. Over 50% [27] of these involved voyages supposedly to Bergen, which was a conveniently located port to the north-east of Scotland. Because of the intensity of apparent 'pretended bound' voyages, it is surprising to discover that a vessel ever arrived there. In this context the collector of Montrose's comment about the return to port of the two tidesmen who had been boarded on the *Friendship* of Crail, John Chiene master, is of interest: 'they say when they left Bergen the *Friendship's* cargo was not all unload'.

Other northern and eastern destinations of these voyages were: Christiansands, Drunton, Stockholm, Copenahgen and Dantzick. On occasions the voyages were in the opposite direction, when Campvere [see Chapter Six] and Lisbon were favourites. Then there were also the Manx and Irish destinations.

The vessel sailed from Campvere in December 1750 and went into Kincardine Road 'load chiefly with prohibited and high duty goods and pretending to be bound for Norway. Enclosed is a copy of the cargo as he [the master] has delivered on this day at the custom house with the intimation of his pretended intended voyage. The surveyor boarded her in Kincardine Road and attended her into the harbour of Alloa and has looked into the cargo, as much as possible, and as far as he can judge the goods in the three first lines are of quality viz. the hogsheads and half hogsheads are wine, the ankers and half ankers are spirits, the forty-three casks fruits and the boxes and bundles tea, cambrics and lawns. The surveyor says that the foresail and jib are so spent that the vessel could not safely proceed upon her voyage till they were refitted. How far it is probable that [she] was bound to Norway at this season of the year I leave to your Honours to judge ... I am well persuaded that the cargo belongs to merchants in Stirling, Alloa and Airth and by the vessel being discovered soon after she came to Kincardine Road the fraud intended has been prevented. I heartily wish a method could be fallen upon to discourage this kind of trade and for my part I see no other but to seize the tea and spirits upon every such occasion'.

The *Nelly*, Thomas Webster master, arrived at Montrose on Saturday, 1 September 1770, from St Lucas in Spain with about 2,000 bushels of Spanish salt and other goods. 'This ship was boarded before she came into this harbour by an excise boat, belonging to Mr Henderson's vessel ... We have required the officers of excise here to do duty on board of the ship along with the officers of the customs, in respect of the large quantity of brandy that is on board, and have examined upon oath James Nicol and Henry Paton, two of the sailors ... who deponed they left St Lucas on the 17th July last and have been since that time at sea, occasioned by contrary winds, and that they were in want of waters, bread and firing and [had] sprung the head of their foremast, which obliged them to come in for a supply of these necessaries and to get their mast mended'.

On 8 September the Montrose collector forewarned Anstruther, Dundee and Aberdeen 'The ship *Nelly* of this place a square-sterned brigantine, having on board a cargo of Spanish salt, twenty-four hogsheads brandy, nineteen hogsheads wine and a barrel of soap ... is ready to sail on her pretended voyage to Dantzick'. The vessel, apparently from Christiansands, came into Montrose in October accompanied by Duncan Aire [commander of the *Royal Charlotte* excise yacht] and his boat's crew. The master reported his ship. During the unloading Mr Aire seized sixteen half hogsheads Spanish white wine and forty ankers and six half ankers brandy, one anker, two half ankers and one stone bottle rum, three ankers and five half ankers geneva, one anker wine and two ankers clove waters. This time there is no clue as to the intended destination of the vessel. Had she been to Dantzick and then Christiansands in the time available? It seems strange that she should have had such a similar cargo on board. And why was she bringing the Spanish white wine from Sweden instead of Spain? [see the story of the *Margaret* of Dundee]

By 1775 the Board was demanding proof of stress of weather. On more than one occasion the collector was instructed to consult with 'shipmasters of character who knew the proper course for Bergen from Holland and who from his journal can prove the state of the winds and weather on the east coast of Scotland' on the particular dates. But this was not as easy as it sounded. 'We are sorry to find there is not a shipmaster either here at the port or at any of our creeks at home just now proper to serve for the purpose you want'.

Sometimes the distress was genuine. In June 1749 the collector at Aberdeen received a letter from the tidesmen at Peterhead about the *Thomas* of Kincardine, William Nicol master, from Rotterdam 'pretending bound for Bergen'. On 14 June the mate brought a certificate to the custom house 'under hand of Dr Gordon of Peterhead attesting the master's not being able to travel'. As the mate 'could not condescend on the quality of the cargo and as master nor mate made no proof of distress' the collector ordered the tidewaiter to stop the vessel. On 17 June William Nicol gave in a protest taken by James Mullikins, his supercargo, saying that they had put into Peterhead 'by reason of a strong northerly wind'. They had an affidavit from William Sim, master of the *Janey* of Alloa, and James Murray, his mate, stating that Nicol was in great distress at sea for want of provisions and had got from William Sim two ankers of water, three dozen biscuit and some coals and that they were put into Peterhead by a strong wind from the north as well.

In November 1765 the *Mary* of Kinghorn, John Dalrymple master, from Gothenburg loaded with tea 'pretending bound for Campvere' went into Peterhead, having lost her mast in a storm at sea. On her arrival at that port she filled with water and sank.

Provisions

On 30 May 1725 Captain Hamilton brought into Montrose the *Friendship* of Crail, John Chiene master. Having headed for Crail to consult with his owners, Chiene returned to Montrose. The collector reported 'He pretends that having been five or six weeks on her passage from St Martins [she] fell short of provisions in the Channel of England, where he put in to Cowes in order to be supplied. But could not procure any credit there to buy victuals for her voyage so that he was obliged to call on this coast before he could proceed to Norway for want of the same. The wind blowing hard at south-west it was as much as he could do to get in to Lunan Bay on Sunday morning the 30th past, when Captain Hamilton found him riding at anchor. On the other hand Captain Hamilton says he had an information some time ago that the above vessel was to be on the coast and offers to prove that on Friday morning, the 28th past, he saw the ship in St Andrews Bay with a boat on board but could not then come up with her (this Mr Chiene positively denies of his being at all in St Andrews Bay) and likewise when he found him lying in Lunan Bay he had a quantity of peas and bread (which Mr Chiene says he bought at Cowes) on board, which Mr Hamilton judged sufficient to have carried him to Norway, the wind then blowing fair for that coast'.

In July the collector reported that the two tidesmen who had attended the *Friendship* to Norway had returned to their duty. 'Enclosed we send your Honours the certificates they have brought from thence of their having delivered the vessel with her cargo into the hands of the officers at Bergen. They found a vessel belonging to Arbroath coming home and got their passage on board her but they say when they left Bergen the *Friendship*'s cargo was not all unload. These tidesmen are demanding their charges therefore we beg to know how much your Honours will be pleased to allow them a day during their absence. They were boarded her the 11th June and returned this day [16 July 1725]'. More is known about the ownership of the *Friendship* than is usual at that date. According to the collector at Perth, the *George* of Leith was sold and renamed the *Friendship* in 1722. The new owners were David Aikenhead, merchant in Edinburgh, James Lesley, David Lesley, Henry Crawford, John Adamson of Crail and Anstruther, merchants, and John Chiene, shipmaster. More details of the smuggling merchants are given in Chapter Seven.

In May 1730 the collector of Dundee forewarned the collectors of Montrose, Aberdeen, Kirkcaldy and Anstruther about the *Gloucester*, James Miller master [see Chapter Two]. This snow, 60 tons burthen, had a cargo of salt in bulk, 14¼ tuns of wine, four hundred and thirty ankers of brandy, one cask of prunes and one cask of indigo from St Martins, 'as the master pretends bound for Bergen in Norway, being put in to the river (for provisions as is alleged) and to sail with the first fair wind, we having reason to believe she intends to run all or part of the cargo on the coast we thought proper to acquaint you herewith to prevent the clandestine landing any part of her cargo'.

Two suspicious vessels arrived at Montrose in December 1720. On 24 December the collector wrote to the Board 'last night the *Middletoun* of Newcastle, Francis Pemberton master, came here from Bordeaux bound for Copenhagen. The master says he is load with wine and brandy in pipes and hogsheads. There's eight men and two boys besides the master and his wife, who all appear to be in good health [customs were also responsible for quarantine regulations]. The master pretends they were obliged to put in here ... having broke their main yard and had not above three days provisions on board but how soon he is provided in what necessaries he wants he will again put to sea. We have allowed no boats to go on board ... the vessel is pink-wise built about 70 tons burthen'. She sailed on 27 December.

Then on 28 December the *Margaret* of Dundee, Andrew Anderson master, arrived. 'The master pretends he is come from Bordeaux and load with wine and brandy bound for Bergen. He says he was forced in here having been long at sea and short of provisions, lost his boat and topmast and that how soon he is supplied in these things he'll put to sea again. The vessel is broad-sterned with one mast, of about 30 tons burthen, with two men and two boys besides the master. Their cargo belongs to merchants in Dundee, as the master gives out. We have caused sentries to be placed to hinder boats going to her or coming from her'. There is the story of another *Margaret* later in the chapter.

Supply of Hands

In August 1755 the *Two Brothers* of Dundee, Patrick Ogilvie master, arrived in the river Tay on his way from Stockholm to Lisbon. His cargo included deals, iron and tar plus brandy, tea, silk, muslin, cotton handkerchiefs, china tea cups and saucers, a teapot, slop bowl and two plates. These were all brought to the warehouse as a seizure by Ambrose Starks, tidesurveyor, who had boarded her on the 14th with four tidesmen and two boatmen and attended her all that night and the next morning. The master's reason for coming into the Firth was 'for a supply of hands, three of his men being pressed by a tender on the coast'. By September 'the merchants considering the danger that might attend the voyage at this critical juncture [an undeclared war had started with France] propose that the master shall report the said vessel here and enter and pay the duty for the deals, iron, tar and silk and to have the muslin, cotton handkerchiefs and china reported for foreign parts'.

On 26 June 1770 the collector at Montrose reported that the *Mary*, Alexander Pearson master, from Rotterdam 'appeared before this town on Saturday night last and continued all Sunday hovering on this coast and at length came into the harbour yesterday about midday. This day about half an hour after eleven the master came to this office and presented an intimation ... that he had twelve hogsheads geneva on board consigned to Messrs **Wallace & Co** merchants in Bergen [the same 'destination' as the cargo of the *Peggy* of Stromness] ... The reason he assigned for coming in was to complete his complement of men, some of whom had run away, which obliged him to put in here, as well as to repair his ship, offering to prove these facts ... there is no mark [on the hogsheads] mentioned in the intimation'. The Board instructed the collector to find his own proof of the facts. 'We examined severally upon oath Robert Durward, Archibald Greig and James Monro, three of the sailors, who all in one voice deposed that they were engaged here by Captain Pearson about ten or eleven months ago to go on a voyage from thence to Charlestown on board of said ship *Mary* and to return to Cowes and from thence to Rotterdam. Captain Pearson insisted to engage them from Rotterdam to Norway, which they refused as they wanted to come to Montrose. One of the crew left them at Rotterdam, in whose place he got a sailor out of a ship which was lying there, belonging to this town, who came hither with the ship. There was no other goods taken on board at Rotterdam but the twelve hogsheads aforesaid but to whom they belong they do not know. The vessel was so leaky on her voyage from Rotterdam hither that she was obliged to be pumped twice every watch and now the carpenters are employed upon her in driving new trenails, the old ones being rotten, and caulking of her. They further deponed that they are not going on the voyage to Norway in the said ship.

'We never doubted but the sailors would support upon their oaths the information given in by the master and therefore we examined no more of the crew, as these three were in our apprehension as likely to tell the truth as any of the rest. We are humbly of opinion that the twelve hogsheads are the property of the master and mate, as what is called portage [the freighters often allowed the master and crew to have their own 'adventures' on board], from the mark upon each of them being DO [as observed by the comptroller and clerk when they inspected the cargo], which are the initials of the name of David Ogilvie, mate ... upon the collector's asking the master why he did not come into the river immediately upon his arrival he declared that the reason of his cruising on the coast from [the] Saturday night that he appeared on it all Sunday and part of Monday was because he expected to be employed on a voyage to Norway to bring home a cargo of timber for the building of the bridge over the water of North Esk and in that event he was not to come to this river at all but to proceed directly to Norway. This shows evidently that he could have gone to Norway without either more men or his ship being repaired and consequently his intention was for smuggling the spirits. The burthen of this vessel is 200 tons upwards'. On 14 July the twelve hogsheads were secured in the king's warehouse for the duties.

Double Entry

Double entries were one of the more concerning aspects of potential pretended voyages. In April 1750 the *Crown* of Airth, David Gray master, from Hlena sailed up the Forth with wine for Alloa and brandy, tea, tobacco and tobacco stalks for Norway. In June 1755 the *Merry Plowman* of Dundee, James Smith master, reported a cargo of salt and wine from Cadiz for Dundee and four hogsheads of brandy and four boxes of white soap for Dantzick. Once the salt and wine were discharged, Mr Palmer, the merchant, proposed to ship off the salt in the same ship for the said port of Dantzick'. The Board's instructions can be guessed because in August the collector forewarned Aberdeen, Montrose and Anstruther that 'The *Merry Plowman* of Dundee a square sterned brigantine about 55 tons James Smith master lies ready to sail from this harbour for Dantzick with a cargo of salt lately imported here and four hogsheads of brandy and four boxes of castile soap reported here in the ship from Cadiz for Dantzick' .

The *Elizabeth* of Dundee

Elizabeth of Dundee was a common name for a vessel on pretended voyages, though it is unclear whether or not it was the same vessel on all occasions.

The *Elizabeth* arrived at Dundee in December 1735. She was laden with 'Holland' goods from Rotterdam 'pretending bound for Norway'. The master had given a hovering bond at Anstruther. 'I am well informed that part of the goods belong to this place but the bulk of the cargo to Inverness. The pretence of lying here a few days is to repair her sails, which were split at sea, and as I have not the utmost confidence in many of our tidesmen I have placed two of the best of them and continued the two belonging to Anstruther as checks on one another for a few days, which is the most he shall be permitted to stay, the Act of Parliament [about hovering] having left that to the discretion of the officers of the customs'. On 9 January 1736 the Board agreed to the collector's proposal of placing 'two trusty tidesmen on board ... and in order to repay their charges you are to advance them £3 each, giving them strict orders to see her to her foreign port. And in case of any delay or opposition in proceeding on the voyage to inform us of every circumstance and to endeavour to get proof of the fact'.

In October 1754 the *Elizabeth* of Dundee, Robert Leslie master, put into Whitby by stress of weather, pretending to be bound for Bergen with a cargo of tobacco, spirits etc. The Board instructed the collector at Dunbar 'as there is cause to suspect the cargo is designed to be run upon this coast we direct you to put all the officers in your district on their guard and in case they shall be found on the coast ... you are to lay your hands upon her acquainting us for our further orders'.

The *Elizabeth*, David Boyter master, between 40 and 50 tons burthen, arrived at Dundee from Rotterdam in April 1755 and 'the master offered to make a double report viz. of linseed flax and other entrable goods for this place and a parcel of stone bottles, boxes, bundles and small casks for Bergen in Norway. But as we suspect these goods pretended for Norway are prohibited goods we have delayed taking the report until we advised your Honours thereof and have your directions there anent'. The directions must have been to let the vessel sail because in May it was reported that William Geddes, supervisor, and Joseph Peck, officer of excise, seized out of the *Elizabeth* 'a considerable quantity of spirits in small casks and stone bottles, which they lodged in the king's warehouse here and which is since condemned by order from the Board of Excise before the justices, which spirits and customable goods contained in the enclosed return they seized in consequence of an information they had on the ship'.

Margaret of Dundee

Although there were also several *Margarets* of Dundee [see the Provisions section], this story refers to one particular vessel. In May 1760 the collector at Dundee forewarned Inverness, Aberdeen, Montrose and Anstruther about the *Margaret* of Dundee, William Cooper master, supposed bound with goods for John Smith, merchant in Christiansands, including red and white French wine, white Spanish wine, brandy, geneva, rum and vinegar. She was described as 'a square-sterned brigantine with two standing topsails, about 50 tons burthen'. Captain Alexander Read, commander of the *Prince of Wales* revenue sloop, attended her off the coast.

On 6 August she returned to Dundee from Norway on her way to Perth with deals and timber. Most of the wine and spirits were still on board and the master reported that these were to be taken to the Isle of Man. He sailed from Newburgh with two Perth tidesmen, James Quarrier and John Cairns, on board. This time the collectors at Dunbar, Dundee, Montrose, Anstruther, Aberdeen and Inverness were forewarned together with Captains Read and Kyd of the revenue cruisers. The *Margaret* went as far as at North Ferry Road, back in the Dundee precinct, where Cooper waited for about fourteen days during which time he tried 'to purchase the connivance of these officers' in smuggling part of the cargo. When this failed, he put them ashore. Early next morning he was boarded by the boatmen at Ferry Pantoncraigs, who found nothing but ballast on board and so brought her back to Dundee. The collector added 'PS We are further informed by the boatmen that they were several times fired at from the vessel near the mouth of the Tay to prevent their boarding her'.

In September the collector at Perth reported 'we have not been able to catch the least hint that might lead us to suspect who are the owners of these goods and the result of all our enquiries is a moral certainty that they do not belong to any person residing in this place. If it is considered what strong grounds there are for believing that the wines and spirits were first of all brought to Dundee from Holland and that the rest of the cargo at that time belonged wholly to merchants of Dundee and were actually entered and landed there, we are persuaded it will not appear surprising that our endeavours to find out the proprietors of these goods in this town should prove fruitless.

'The only persons within our district who we have been able to learn had any dealings with the master of this vessel are John and Thomas Anderson, to whom the wood and three tierces of vinegar were consigned, and even these goods we are assured at the very time when the vessel was first entered here had not been commissioned by the merchants but were sold or pledged to them by the master after he came to this port'. In October 1760 the sheriff of Forfar was sent two writs of capias for the arrest of Robert Geary, merchant in Dundee, and William Cooper, the master of the *Margaret*.

Not all the pretended bound voyages involved long overseas trips. Some of them were part of the coasting trade. According to a petition from the master, dated August 1775, 'I sailed with my vessel, the *Betsey* of Leith, from Greenock the 26th July last with a cargo of beef, iron and staves for Leith and was yesterday, the wind blowing hard from south-west, obliged to put into this port'. She was rummaged by the comptroller who found seven casks of butter hidden among the staves.

He also tried to seize several bottles of geneva. One of these contained about 7 gallons. 'This the comptroller handed up to James Miln, tidesman there on duty, from the cabin, which immediately was broke to pieces with a handspike, while Miln was holding it, and the spirits all lost, by one of the crew of the vessel'. Neither the master nor crew would name this man. The collector wrote 'We beg liberty to observe that the master's obstinacy in refusing to part with or suffer the geneva to go out of the ship till Mr Kennedy was obliged to get a party of dragoons to his assistance and then in refusing to tell the man's name who broke the large bottle is blamable, the more especially as he told us that he is a master of one of His Majesty's ships of war and that as such he is presently on half pay'.

The significance of the party of dragoons being present is discussed in Chapter Ten. The tailpiece to this chapter describes a typical charter party.

The Story of the *Benefactor's* Charter Party and Bond

A charter party was the agreement between the freighters [who were not necessarily the owners] and the master of a vessel for a particular voyage. The charter party for the *Peggy* of Stromness mentioned earlier in the chapter was from Orkney-Leith-Newcastle-Rotterdam-Bergen-Orkney, on paper.

On 7 October 1710 a charter party was drawn up between various merchants in Edinburgh and Robert Kincaid, master of the *Benefactor* of Bo'ness. According to this Kincaid was to let his vessel to the merchants. She was currently lying at Leith, where she was to load with victuals and other goods 'and immediately upon receipt of wind and weather serving to sail' to go to Bergen in Norway. There she was to unload her cargo and take on board deals and other goods and wind and weather serving again, return to Leith.

Attached to the charter party is the following bond, which is of more interest in the context of smuggling:

'We Patrick Chalmers, William Cochran, John Hutchison, John Hislop and John Parkhill, merchants in Edinburgh, and Andrew Wilson, writer in Bo'ness, for as much as we have freighted the *Benefactor* of Bo'ness, whereof Robert Kincaid is master, from this to Bergen in Norway, where she is to load what goods we or our constituents there shall ship as the Charter Party betwixt Robert Kincaid and us of this date bears. And in regard we design (if opportunity offer) to ship at Bergen a parcel of brandies or other liquors, which cannot be admitted to entry, not being allowed by law to be imported. And that the shipping thereof will endanger the ship. Therefore and to the effect Robert Kincaid and the owners of the ship may no ways suffer or lose by any undertaking or proposal of ours we hereby oblige us and our heirs ... that in case the ship shall be seized by any of the officers of Her Majesty's customs for importing in her goods not allowed to be imported or she be exchequered therefore to content and pay to Robert Kincaid for the behoof of his owners the sum of three hundred pounds sterling, as the value thereof, and to reimburse the master of all charge he may be at in case of the ship's being seized and his capitulate with the seizure makers and to free the master of all hazard he may incur there through any manner of ways, consenting to the registration hereof in the books of counsel and session or others competent to have the strength of an doit interponed thereto that letters of horning on six days charge and others needful may pass hereupon in form as affairs and these constitutes'.

CHAPTER FOUR: SMUGGLED GOODS

'In cases of seizures of spirits you are to endeavour by all means in your power to discern the persons engaged in the business. They must be immediately arrested and taken before a justice of the peace to find security for the penalty or put in prison ... I have no doubt but there will be a great deal of smuggling this winter so I beg your attentions to those matters sending us an express when a seizure (where any of the parties are detected) does happen'. [From the Board to the outports 4 December 1807]

A wide range of goods were smuggled into the Montrose to Dunbar area during the eighteenth century. The following list has been produced from the custom house letter-books:

aniseed; cassia [the source of senna]; pepper; aqua vitae; brandy; cordial waters; geneva [gin]; rum; wine - sweet, white, red, claret, French, Portugal, Spanish, canary, Malaga; vinegar; butter; chocolate; currants; figs; liquorice - ball, juice, succus; prunes; raisins; sugar candy; syrup of maiden hair; cambric; damasks - Indian; handkerchiefs - Dutch cotton, Spanish silk, black silk; lace - thread, bone; linen; muslin; silks - Indian; candles - tallow; china; coal; combs - bone; feathers; gunpowder; paper; pearl ashes; playing cards - foreign, Dutch, French; salt - great, foreign, French, Portuguese; soap - hard, soft, black, castile, Flemish; starch; train oil; wool; coffee berries; tea - coarse, fine, green, black, bohea, congo, ageover; snuff - rappee [coarse]; tobacco - leaf, roll, stalks.

These goods were seized in stone bottles, half ankers, ankers, casks, tierces, hogsheads and pipes; boxes, parcels and canisters; firkins and rolls or matts. As there were no standard weights and measures, especially in terms of containers made by the smugglers themselves, it is difficult to estimate the exact dimensions of some of these containers. The most obvious calculation of dividing a seizure in terms of gallons by the number of containers produces a significantly different answer each time. The following approximations are given as a guide: half anker - 4 gallons, anker - 8 gallons, tierce - 30 gallons, hogshead - 50 gallons (or in the case of tobacco 1,000 lbs), pipe - 105 gallons and firkin - 8 or 9 gallons.

Only a small selection of these goods: wine, spirits and coal, are discussed here, although examples of the smuggling of a wider range of goods are found throughout the other chapters in the book. There is one particular story from 1718 which illustrates wine smuggling, the returns to an enquiry from the Board give a picture of spirits smuggling in the 1780s while the Alloa collectors of the 1730s described the different types of coal smuggling.

Wine

According to a forewarning from the Board in February 1710 'The season of the year now approaching in which we are to expect wines to be imported from Portugal, Spain and the Levant and there being great reason to believe that the merchants will use the same endeavours and industry as they have formerly done to import French wines under the denomination of wines of those countries we therefore think fit to give you this timely advise for your government and for preventing the damage the revenue has hitherto suffered by irregular proceedings of officers. When any ship arrives with wines, after the wines are entered and landed (and not before) you are with great care and circumspection to view and taste. All the wines you find cause to believe are French or have any mixture of French wines in them you are to lay your hands upon them and give us notice thereof with the particular circumstances of the case'.

The concern over the origin of the wine was based on the fact that French wines should pay a higher duty and, at various times during the eighteenth century, were considered as prohibited goods. The story of the *Greyhound* is an example of the merchants attempting to enter French wines as Spanish.

In early April 1718 the *Greyhound* of Bo'ness, John Izatt master, sailed up the Forth. The Board forewarned the collector at Alloa that she had on board 'several prohibited goods which are designed to be run'. But the vessel had arrived already. The Bo'ness surveyor had seized some goods under the cabin and, as the collector at Alloa commented bitterly, 'he should have sent us notice by an express that such a ship was coming up and that there was contraband goods aboard of her, which would both have been acting neighbourly and effectually preventing their running'. Instead he put one of his tidesmen on board.

'It was mere chance that our surveyor happened to be at Airth and got sight of her or she might have been there till she had run her whole cargo'. Instead he boarded her at Higginsnook and sent the collector an express. He in turn sent 'one of the landwaiters with some others in a boat at midnight to observe her and had bespoke the captain to have a party of men [soldiers] ready at a minute's warning to go done in case the surveyor and landwaiter should have made such a signal as was agreed upon'. The collector sent an express to the surveyor 'to signify to the master (who had pretended not to know where was to be his landing port) that unless he immediately repaired to some harbour that I would bring down a party of soldiers and force him to it'. The vessel arrived at Alloa in the daytime and 'nothing can be done aboard of her but what we can see out of the windows of the custom house. I applied to the captain for a party to watch along the shore the whole night, which was accordingly done'.

On Friday night a corporal with four men were boarded on the *Greyhound* and on Saturday morning the merchants came to the custom house 'and desired that we should go aboard and rummage the ship and if there were any contraband goods aboard that we should seize them. For they knew of none nor had commissioned any. Accordingly we went but found nothing and the hold full and in good order'.

The vessel was reported from Bilbao in Spain yet the Board had 'certain information she came directly from Bordeaux in France', which meant that the wines were probably French. 'You are nevertheless to allow the merchants to enter the wines under what denomination they please. But if entered under a wrong denomination you are to seize and secure the same in His Majesty's warehouse and put a sentry on it. If there should not be sufficient room in the warehouse for holding the quantity of wines then you are to get a good and sufficient cellar with sentries on it thereby to secure the same'.

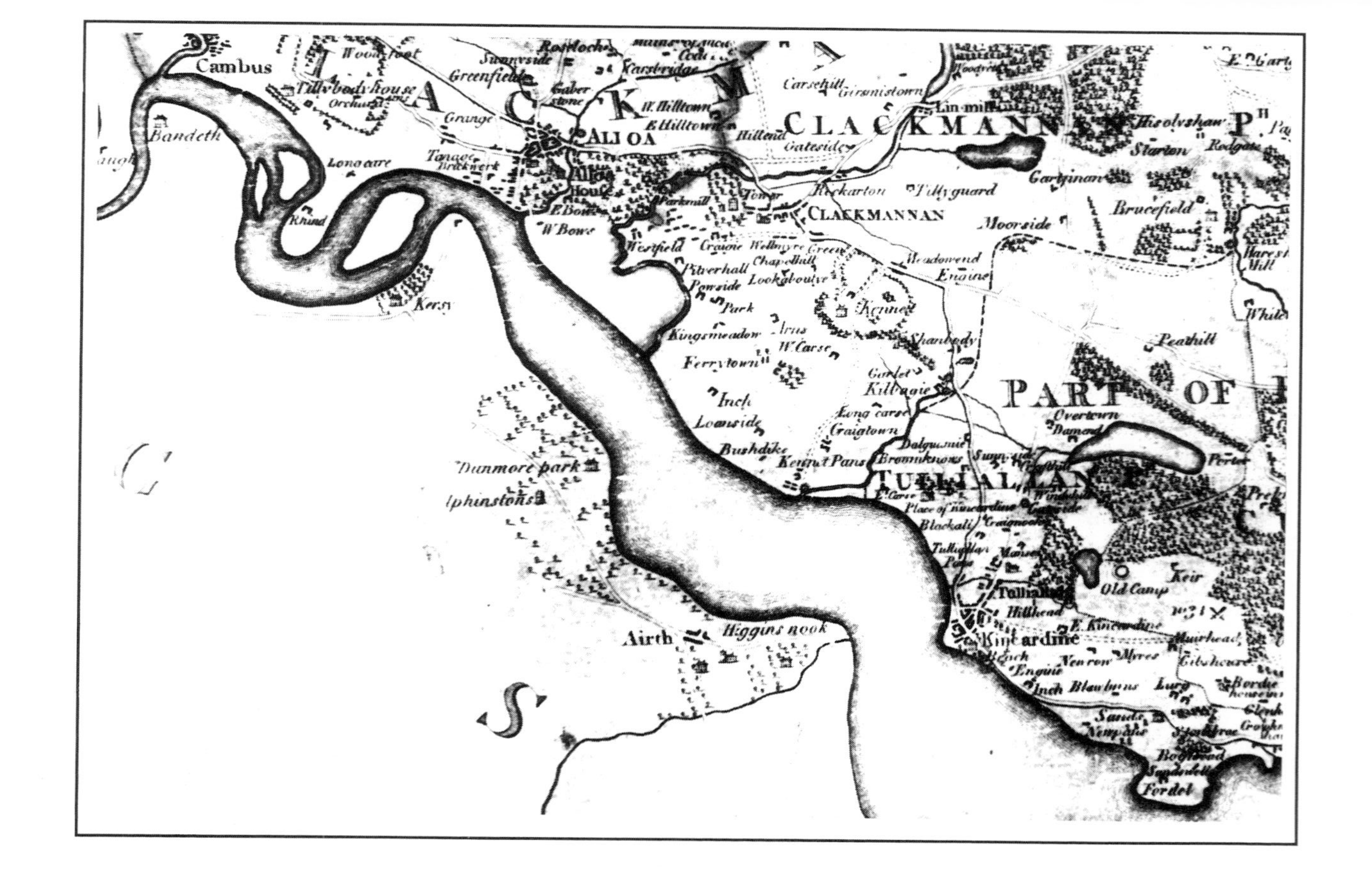

Cambus
Bandeth
Tillybodyhouse
Grange
Greenfield
ALLOA
Alloa House
CLACKMANNAN
Clackmannan
Kersy
Kingsmeadow
Ferrytown
Inch
Loanside
Bushdike
Kennet Pans
Kennet
Kilbagie
PART OF
Dunmore park
Airth
Higgins nook
Tulliallan
Kincardine
Old Camp
Peathill
Brucefield
Moorside
Tillyguard
Rockarton
Fordel

Figure 7: The Alloa district in the Eighteenth Century

This map shows some of the main Alloa locations: Airth, Elphinstone, Higginsnook, Kennetpans and Kincardine. It explains why so many of the deforcements listed in Chapter Ten were at Airth, where the collector depended on Mr Graham, the judge admiral, to intervene so that his officers could do their duty without constant abuse [see tailpiece to Chapter Ten]. The somewhat unexpected behaviour of Lord Elphinstone, the senior member of the local justices, is described in Chapter Seven.

In October 1741 the collector at Alloa reported 'On Tuesday morning early arrived here the *Clementina* of Airth, James Duncanson, master from Oporto. When she was boarded by the surveyor who upon rummaging her found as near as he could reckon twenty-nine pipes, seven half pipes and five quarter pipes of wine on board. As a great part of her hold was empty, he went out in the boat that night as well to visit the officers on board as to see if he could discover any boats with goods upon the water. Accordingly he found an open boat, Robert Haiggen [Higgin?] master, on board of which he seized four pipes, four half pipes and four quarter pipes of zerry [sherry], two hogsheads claret, two hogsheads foreign spirits and a quarter pipe of vinegar, all which he lodged this day in the king's warehouse here.

'We have only to observe that though this vessel frequently drives the wine trade the surveyor assures us that she never has once been boarded by the surveyor at the Ferry [Queensferry] when load with wine and that she has seldom if never come to this port with above one half or two thirds of her cargo.

'We are informed that this time she passed the Ferry on Sunday about midday and came to an anchor about Carron Mouth, in the district of Bo'ness, where she lay till Tuesday morning, which gives us reason to believe the goods now seized were part of her cargo and that had she been duly boarded this fraud might have been prevented. She is a vessel about 28 or 30 tons burthen and by the surveyor's report to us it appears that about two fifths of her cargo has been run ashore'.

James Duncanson's signature is reproduced in Figure 4.

The following postscript to the Board's letter dated 8 April surprised the collector: 'PS Having considered yours of the 7th inst ship ... which mentions your communicating to the merchants that if the entries were made of their wines as from Spain that you would seize them, you ought to have kept that part of your letter secret and allowed the merchants to enter the wines as reported and to have seized them, when discharged'. One has sympathies with the collector because, providing the copy of his letter in the letter-book is the true transcription, then it is impossible to understand why the Board had taken exception to his actions. He replied on 10 April 1718 'Now I beg your Honours may be pleased to peruse that letter again. For I communicated no such thing. Neither could I for your Honours gave me no other reason (and I knew nothing about it) when you ordered me to secure the ship and wines than that there were several prohibited goods aboard ... the merchants have not been here since Saturday and I hear they are at Edinburgh'.

The merchants finally entered the cargo on oath as Spanish wine and it was seized. At this stage the collector believed that he would be able to distinguish between the two types of wine and he wrote 'I desire you may put in William Polgreen and John Liddell, landwaiters, for appraisers, if you desire to have custom house officers, and if merchants, William Nurle and William Hutton of Alloa'. Instead on 7 May the Board directed the collector 'to take to my assistance the surveyor' and taste each hogshead before reporting the result. A week later he wrote 'nobody here pretends to know the difference of French and Spanish wines. Neither is it possible for me to procure so many bottles here as to take samples of them all'.

On 5 June the collector stated that he was not happy to prosecute the seizure 'on my own charges'. But the Board must have thought that they had a sufficiently strong case because on 25 November they wrote 'whereas there was some time since seized at your port a quantity of wines the growth of France, which had been entered as Spanish, and several merchants claiming the same in His Majesty's court of exchequer, the court thought fit to inflict a fine on the merchants by way of composition for the French duty after the rate of 4d per tun and having good reason to doubt whether or not the fine was collected upon delivery of the wines' the collector was to check his records and report.

Spirits

On 7 August 1786 the Board circulated collectors and captains of customs cruisers with a series of queries about spirits smuggling, which included the following questions: what quantity of spirits had been fraudulently landed in the district within the space of the last year; what was the price smuggled goods were sold at compared with spirits of the like strength and quality and what was the rate of profit to the smuggler?

The collector at Alloa's response was straightforward - a nil account of spirits fraudulently landed. However, Captain Brown of the *Princess Royal* sloop and Captain Kyd of *Osnaburgh* did not agree. This was Laurence Brown's response 'I am of opinion from my observations upon the manner in which smuggling is carried on upon the different parts of the east coast that 10,000 gallons may have been landed in your [the Alloa] district in the period above-mentioned and that the difference in price between smuggled spirits and spirits of the same strength and quality or reduced to the same strength legally imported may be 80% or even 90%.

'It is impossible to be exact as to the receipts the smugglers may make, as that must depend upon their expense, which must vary greatly from circumstances and from the hire of boats, carts, horses and porters etc differing very much in different parts of the country. But I apprehend they never would carry on a trade of that nature and continue it at such a risk and have so much trouble and anxiety as they must naturally have, if they did not clear a profit of at least 60%. I believe two thirds of the spirits smuggled upon this coast is geneva. This is what occurs to me upon this subject'. Four days later the collector forwarded this to the Board with the following comment 'We pray leave to take notice that what Mr Brown represents does not consist with the knowledge of us or any of the officers in this district and [we] are of the opinion that Mr Brown has mistaken the limits or creeks of the district and thereby been led to throw into his calculation spirits smuggled somewhere else. For we cannot from all our enquiries find that **any** smuggle of spirits has happened in this district the last year'.

Captain Kyd's return arrived a few days later. He also quoted the figure of 10,000 gallons of spirits. The smuggled geneva was sold at 4s

6d per gallon compared with 11s to 12s for 'legally imported' spirits. 'The smugglers profit by those prices is at least 100%'. Brandy sold at 6s to 7s per gallon compared with 12s to 13s. 'Foreign rum cannot be legally imported. That smuggled is commonly sold at the same price as the brandy but it bears a very small proportion to the other spirits smuggled'. As this information was 'much of the same tenor as that of Captain Brown's' the collector's instinct was to dismiss it as well.

The Perth collector's reply was dated 23 August 1786. Once more his view was 'we have no reason to suppose that spirits have been fraudulently landed in our district in the course of the year 1785 ... In order to show your Honours on what grounds we make this report we here transmit an account (taken from the journal of Mr Laing, our tidesurveyor at Newburgh) of the arrival of all vessels from foreign parts in this port in 1785, distinguishing the vessels which arrived having revenue officers on board from those which were only boarded and rummaged before their arrival. From this account your Honours will see that in 1785 we have had forty-two arrivals from foreign ports: 19 whereof had revenue officers on board; 18 had been boarded and rummaged; 1 had discharged part of her cargo at Kirkcaldy; 1 had been sometime in Dundee harbour and 3 came up without any officers or being boarded, but it is probable they were boarded at Dundee, although the journal does not say so'. [These figures have been included as a comparison with those for Dundee quoted in Chapter Two.]

'In the whole of these vessels there was not a single gallon of spirits seized and we apprehend that our port is too much inland for any vessel to attempt the landing a smuggled cargo. Indeed as far as we can learn any smuggled spirits which are brought here are by land carriage. Another channel of landing smuggled spirits has occurred to us which is by the coasting vessels bound for this port, who might happen to fall in with smuggling vessels at sea and purchase part of their cargo. But as in the year 1785 no spirits have been seized here from any of the coasters we think that we are well-founded in presuming that nothing of that kind has been attempted'.

He had also received comments from Captains Brown and Kyd, which he transmitted to the Board. 'In these letters they give their opinions that 60,000 gallons [40,000 gallons less than in the Alloa district] may have been landed in our district in the above-mentioned period but we are ignorant upon what grounds they have formed their conjectures and they have furnished us with no reasons for altering our report. We have only further to observe that as these gentlemen both agree in thinking that the greatest part of the spirits smuggled on the east coast is geneva, the suspicion therefore we apprehend should lie chiefly on the vessels from Holland. But your Honours will see by the enclosed account that ten vessels from Rotterdam arrived here in 1785: 1 whereof came from Bo'ness with 1 tidesman on board; 1 had a Dundee boatman; 1 had 6 yachtsmen [from an excise cruiser]; 1 had 6 ditto; 1 had 3 ditto; 1 was boarded and rummaged by Captain Brown; 2 had 3 yachtsmen and 2 had 2 Dundee boatmen. As these people remained on board until the vessels were discharged it is clear there were no spirits on board any of them'.

The spirits smuggling continued. On 18 March 1805 the collector at Anstruther transmitted an anonymous letter to the Board 'In consequence thereof we made particular enquiry into the circumstances set forth, all of whom we had a knowledge of previous thereto. The quantity of foreign gin there said to be smuggled into Fife from the opposite county of Angus is, we humbly conceive, considerably exaggerated when it is taken at 1,500 ankers in the course of that winter. We have obtained, as we thought, a very accurate account of 540 ankers being smuggled into St Andrews and other places as far as the district of this port extends, a hundred ankers of which ... were seized by the officers of the revenue. But what may have been smuggled into Leuchars and those parts of Fife north of the Eden water in the district of Dundee we cannot pretend to say'.

Coals

It is easy to forget the high duties payable on certain goods exported from Scotland. These attracted all the wiles of the smuggler, as much as the more familiar import smuggling. The main point was that according to an order from the Board dated 22 July 1724 no open or small boats trading to ports along the Forth 'were obliged' to take out clearances, indicating exactly how much coal they had on board, but merely a sufferance, on the oath of the master.

In January 1730 the Alloa collector was asked to examine 'how far the revenue has or may suffer' as a result of this order. He replied 'we find that under the pretence of going to Leith several vessels have carried abroad the whole loading of coals without payment of duty or clearances'. He cited two examples of this from 1728: the *Primrose* of Elphinstone, Andrew Ross master, [see Chapter Figure 4] and the *Godsend* of Dundee, John Wyllie master.

Before these frauds can be fully understood, a word of explanation is necessary. There were three different documents involved in the coasting trade: a sufferance, a clearance and a cocket [collectively referred to as dispatches]. Basically one allowed goods to be transported, the next confirmed that they had been cleared and the third should tally with the cargo on board. In other words these documents taken together should record the exact amount of coals on board and where they were supposed to be going. A further safeguard was the merchant or master's bond, a security that he was going to land the coals at the correct destination, and in theory only claimable once this had been confirmed.

If it were discovered that a boat had sailed directly to a foreign port, without paying the overseas duty, the master pretended 'they were put past their designed port by a storm'. In March 1784 the *Jean* of Kincardine, Andrew Ellis master, cleared from Alloa for Dundee. But according to the affidavits of both the master and the mate the vessel was 'forced over sea with the cargo of coals', which she actually landed at Clysholm in Sweden. This is reminiscent of a pretended voyage but in reverse.

Sometimes the collectors could only guess at a fraud. In March 1755 the collector at Perth reported to the collector at Kirkcaldy that 'the 25 tons of great coals shipped at Methil by permit dated 23rd September last on board the *Isobel & Jean* of Newburgh, Robert Blyth master, were not brought to this port [so that the master should not be able to claim his bond]. We likewise find that the ship was reported here the 18th November 1754 from Rotterdam'.

This was a comparatively straightforward fraud. At the same time the boats were taking in more coals than they claimed, by having at least one third or a half more on board than listed in the sufferance. The collector could see one way of stopping this. The coal overseer should make the oath that the sufferance was correct as 'it is well known that the generality of masters have very little regard to what they call a custom house oath and therefore will more readily make free therewith for their own advantage than an overseer of the coals, who beside having probably another way of thinking can have no benefit thereby'.

Once they had more coals on board than were in their papers, the masters took various advantages of this fact. One method was to sail to Bo'ness, produce the sufferance, say that their voyage had been changed by their merchants and that they were now to go overseas. They would then pay the required duty - but only on the coals in their papers rather than on the whole cargo. In November 1737 James Jamieson, master of the *Hopewell* of Leith [see Chapter Six], took out a clearance at Alloa for 32 tons, half the coals he had on board. He then went to Bo'ness, where 'upon pretence of having altered the voyage proceeded to foreign parts'. When he returned to Bo'ness, he claimed a drawback of the duty on the 32 tons exported. He then went to Alloa and pretended that the 32 tons had been unloaded at Bo'ness, where no duty was payable. 'If we had not accidentally got notice of the coal being exported we should have discharged the bond upon this certificate without further enquiry'.

James Cassells, master of the *Owners Good Will* of Leith, took out coast dispatches for 62 tons in March 1738 and went to Bo'ness. There he took out a sufferance to unload 22 of the 62 tons contained in his coast clearance. 'And thereafter upon pretence of having changed her voyage ... and paying duty for the remaining 40 tons proceeded to foreign parts, as appears by the enclosed certificate given in here by Cassells to discharge his coast bond'. The collector could only guess how much coal had been exported. These two Bo'ness examples emphasise the loss of the records from that outport.

The customs officers would become suspicious of particular masters. In 1730 the collector at Alloa reported he had refused to allow Robert Walker, master of the *Agnes* of Bo'ness, to load coals for Leith 'without giving security to land them since he had gone several times abroad formerly, when he had no clearance. Upon which he protested against us for not complying with the [Board's] order. However we refused letting him go until security was given and he finding that his intention was discovered took out a coast permit for 25 tons coals for Dundee but went no further than Bo'ness, where he was allowed to enter his coals outwards, and only paid duty for the 25 tons. By which means if he failed in his first intention he had it in part by defrauding the revenue of one half or one third of the duty'.

Another system was for the masters to persuade other small coasting vessels to meet up with them in the Forth and load more coals on board. In 1738 the collector at Alloa reported 'There is a particular instance of this kind of one Thomas Boswell, who entered his ship outwards coastwise for London and took out a sufferance for about one third of the cargo. So soon as his sufferance was endorsed, he went out of the harbour to the Road, where the officers observed two small vessels, one on each side, unloading their coals aboard of him'. The master then returned to the custom house 'pretending to have altered his voyage to foreign parts and offering to pay duty for the coals in the sufferance but finding that he was discovered he paid duty for these two cargoes also'.

Finally, not all the additional coals were headed overseas. 'There are others again who take out coast clearances for ports in the Firth, where no duty is to be paid, and take in double of what is contained in their coast clearance. Then [they] proceed to ports in the north where the duty is payable and pay duty for no more coals than is contained in their coast clearance. This is what is daily practiced and may be effectually prevented if the officers at the ports where the duties are payable did their duty in taking care that all coal coming thither paid duty without regard to the coast clearance that accompany them'.

This was a case of passing the onus of accurate weighing of the coal elsewhere. One of the problems at Alloa was staffing. 'As it is impossible for a shipping officer to look after above one vessel at a time and do his duty as he ought to do and it frequently happens that twenty, nay sometimes thirty, vessels are taking in coals at one time at this port and creeks. If the same care were taken in shipping coals coastwise as for exportation, ten officers more than our present establishment would hardly be sufficient for that purpose '.

As if to confirm the collector's comments, in 1746 the *Mary* of Stirling, James Duncanson master [see Figure 4], was involved in a tobacco/coal fraud, which is described in Chapter Six.

The tailpiece to this chapter describes a deforcement when the officers at Dundee attempted to seize some smuggled spirits.

A Story of Smuggled Spirits

In January 1788 Leslie Douglas, tidesurveyor, with William Imrie, Charles Stewart, Mathew Balderston, boatmen, and Alexander Murhart, employed as an extraordinary boatman, while making a seizure of spirits about a mile and a half north-east of Dundee 'met with very obstinate resistance from Andrew Duncan and three other persons, who accompanied the cart. William Imrie and Charles Stewart are much bruised and Mr Douglas received a very severe contusion in his head.

'Although they all had arms, the onset of the smugglers was so instantaneous and violent, after they [the smugglers] had been desired to stop the cart that they had not time to use them. But while William Imrie was struggling with a person who had overpowered him and brought him to the ground, a blunderbuss which Imrie carried, loaded with small shot, went off by accident and mortally wounded Andrew Duncan, the driver of the cart. To this accident alone Mr Douglas and Imrie declare they owe their lives. Whilst Mr Douglas and William Imrie were engaged with two persons and Charles Stewart secured by a third, the cart and horses were carried off by Alexander Murhart. Mathew Balderston, previous to falling in with the seizure, was dispatched to watch at a certain place which happened to be at a distance from the part where the scuffle took place and did not join the party till all was quiet'.

The collector added 'The officers have real merit in the service they have performed for they had three of the most determined blackguards in this part of the country to contend with, especially when it is declared that two of Mr Douglas's officers are infirm men and that another of them was absent during the affray'. [One becomes surprised that any seizures were ever made by this group].

'PS Since writing the above we are informed that Duncan died this morning of his wound and further that two of the three other persons who attended the carts are one Baird and Steen, residenters in Monifieth, two noted smugglers. Steen it is said is wounded by the strokes of a sword'.

Note: The name Baird reappears in connection with smuggling in the tailpiece to Chapter Seven.

CHAPTER FIVE: SMUGGLING VESSELS

'Having received information that the smuggling trade from Holland is increased to an enormous height upon the coasts of Scotland and particularly that considerable quantities of high duty and prohibited goods such as cambrics, tea and nutmegs are concealed in matts of flax, casks of flaxseed and between the timbers of the ships and in their cabins, we therefore direct you to put all the officers in your precincts on their guard and strictly to enjoin them to exert their most vigilant endeavours to prevent or detect the frauds complained of. You are in a particular manner to recommend to the landsurveyor and landwaiters carefully to examine bags, trunks and matts of flax, hogsheads of flaxseed or other barrels of goods for discovery of false packages, double bottoms or other concealments and to the tidesurveyor to rummage in the hold to search for false bulkheads or private places for concealed or prohibited goods, as likewise in cabins and chests for loose packets or portable goods subject to seizure as being a material part of their duty and more fully pointed out to them in printed instructions'. [Instructions from the Board dated 17 August 1768]

Some smuggling vessels hovered off the coast, others arrived with a clearly visible legal cargo but with the goods to be smuggled hidden in specially designed 'concealments' while the majority of the smuggles came from on board vessels which 'chanced' getting rid of part or all of their cargoes without being discovered.

The Hoverers

Vessels hovered for two different reasons - they were waiting for a pre-arranged message so that they knew when to come in to land goods or that smaller boats were ready to come out to them for goods. Alternatively sometimes the vessels acted as floating warehouses, hoping for contact with potential buyers on the land.

In November 1785 the Board instructed collectors to transmit 'as accurate an account as you can possibly procure of the number of smuggling vessels now employed on an illicit trade'. Further north, Aberdeen actually presented a detailed list. Montrose explained that there were no smuggling vessels owned within the precinct of the port 'although we have reason to believe that a contraband trade is carried on to an alarming extent within its limits as luggers and cutters are frequently seen hovering on the coast. But as they never come into port it is not in our power to ascertain their number'. The 1785 letter-books do not exist for Anstruther, Dunbar, Dundee or Leith while both Perth and Alloa, probably because they were so far up the Firths, submitted straightforward 'nil' returns.

Thomas Currie and John Ferrier, respectively commanders of detached boats belonging to the *Osnaburgh* and *Princess Royal* revenue cruisers, went out from Arbroath in January 1790 after a lugger's boat, which they had seen heading towards the north to land goods. When they caught up with the boat, she was on her way back to the lugger. They ordered her to stop, then fired shots over her 'which not having had the desired effect, they then fired into her and wounded one of the men, which caused them return, when the boat was seized. William Butcher [see Chapter Seven] having made a signal for the lugger to come close up where the boat lay, they could not get her brought off'. Instead they had 'been obliged' to stave and sink her, after taking her dimensions: length of keel 29 feet, breadth 9 feet and depth 4 feet. The problem was that as there were no goods in the boat when she was seized nor any proof that she had been involved in a fraud, technically the officers had no right to seize, let alone sink her.

The collector at Montrose explained to the Board in September 1775 that the seizure-makers of 44 gallons of geneva knew that this had been smuggled from a large three-masted lugger, which had been lying off the coast, because it was 'notoriously known' that this 'Flushing cutter' had 'opened a sale for geneva on board'.

There were other examples of these floating warehouses. In November 1800 the Board received information that 'there is not now a Norwegian ship arrives from the coast of Holland but what smuggles foreign spirits, which they effect in the following manner. How soon the ship arrives at her port, the pilot comes on board and enquiries what contraband goods they have to dispose of and for what price ... and the Danes [Norway, which had been part of Denmark for over four hundred years, was ceded to Sweden in 1814] have nothing to do but come ashore and pocket their money, by which means these foreigners derive advantages from this country which are rigidly withheld from our native seamen, who are infinitely more deserving'.

The Seizure Three Fishing Boats

A supply of fishing boats, ready and willing to unload a hovering vessel, were an essential part of the hovering scheme. In January 1805 the collector at Anstruther reported 'we have been informed by Peter Adam, master of the sloop *Young Eagle* of Anstruther, then lying in Arbroath, that on Friday morning ... a smuggling lugger lay off the Red Head and from the three above mentioned places [Auchmithie and East and West Haven], but particularly the first, fifteen boats went off and were loaded from her, some part of whom landed their cargoes in that neighbourhood and part went to this district'.

Three of these boats landed their cargoes at St Andrews, some of which was seized [see Chapter Seven], one at Boarhills, one at Anstruther and a sixth headed for Elie harbour but 'finding an excise cutter lying there she put off and proceeded up the Firth, supposed for Burntisland'. Further information about one of the boats was obtained from James Melvill, master of the *Dainty Davie* of St Andrews, and formerly belonging to the *Princess Royal* [under Captain Brown]. He informed the collector that 'on Monday morning the 31st of December last he was awakened about four in the morning with the noise of a smuggle in the West Sands of St Andrews. He took a walk that way and found a large fishing boat lying there aground with four or five men, who had smuggled their cargo about two or three hours before that time. They informed him that they belonged to the East Havens and that the master's name, he thinks, was John Scott ... the master requested him to assist them in the launching their boat but which he declined on account of the great cold. He knows most of the people of the Havens but he did not know any of them in that boat'.

The collector was convinced that Melvill's evidence would lead to the conviction of Scott. But according to his letter to the Board's solicitor in February 1806 'I regret that the declaration of James Melvill ... was not thought by you to contain sufficient grounds for a prosecution against

Braid [see Chapter Seven]'. He had hoped that if Scott did not tell the truth 'he should be sent on board a man of war and his boat broken up'.

Robert Boyack, tidesman at St Andrews, seized three of the boats at Boarhills and the collector was sure that more would be found out about the crews 'who it would appear are daring, lawless felons [who] pursued an excise officer on the morning of the day of their seizure upwards of an hour at Tentsmuir, with their boat-hooks in their hands, and finding themselves discovered at that place they put off to sea and in making across St Andrews Bay for Boarhills were discovered by Boyack and Mr Brodie, the supervisor of excise. The men belonging to them, assisted no doubt by the people of Boarhills, concealed part of the tackling of the boats. This circumstance along with the daring conduct at Tentsmuir of the crew of the boats induced us to bring them round to Anstruther as a place of security, Boarhills, where they were seized, lying nearly opposite to Arbroath, in which neighbourhood these boats are owned. From all we have been able to learn these are the boats that have been usually employed this winter in bringing smuggled gin from the Angus side to the coast of Fife'.

As soon as Boyack seized the boats, he had disabled them by knocking holes in their bottoms [see Chapter Eight]. When it was decided that they should be brought round to Anstruther, repairs were necessary. 'in order that they might swim that distance [nine miles]'. This resulted in expense, including 'the refreshments furnished to the people. This we confess is the first instance of the kind that has occurred at this port but it could not have been avoided owing to the peculiar circumstances of the case. The men had been employed from two o'clock in a winter morning until five o'clock the same night, a great part of the time in the water, and were numbed with cold. Had these refreshments not been paid for by Mr Hodge [tidesurveyor] the payment for the men would of course have been more'.

Following exhaustive enquiries by the collector, two further names were added to the list of masters: James Pink and James Hilton [their names had been obliterated on the boats that had been seized], both belonging to Auchmithie. As with the case of Scott, nothing more is heard of their possible conviction. This story ends with a report dated 30

July 1805 that 'after due intimation made, we yesterday exposed to public sale three boats and their tackle and apparel ... for which no offers were made'.

The Concealments

In December 1737 the collector of Alloa received information of a secret hiding place on board the *Success* of Stirling, William Virtue master, from Bremen. 'I have been on board the ship ... and find the fore breast of the hold cut through with a saw, the breadth of two deals cut clean out, the third sawn half through and then broke through the middle by the length, where at the entrance there has been some small oak pieces stopped to prevent the officers from getting access ... the cavity in the hold I think is above 12 foot long, 5 or 6 foot wide and about 3 foot high'.

The arrival at Perth in 1735 of the *Elizabeth & Ann*, John Westwater master, from Rotterdam, was described in Chapter Two. The letter from the collector continued 'After we were aboard the surveyor fell arummaging and we found a passage from the steerage to the hold, artfully covered over with a hogshead and the party's arms lying upon it, which the surveyor had put aboard to prevent smuggling ... upon removing the hogshead the surveyor got easily into the hold and found a void place that might have contained two or three tons of goods. Upon the collector's going down he observed the goods in such confusion that it was impossible she could [have] come from sea in that condition, which convinced us that goods had been run out of her since her entering into the river. After the surveyor had taken an account as far as he could of what goods still remained aboard we went into the cabin and examined James Young, tidewaiter at Dundee, and David Randie, tidesman at this port, anent the goods we supposed had been run out of her'. [The rest of the story is told in Chapter Nine]

On 30 August 1822 the *Melville* revenue cruiser seized the brig *Fortune* in Burntisland road. She had a cargo of wood and a 'false bottom', access to which was by way of the stern [see Figure 8]. This was a significant seizure: one hundred and ninety-nine bales containing 4,830 lbs roll tobacco, three bags and two parcels containing 323 lbs roll tobacco, one keg containing 10 lbs snuff, three hundred and three kegs

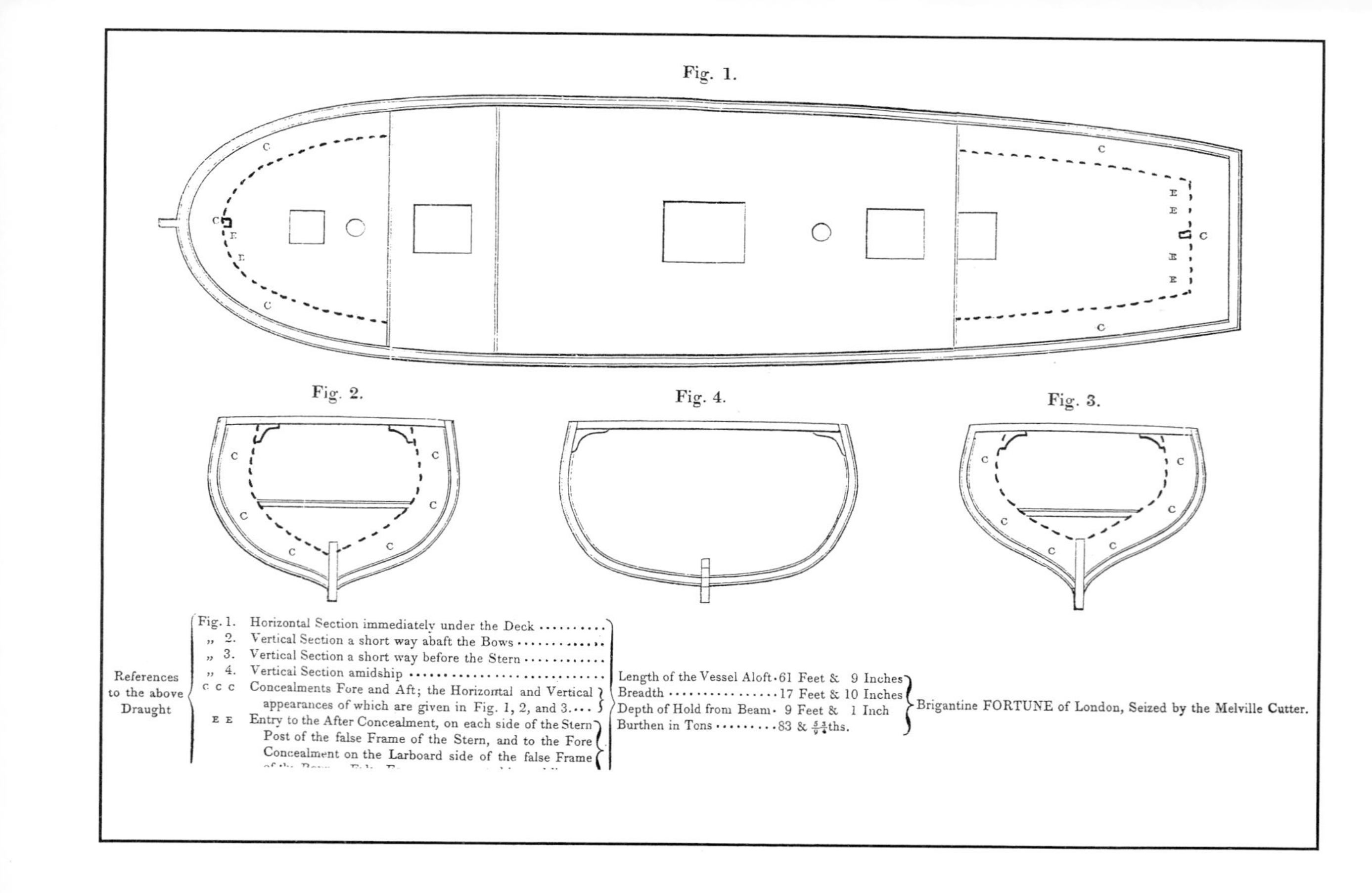
Fig. 1.
Fig. 2.
Fig. 4.
Fig. 3.
References to the above Draught
Fig. 1. Horizontal Section immediately under the Deck
„ 2. Vertical Section a short way abaft the Bows
„ 3. Vertical Section a short way before the Stern
„ 4. Vertical Section amidship
C C C Concealments Fore and Aft; the Horizontal and Vertical appearances of which are given in Fig. 1, 2, and 3.
E E Entry to the After Concealment, on each side of the Stern Post of the false Frame of the Stern, and to the Fore Concealment on the Larboard side of the false Frame
Length of the Vessel Aloft 61 Feet & 9 Inches
Breadth 17 Feet & 10 Inches
Depth of Hold from Beam 9 Feet & 1 Inch
Burthen in Tons 83 & $\frac{53}{94}$ths.
Brigantine FORTUNE of London, Seized by the Melville Cutter.

Figure 8

Description of the Brigantine "Fortune," seized by the Commander of the Melville Cutter.

THIS Vessel, in her outward appearance, is like any other common Merchant Vessel.

The Concealments, as will be seen upon reference to the Draught, are confined to the Bow and Stern parts of the Vessel, and are formed by constructing on the Kelson fore and aft, the Body of another Vessel within the real one, which false Vessel being fitted with Timbers and Planks, and with Beams and Knees, appears, upon entering into the Forecastle and Cabin, to be a part of the real Vessel.

These Concealments, it will appear from the Draft, only extend about 12-feet aftward from the inside of the Bow, and about 16-feet foreward from the inside of the Stern of the real Body of the Vessel, but they diminish towards the Main Hold, and extend downward on both sides towards the Kelson, being 3-feet and 2-inches at the widest part at the Stern, and 2-feet and 2-inches at the widest part at the Bow, and they are terminated at the ends nearest the Main Hold by fixed Bulkheads, which separate them from the same.

There is an Entry to the Bow concealment, and two to the Stern concealment, as will be seen upon reference to the Draught, and these entering Places are secured by false Treenails about 2-inches long, which, upon being removed, discover Screw-bolts in the Timbers that are unscrewed, by Keys made for the purpose, and loosen certain Pieces of the Timbers, which being removed discover Scuttles on small Hatchways within, which enter to the Concealments.

containing 1,096 gallons geneva, thirty-three boxes and two hundred and thirteen bags containing 1,512 lbs tea and one box containing seventy-two packs of playing cards.

The Chancers

On 11 March 1730 the *Margot* of Dundee, James Davidson master, sailed up the Tay with the first part of the flood and anchored without lights 'designing to lay till night that he might have an opportunity to run [his cargo]'. As Finlayson, the tidesurveyor at Dundee, had been watching the vessel, he set off in the king's boat and boarded her 'with a very lofty sea' about two o'clock in the morning.

'I was not long aboard till one Harris Sholl in North Ferry came aboard with seven hands in his boat. Doubting [but] he had letters from the master's employers we took hold of the villain, when [he] entered the ship and was searching him at which time the rogue took out his letter directed for the master and threw it into the water. I have kept him prisoner aboard ... I have brought the ship up to the Ferry road and will stay aboard till I receive your instructions'.

This is not one of the standard letters transcribed in the records but the original letter, actually signed by Finlayson, and written on board the *Margot* as he had 'spoiled my right leg in entering aboard the ship, she being so lofty'. Finlayson recovered but nothing more has been found about the incident, as yet.

In March 1740 Captain Stark's mate seized four small casks of wine and a small cask of vinegar on board the *Marishall* of Arbroath, John Wallace master. At this stage there were eighteen hogsheads and some half hogsheads of wine on board. On 2 April the vessel sailed from Arbroath Road but was back in that harbour on the 4th, at night, 'without having any of the casks on board only some pieces of linen and woollen cloaks and a small bag of hops. The reason the master gives for this fraud is that his vessel proving leaky at sea he met with a ship bound for Norway and put the wine on board of her and returned with his own ship not being able to perform the voyage'.

On 30 September 1755 the collector at Dundee reported that the previous Sunday afternoon the *Good Intention*, David Gray master, from Norway, had sailed from his port 'pretending bound to Perth'. That night the two tidesmen boarded by the tidesurveyor were deforced by the mate and ship's crew and 'a considerable quantity of goods run'. As the collector commented, 'it seems to be a pretty bold attempt within a quarter of a mile of the pier head and the custom house boat lying that night in the harbour. I'm told the goods carried away were ten hogsheads wine ... This new way of running goods will be of very bad consequence if it prevails which it infallibly will if the actors are not prosecuted'.

In September 1800 the Board received a letter from Eyemouth about goods being run up the Forth. These were invariably landed initially in Northumberland. Previously they had been brought overland into Scotland but 'since the removal of the king's boat' three fishing boats had been 'in constant practice' of going to Bowmore, taking in large quantities of spirits and tobacco and running them straight up the Forth. During the previous winter they had returned frequently from fishing in the Firth 'upon frivolous pretences' and went back to Burntisland with their boats 'almost loaded with ankers covered across with their fishing tackle'. It was estimated that at least 900 ankers had been disposed of this way.

The Prime Story

The *Prime* was described as 'a square-sterned, low and flat built sloop; neither has a galley or head; is in length from the fore-part of the main stern to the after-part of the stern-part aloft 42½ feet 2 inches; depth of hold 7½ feet; admeasures 40 1/3 tons; has a plain sloop rig and like all the sloops in this district has a running bowsprit for the purpose of hauling in when in harbour. From information of nautical people we pray leave to give it as our opinion, in which the surveyor joins, that the sloop has been built and is calculated for the coasting trade only'.

On Friday, 22 August 1788, the *Peggy & Agnes*, Alexander Sands master, the *Neptune*, Hugh Dawson master and the *John & Christian*, Alexander Wishart master, all of Kincardine, sailed down the river Tay. They passed the *Prime*, John Miller master, hauling on to the beach at

Parknook. They thought that she was sinking because she was so deep in the water.

Wishart hailed her and Miller told him that he had come from Sunderland. 'Wishart, seeing evidently that the *Prime* was leaky and knowing that limeshells was the only cargo brought from Sunderland to the Tay, was surprised that the vessel was not on fire. But Mr Stewart [landwaiter] having since seen the lime, it appears there was no danger of this accident happening for the small quantity of lime, which was landed, is rather like slaked lime or lime rubbish, mixed with small stones.'

There were several people prepared to give evidence that the *Prime* had gone aground at Parknook not only because she was leaky but also to run her cargo. Peter McGregor, farmer at Camcase Mill, about 200 yards from where the sloop grounded stated that she had discharged her cargo of foreign spirits and tobacco on Friday, 22 August and Saturday morning 23 August. McGregor's wife confirmed this. David Melville, weaver, and his sons Robert and John, who lived about 100 yards from where the sloop lay, 'having the key of the lint mill in their possession, opened the doors of the mill and assisted in landing the cargo and lodging part of it in the mill'. William Robertson, a weaver in Newburgh, who had been helping with the harvest, together with several others, had helped to unload the goods and hide them in the mill.

'When the farmer to whom the mill belonged heard what had happened, he sent his servants with orders to turn the spirits and tobacco out of the mill, which they did accordingly, turning them out upon the green, where McGregor, his wife and daughter saw them lying. McGregor declared also that there was no other sloop on shore there at that time but the one commanded by Miller'.

It was essential for Miller to move the goods again. Alexander Anderson, merchant in Newburgh, 'was informed that a person calling himself a shipmaster had applied to several farmers of Mr Anderson's acquaintance, asking the assistance of their horses and carts to carry off his cargo and telling them that Anderson had a concern in it. Some of the farmers, thinking they were doing a favour to Anderson, did send their carts. Mr Anderson was exceedingly angry when he learned that his name was made use of as an inducement to the farmers to furnish their carts, he having no concern in that or any other smuggling cargo whatever'. McGregor added that on the Saturday, after the goods had been run, he helped unload part of the lime and there were several feet of water in the *Prime's* hold. Her 'people [were] busy in stopping the leak with canvas'. Shortly after this the *Prime* was seized.

Andrew Anderson, master of the *Elizabeth & Ann* of Kincardine, had spoken to Miller, after the *Prime* had been seized and had been told of the smuggle, Miller 'saying that it must have been blown by the farmers, who assisted in unloading the cargo, his merchant having fallen out with them about their payment'. According to her original register, which Miller took to Leith and gave to John Hutton, ropemaker, and Alexander Hill, boatbuilder, [one wonders if they were involved in the smuggle], he was one of the owners, with David Martin also a shipmaster from Kincardine.

After condemnation in the exchequer court [for having been involved in smuggling] the *Prime* was appraised at £135 and, in April 1789, sold to David Peacock for £101. According to her new register, he was the sole owner and master. In July 1800 she cleared for the white herring fishery and in August 1801 was sold to Ayr, where she was registered de novo. Sadly the Ayr registers do not exist for this date so there is no information about her final fate.

The following tailpiece, though somewhat long, has been included because it provides the intimate details of a smuggle - recorded in the minutes of the University of St Andrews.

The Story of the *Dorothy* of St Andrews

These extracts, taken from the Minutes of St Andrews University, have been reproduced to give the full flavour of this smuggling story.

February 19th 1728

'The University considering that it is the duty of all good Christians to give unto Caesar what is his due, and that it is a wickedness against the Laws of God, and the good Laws of our country, to defraud the King of the duties of Customs or Excise allowed to him by Parliament or deforce His Majesty's officers in the execution of their office, and particularly that it is most unbecoming the students of this University to give any assistance to the running of goods or to threaten and impede His Majesty's officers in making of seizures. And the University being informed that some few students have been so weak and foolish as to suffer themselves to be enticed and misled into this evil practice, by forcibly detaining some of His Majesty's officers of the customs in the cabin of a ship in this harbour, while the goods therein were carried off. Therefore for preventing the like practice in time coming they do hereby strictly prohibit and discharge all students of this University and everyone of them to give any countenance or assistance unto the running of goods or any manner of way to hinder or disturb any of His Majesty's officers in making of seizures of such goods by threatening or opposing or using violence to deforce them in the execution of their office with certification that the contraveners of this statute shall be declared infamous and deprived of all degrees and promotion in this University and extruded therefrom'.

As the University had been informed that the Board were to take out a criminal process against some of these students, they sent a letter to Edinburgh.

February 26th 1728

The Board's reply gave 'encouragement to expect that they will not proceed any further in the criminal process against the students, if they shall ingenuously declare who were the persons that seduced them'.

A committee was set up to examine the students. This included Principal Drew, the Rector, Provost Ramsay, Masters James Duncan, Charles Gregory, Henry Ramsay, Henry Rymer and Francis Pringle.

contd.

The Story of the *Dorothy* of St Andrews contd.

March 11th 1728

The Committee appointed on 26 February 1728 had held two meetings.

February 28th 1728. The Committee called before them the students who were said to have assisted in running of goods out of Greig's ship, the *Dorothy* [see Chapter Two: France] As a result of their detailed examination of the students they discovered that on 27 March 1727 'when William Greig's ship was come into the harbour, John Stuart, Alexander Ayton, Alexander Macdonald and Alexander Nairn, students, happened to go aboard another ship there belonging to one Abercrombie in Dundee [see Chapter Three], which was taking in a loading of victuals, on board of which was one James Haldane, a waiter, but was fast asleep, being as they suspected overtaken with drink. That the mate of Abercrombie's ship represented to them the great loss Greig and his merchants would suffer if they got not help and called Greig on board, who solicited them for their assistance, telling them that he and his merchants would be ruined if they got not the goods run out of the ship and told them also there were valuable goods in the cabin and gave to John Stuart (as he owned) a note of directions where to find them ... That soon after they had come up to the town. Some of them were invited to the house of Laurence Gibb, tavern keeper. That John Stuart and Alexander Nairn went thither, where they found David Rutherford, merchant in Cupar, and John Morrison, merchant in St Andrews, who gave them a glass of wine ... That the above-mentioned four having engaged other students [James Halket, Robert Hamilton, David Lindsay, John Menzies, David Scot and John Tod] to join them went down toward the harbour betwixt eight and nine at night and by the way near St Leonards College they met Mr Aikenhead, the surveyor, coming from the shore ... That when they came to the shore they received some two or three swords and pistols from Abercrombie's ship ... That before they went on board Greig the master desired them to thrash him heartily and to call for ropes to bind him that he might not be suspected ... That it being low water they went by the boat to Greig's ship and mounted the deck by ropes without any opposition. That upon their entering the waiters on board retired to the cabin and shut the door, which they quickly beat upon ...

contd.

The Story of the *Dorothy* of St Andrews contd.

'That they found in the cabin two waiters who reside in this town viz. John Auld and John Ogilvie and another they did not know, but learned his name was Campbell, and Greig the master of the ship ... John Stuart added that upon his entering the cabin John Ogilvie struck him over the head with his cane and that he returned the blow.

'That the waiters sat down at the table and drank beer and did eat bread and cheese with them. That some of them by previous concert with Greig asked the keys from him which he delivered to them. That they opened some of the lockers and presses at his direction and he himself opened some of the lockers, which they could not open, and that they handed out the goods that were in them to the sailors and others on deck who handed them ashore ...

'That meanwhile there were people with horses and carts on the shore receiving the goods that were pulled up out of the hold by the ship's crew ... That they heard the goods belonged to Mr Rutherford and Mr Morrison and to Greig himself ... That they saw Rutherford and Morrison and the carters and whiplickers on the shore ... That Rutherford behaved as interested by helping to lift the goods into the carts and giving orders ... That there was a barrel of figs broke open on the shore and the students as they came out of the ship were invited and allowed by Rutherford to take of them what they pleased ... Alexander Ayton further declares that after he returned to the town about eleven o'clock Mr Rutherford carried him in to Gibb's house, gave him a glass of wine and thanked him for the goods and kind service they had done him.'

March 10th 1728 The students confirmed that their declarations were true.

The University agreed that a letter 'framed from the declarations' should be forwarded to the Board.

March 18th 1728

The Board had received the letter and promised to reply 'after they had taken advice of their solicitor'.

contd.

The Story of the *Dorothy* of St Andrews contd.

April 15th 1728

The Board had replied 'desiring the University may send them over a list of the names and designations of the students who were seduced to deforce the king's officers in order to a prosecution against William Greig, master of the *Dorothy* and David Rutherford merchant in Cupar'.

April 22nd 1728

The full declarations had been sent to the Board with a letter 'thanking them for the respect they have shown to the intercession of this University in favours of the students in dropping the designed process against them and desiring they may show as much tenderness as possible to the students that they may not be put to needless attendance as evidences, which may bring them not only to expenses but divert them from their studies. As also they overtured that the designations of the students that were examined may be added to their names, which being considered by the University they approved thereof and appointed accordingly'.

The author is grateful to Mr Smart of the University of St Andrews for producing the following information about these students: Alexander Ayton; born 1710 son of John Ayton of Kinaldie, matriculated 1725*, succeeded to Kinaldie, soldier, died without issue 1766; James Halket: his father either landed or a professional man, matriculated 1725*, MA 1729; Robert Hamilton: son of Hamilton of Kilbrachmont, matriculated 1727**; David Lindsay: son of Robert Lindsay of Glenqueech [sic], matriculated 1724**, MA 1728; Alexander Macdonald: son of Sir David Macdonald of Sleat, matriculated **, succeeded 1720, died 23 November 1746; John Menzies: son of a tenant farmer or artisan, matriculated 1725*, MA 1728; Alexander Nairn: matriculated 1726**; David Scot: born 1710 of artisan stock, matriculated 1726*, MA 1729, licensed St Andrews Presbytery 1737, Minister Channelkirk 1752 to 16 April 1792 (died); John Stuart: son of Francis Stewart of Camilla, matriculated 1726**; John Tod of artisan stock, matriculated **.

Key: * St Salvators College
** St Leonards College

contd.

The Story of the *Dorothy* of St Andrews contd.

Note: The 'Smuggling Act' was in the version of the University laws in 1747, was probably dropped about 1780 (but not minuted) and was not in use in 1826 or for some time previously.

CHAPTER SIX: THE TOBACCO STORY

'Having this day received intelligence that a ship from one or other of the plantations in America is daily expected to arrive here with a cargo of tobacco belonging to the merchants along this coast, I thought it my duty to inform your Honours thereof that the smuggling [of] any part of it, which has been too frequent in this part in the like cases, may be prevented as far as possible'. [Collector at Montrose to the Board dated 24 December 1770]

Each stage of the tobacco story can be found in the custom house letter-books from importation to re-exportation to seizure. Several of the main tobacco merchants in the area during the eighteenth century can be identified [see Figure 9].

Tobacco leaves and stalks were imported from Virginia in hogsheads, each containing approximately 1,000 lbs. Before these could be imported into Europe, they had to be landed at a British port and the duties paid, or a bond given that the tobacco was to be exported. The first landfall was the west coast and this explains the rise of the tobacco lords of Glasgow. In 1724 Daniel Defoe, describing the Firth of Forth, wrote 'as they tell us, the Glasgow merchants are resolving to settle a trade to Holland and Hamburg in the Firth, by bringing their foreign goods, (viz.) their sugars and tobaccos by land to Alloa, and from thence export them as they see occasion. I say, in this case, which is very probable, the Bo'ness men will come into business again; for as they have the most shipping, so they are the best seamen in the Firth; and particularly they are not sailors only, but even pilots for the coast of Holland, they are so acquainted with it, and so with the Baltic, and the coast of Norway also'. [See comment in Chapter One about the loss of the Bo'ness records in the custom house fire]

Defoe mentions this proposal again in his next letter, under the section about Glasgow. 'Now, though this may be some advantage (viz.)

carrying the tobacco from fourteen to fifteen miles overland; yet, if on the other hand it be calculated how much sooner the voyage is made from Glasgow to the Capes of Virginia, than from London ... the difference will be found in the freight, and in the expense of the ships, and especially in time of war, when the [English] Channel is thronged with privateers, and when the ships wait to go in fleets for fear of enemies; whereas the Glasgow men are no sooner out of the Firth of Clyde, but they stretch away to the north-west, are out of the way of the privateers immediately, and are oftentimes at the Capes of Virginia before the London ships get clear of the Channel. Nay, even in times of peace, and take the weather to happen in its usual manner, there must always be allowed, one time with another, at least fourteen to twenty days difference in the voyage, either out or home; which, take it together, is a month to six weeks in the whole voyage, and for wear and tear, victuals and wages, is very considerable in the whole trade'.

Despite this, there are frequent references to the arrival of the tobacco ships from Virginia on the east coast. The *Concord* appears to be one of the more common names for a tobacco vessel, which can cause problems when trying to trace the history of a particular importation. The following references help to indicate the complicated nature of the tobacco trade. In July 1730 the *Concord* of Glasgow arrived at Dundee and on 30 November it was reported that eighty-seven hogsheads from this cargo had been exported to Rotterdam on the *Margaret* of Dundee, Robert Philp master. On 15 December John Smith, merchant in Dundee, demanded his debenture expede [expedited]. The *Concord* of Leith arrived at Dundee in 1733 and again in 1734, James Brebner master. Thomas Kyd & Co 'had occasion to break up their warehouses to make room for that cargo and in so doing Mr Colville stopped in the streets of Dundee six hogsheads containing 4,878 lbs, which they claimed was part of the fourth [1733] cargo'. The *Concord* was back in Dundee with another load of tobacco in 1735. The *Concord* of Arbroath, John Spink master, arrived at Montrose in 1740. The Board instructed the collector 'to proceed to the discharge thereof in the exactest manner and when finished to send us a copy of the blue book so far as relates to the tobacco, taking care that the security be good and sufficient'.

The full tobacco story is now described stage by stage.

As can be seen from the introductory quote, tobacco ships arriving from the British Plantations were always suspect, as they often ran part of their cargoes before unloading at their destination. In 1734 the *Rebecca & Mary* of Montrose, George Ouchterlony master, obtained a British Plantation bond allowing her to go to Virginia for a cargo of tobacco. She returned to Montrose in February 1735 with thirty quarter casks of rum and one hundred and fifty hogsheads of tobacco. At first it was unclear whether she was to discharge the cargo at Montrose or Dundee. Three days later the master reported that he had been instructed by his merchants 'to proceed to Alloa the first fair wind to discharge her tobacco there'. Both the collector at Montrose and the Board forewarned the Alloa collector who reported, possibly to everyone's surprise, one hundred and fifty hogsheads of tobacco unloaded there. But in July 1735 the collector at Montrose wrote to the Board that there had been no certificate from Alloa for discharging the Plantation bond 'as yet produced to us though we have frequently called upon the master for it, who always promised to procure it'. Nine hogsheads of this cargo were subsequently exported by David Fotheringham, merchant in Arbroath, and a further one hundred and eighty hogsheads by James Colhoun & Co of Dundee.

Once the tobacco was landed and weighed, security had to be given that the duties would be paid or that the tobacco was to be re-exported. The amounts of money involved were considerable [remembering that inflation since the eighteenth century is some fifty times] and it is often the non-payment of the bonds that produces information about the individual merchants concerned [see Table 9].

In 1735 John and Thomas Wallace of Arbroath were owing £201 19s 13¼d, some of which was offset by subsequent re-exportation. Ten years later Patrick Wallace and James Milne owed £57 4s 3¾d by two bonds dated 23 and 31 May 1743, payable 23 and 31 November 1744, for duties on tobacco. Patrick Wallace had recently exported the remainder of the tobacco and the debentures now due extinguished the principal sum. However, he refused to pay the interest, stating that according to common practice in Port Glasgow this was not payable when the tobacco for which the bonds had been granted was exported within three years. James Milne was also involved with David Skinner, who on 28 September and 5 October 1749 entered tobacco out of the *Thetis* of Glasgow, William Andrew master, from Virginia. By March 1750 they 'became due to His Majesty in two bonds on which there is a balance owing of £2414 4s 9¾d sterling ... David Skinner one of the persons bound in said two bonds being dead [the collector wanted to know how to ensure that the money would be paid]'

When the merchants applied to re-export the tobacco, the local collector would inform the Board who in turn would forewarn the other outports - 'we direct you to put all the officers in your district on their guard to prevent the running or relanding any part of the tobacco'.

According to forewarnings sent by the Board to the collector at Dundee, in 1735 the following tobacco vessels cleared out of Alloa: the *William* of Airth, John Adam master, for Norway; the *Hopewell* of Leith, James Jamieson master [see the coal section in Chapter Four], for Rotterdam; the *Primrose* of Elphinstone, Andrew Ross master [see Figure 4], for Gothenburg; the *Joannes* of Gothenburg, Peter Sweden master, for Gothenburg and the *James* of Airth, John Connochie master, [destination not recorded] - [see Figure 4].

In October 1746 the Board forewarned the outports that the *Mary* of Stirling, James Duncanson master [see Figure 4], had cleared outwards from Bo'ness with tobacco for Campvere. 'At that time both the tidesmen at Stonehaven being suspended ... we were obliged to supply that creek with a tidesman from the port monthly, and all the tidesmen at the port being on duty on board of ships we sent out William Freeman, boatman, to take charge of that creek'. It was Freeman who received the Board's order about the *Mary*. He was relieved by William Brown, tidewaiter, who 'received from him all the orders he had got from us and particularly the one concerning the ship'. But as yet there had been no sign of her. James Mercer succeeded William Brown but was not given the crucial letter. 'He [Brown] says he quite forgot he received such a letter and that he has certainly lost or mislaid it'. Then, on 24 December 1746, the *Mary* put into Stonehaven. Mercer boarded her but 'did not go into the hold by reason the boat was upon the hatches, which were chalked [to show that it had been checked by customs officers], but looked through a hole in the steerage to the hold, the very same day she came in, and could see nothing but coals'. The master produced a clearance for coals from Bo'ness to Campvere [see Chapter Four] and Mercer had no reason to doubt that this was her only cargo. She sailed on 31 December 1746. The Board, suspicious that there had been a smuggle of the tobacco, wrote to the Aberdeen collector on 28 January 1747. He had to admit that it was very probable that the tobacco was not on board 'we are extremely sorry to incur your Honours displeasure in this affair, since it was the furthest thing in the world from our intentions to contemn your Honours orders or give you unnecessary trouble'.

On 6 November 1740 Mr Fyfe of Perth demanded a coast clearance for 17 cwt of leaf tobacco for Newcastle. 'We told him that he must make oath to the identity [of the tobacco] ... or make oath that he bought it in a fair way of trade and actually and truly believed the duty was paid at importation. He said he did not think he was obliged to make any such oath for ... he had bought the tobacco he was to send to Newcastle from one Hugh Hardie, a tobacconist in this place, who owed him money and whose affairs had some time ago gone wrong and he had now taken it for his payment. Therefore [he] did not incline to make oath, although Mr Hardie, as he supposed, had credit sufficient in our books for that quantity. He designed nothing but what was fair because had he designed any other thing ... there were several in town who had credit enough to have spared him besides what himself had lately compounded for in the exchequer [i.e. a previous seizure of his tobacco] yet he had made use of no mans credit for it but Hugh Hardie'.

In July 1749 the *Janet* of Dundee, Robert Finlay master, sailed from Aberdeen with thirty hogsheads of leaf tobacco for **Henry Wallace** [see Chapter Three] and George Ross, merchants in Bergen. Two days later Finlayson and Boyer, excise officers at Aberdeen, seized one hundred and fourteen matts of tobacco, supposed to have been run from the *Janet*. 'But whether it is the identical tobacco with which Finlay sailed from this harbour or that the same was not landed in Norway, they cannot take upon them to prove'. William Copland & Co demanded to have the thirty hogsheads discounted on their debenture and had produced a certificate from the Bergen merchants, proving that the tobacco had been landed there. The *Janet* returned from Norway in August with a cargo of salt, deals and harrow bills.

An Account of Tobacco Stalks Seized at this Port, Condemned and Sent to the Coll^r and Compt^r of the Customs at Leith, there to be Burnt as the Law directs; in the Molly Leighton, Robert Napier, Master, Shipt the 6th April 1795

Date of Seizure		When condemned	Number of Return of Seizure	Seized By	Seized For Behoof of	Quantity and Quality When Seized: Matts		lb.	Repacked into Matts	When Delivered	lb.
		In Exchequer							No. 1	Sound Tobacco Stalks	203
									2		150
									3		123
1794 Septem^r	19	1795 Candlemas Term	202	William Bleis	William Bleis	6	Cont^g Sound Tob^o Stalks	495		Gross Weight	476
				Thomas Bouchart	Thomas Bouchart		Damaged d^o	182		Tare 5 lb. per Matt	15
										Net	461
									4	Damaged d^o Gross	157
										Tare	6
										Net	151

An Account of the Charges incurred at Montrose, on the sound and damaged Tobacco Stalks above mentioned

	£	s.	d.
To Paid for Four Russia Matts for Packing the Stalks, the Matts in which they were contained when seized being all Torn	..	2	..
To Paid for Weighing and Packing	..	1	3
To Paid for Carriage from the Warehouse to the Ship	..	..	6
To Paid for Shore dues	..	..	4
To Paid Two Appraizers for the Proportion of the dues of Appraizement, on the Stalks the rest vizt 7^d being chargeable on the Cart contained in the same Writ of Appraizement	..	4	5
	..	8	6
To Warehouse Rent on 4 Matts at 4^d per Matt	..	1	4
	£ ..	9	10

Figure 9: An Account of the Tobacco Stalks seized at Montrose in 1794

This table records the seizure in September 1794 of 495 lbs sound tobacco stalks and 182 lbs damaged tobacco stalks, by William Blues and Thomas Bouchart, officers belonging to Montrose, condemned in the exchequer court Candlemas Term 1795 and shipped to Leith to be burned on the *Mally Leighton*, Robert Napier master, on 6 April 1795. The account of the charges listed at the foot of the table totals £9 10s. Several similar tables are found in the letter-books. On three separate occasions in 1765 seizures totalling 5,114 lbs leaf tobacco, 14,720 lbs tobacco stalks and 30 lbs snuff were burned, again at Montrose.

Below are listed some of the tobacco merchants who have been identified in the letter-books:

Alloa: Mrs Beny, Thomas Blair, William Henry (Cambus), Andrew Mitchell, John Ogilvie (Airth), Henry Pattullo, Patrick Stevenson (Stirling), John Watson

Arbroath: David Fotheringham & Co

Dundee: James Colhoun & Co, Thomas Kyd & Co, William Little & Co, Thomas Nimmo, Mrs Prophit, John Ramsay, Thomas Robertson, James Stewart, George Yeaman

Montrose: David Buchanan for John Grant, Richard Dickie, Thomas Douglas, John Grant, James Milne, Alexander Morrison, David Skinner, The Wallaces: John, Thomas and Patrick

Perth: Mr Fyfe, Thomas Marshall, Messrs Peat & Burt, George Ross, Alexander Simpson

As a precaution to avoid relanding of the tobacco, tidesmen were placed on board the vessel. But on 1 September 1725 the collector at Dumfries wrote to the Board 'The bearer, John Hunter tidesman at Alloa, came here this morning being put ashore at Heston the 30th past in the evening out of the *Providence* of Alloa, Alexander Haig master, from Alloa to the Isle of Man with tobacco. When I asked him why he did not go to the Island with the ship, he told me that the master threatened to throw him overboard if he would not go ashore, which makes it plainly appear that they have a design to run the cargo. I have written to the collector at Kirkcudbright and given him the marks of the ship as near as the tidesman could tell that he might take all care to prevent the relanding of that ship's cargo'. By 1795 the Board had accepted the problem of single tidesmen on 'suspect vessels' and instructed that unless two could go together then the practice was to be discontinued.

In May 1750 the *Fortrose* of Leith was at Alloa with tobacco for Norway. David Heugh, tidewaiter, was walking on the deck when he was 'struck on the head with a stone thrown from the shore, which not only made a large wound but also a contusion on the skull. Endeavour has been used to discover the sender but to no purpose. Mr James Haig, one of the best surgeons in town, has attended to him and now completed the cure and has applied to us for his payment. He has agreed to accept of 3 guineas for his medicines and attendance ... which sum we humbly think he deserves for performing the cure of such a dangerous wound. We have no doubt but the person who committed the crime did it out of malice to Heugh, for his diligence and exactness in his duty'.

Another source of information about the tobacco trade is confirmation that the duties inwards had been secured. These vessels all cleared out of Montrose in 1750: the *Jean* of Arbroath, Thomas Herring master, with twenty hogsheads of tobacco for Campvere; the *Argyle*, Robert Scott master, with thirty-five hogsheads for Campvere; the *Margaret*, James Leslie master, with thirty-five hogsheads for Christiansands and the *Katherine*, Robert Ferguson master, with three hogsheads for Hammonds Island in Norway.

The problems of proving what tobacco had been exported, were summarised in a long paper to the Board from the collector at Alloa, dated 1 July 1738. 'When tobaccos have hitherto been stopped passing without clearance or on suspicion of their being relanded or reimported, upon the proprietor making oath ... that the tobaccos under seizure are the identical tobaccos for which he (or the importer) paid and secured the duty upon the importation and that no part thereof has been since drawn back ... it has been hitherto found that there was no foundation for carrying the goods into condemnation [in the court of exchequer] and of course have from time to time been given up by Your Honours orders. Now what I am to lay before your Honours is to show that the importer or purchaser ... may safely make ... affidavits, though at the same time they are really and truly defrauding the revenue, and then humbly to propose a remedy for the preventing thereof'.

He gave an example in which **NB** was the importer and **CD** the purchaser of 30,000 lbs of tobacco. This purchase was disposed of in three different ways. 10,000 lbs was classed as 'inland sale', bought by tobacconists 'in different parts of the country'. 10,000 lbs was exported by **CD** 'fairly' and a further 10,000 lbs had already been exported by **NB**, who had drawn back the duties, but was still unsold in Holland or Norway. **CD** then reimported 10,000 lbs, which was seized by a customs officer. But he could prove that as yet he had not claimed draw back so that the tobaccos were released. The ruse was 'the practice of exporters of tobacco dealing in this way not to expede or make out their debentures for several months, nay sometimes a year, after the tobaccos are exported. Should their tobaccos be seized after they are reimported, before the debenture is fully expede, they may easily swear (at least they think so) that the duties are not drawn back because they have not at that time actually exped their debenture or received repayment of the duties nor are they in any difficulty with respect to the oaths of exportation in the debenture seeing the tobaccos were once fairly exported'.

He then proposed a method 'which in my humble opinion may be of service to prevent the revenue being defrauded for the future in this way'. He believed that an additional oath that 'to the best of his knowledge and belief no part of these tobaccos have ever been drawn back or entered or shipped for exportation' should make all the difference. It appears that the collector's suggestions were not accepted because in October 1740 he reported to the Board's solicitor that William

Henry 'trades in run tobacco from the north and within this six months bygone he offered a certain tobacconist of this place one penny per lb for all the credit he could claim at this place, provided he would procure a permit to carry the same to Arbroath'.

Thomas Robertson and James Stewart were tobacconists in Dundee with a snuff mill at Baldovie. At different times they brought tobacco by sea from Aberdeen. For example in November 1755 5946 lbs in the *Janet* of Dundee, Peter Gawn master. On 3 July 1755 William Geddes, supervisor, and Thomas Donaldson, excise officer at Dundee, went to Baldovie, where they seized and brought to the king's warehouse twenty-nine matts of tobacco stalks, which was returned as a seizure. 'At the time [they] told us that there was a great parcel of tobacco lying [there] which they intended to seize but the proprietors had assured them that they had credit in the custom house books for a much larger quantity. Upon which they came in company and applied for a sight of our books, which was allowed them. But the date of the last certificate from Aberdeen proved to be more than two years old. Notwithstanding Mr Geddes ... said that he did not think it advisable to bring the revenue and himself to an unnecessary charge and at the same time took off his hands of the tobacco, which he had been in possession of by a military force, upon these gentlemen paying his expenses. What other agreement was between them we know not'.

Under instructions from the Board, Gideon Schaw, assistant register general of tobacco, went to Baldovie and seized the parcel of tobacco. The costs of this were considerable. Schaw's personal expenses totalled £5 0s 9d. Hogsheads had to be borrowed from Mr Holden, proprietor of the mill, to transport the tobacco to Dundee, where it then had to be re-packed - the porters were paid 11s 9d. In the meantime Robertson and Stewart were told that the tobacco would be returned 'upon their making oath to the identity of the tobacco and that it was really and truly a part of the tobacco which had come to them by certificate from Aberdeen and for which they had credit on our books ... But this they flatly refused to comply with and answered that they would lead no such practice and that they would take their own way [to recover the tobacco]'. The end of the story has not been identified as yet, but one imagines that the tobacco was returned to the merchants.

In 1760 the collector sent the Board eight certificates for twenty-eight hogsheads containing 29,939 lbs of unmanufactured tobacco brought coastways to Dundee in the *Seaflower* of Kincardine, John Brown master, from Aberdeen. He reported that 'Thomas Robertson proposes to dispose of some part of his tobacco mentioned in these certificates to people in neighbouring towns'. In 1785 Robertson sent 267 lbs of tobacco by William Drummond carrier to Alexander Morrison in Montrose. This was seized by James Mitchell, supervisor of excise. The tobacco weighed 87 lbs more than Robertson had credit for and the collector reported 'I am well informed that this carrier frequently carries both tobacco and stalks in that private manner blended among yarn and other goods. I am also told after this seizure was made he said that had he known he would have set his dog to Barclay the officer when he attempted to make the seizure'.

As part of the attempts to keep the records straight, from time to time the collectors would check the identity of the tobacco in the merchants' cellars. In January 1740 the collector at Dundee 'Having received an information that considerable quantities of tobacco ... were lodged in different cellars here and observing by our books that the credit for that commodity is but small I proceeded to a search and have lodged in the warehouse twelve hogsheads and sixty-seven matts. As the day is short and work of this kind dilatory, considering the interruptions we meet with on such occasions, I was forced to put it in without weighing but I compute there may be about 20,000 lbs of it. I have received a bill of parcels from Thomas Blair for twelve hogsheads and a protest by Henry Pattullo for the sixty-seven matts. As I imagine they will make immediate application to your Honours in order to show how the duties of this tobacco were paid, I propose to let it lie without weighing or returning till I have your directions in regard it's too bulky a commodity to be stole away from me and time enough for being condemned this term'. Ten days later the two merchants had not been able to prove that they had credit for the tobacco, which was seized.

According to the new collector at Dundee, it was possible that a local fraud had developed. In March 1735 he wrote 'There was brought here from Leith in Mr Dent's [the previous acting collector's] time, twelve hogsheads tobacco, which were regularly discharged at the quay and then carried over the water by a permit to a warehouse in Fife, directly opposite to this town, under pretence that the storehouses here were all full. This tobacco is now to be brought back here by another permit in order to be cleaned and repacked for exportation. I must confess I don't know how a permit in either case can be refused, though I am sensible it may and I believe does cover a notorious fraud viz. the tobacco so carried over the water is consumed in the country and an equal quantity either run or relanded from Holland placed in the room thereof and exported again'.

On 11 September 1739 the collector at Perth was informed of seven horses loaded with goods 'having passed about three miles from this place westward. [I] immediately called a sergeant and ten men and followed. When I came to Collon, I was informed six of the seven horses were lodged there [so] I caused be searched the houses and found the horses in the stable. But after a most strict search, which took up most part of the night, could not find the goods'. The search continued the next day, when the collector succeeded in seizing six loads of tobacco. 'As it rained the whole time and the party were very alert and were out part of two days and a whole night they were paid extraordinary'.

This tobacco was claimed by George Ross but the collector was determined to bring it to trial. The circumstances on that night had been suspicious because 'the carriers travelled in a very rainy day at night. When they came to their quarters in the Collon, two miles from this, though the rain still continued very heavy, they hid it in a dunghill in the open fields and built a stack of whins upon it, though they had a good dry barn belonging to the house where they lodged to have put it in. Indeed there were some packs belonging to the carriers themselves, which I found hid in the house amongst peats. I humbly think it is evident from this circumstance that they were conscious to themselves of its being run tobacco. Otherways they would have put it in the barn where it might have been safe and not have hid it in a dunghill'.

This case emphasises the delays over bringing seizures to trial. The tobacco was seized in September 1739, yet in November 1740 the collector wrote to the solicitor's office 'I had yours of the 17th wherein you tell me that the Ross trial is put off till next term. I'm sorry for it because I'm afraid of losing some of my witnesses. However, it is not so bad as Ross gave out when he was last in town, that he was to get up his bond and no further enquiry to be made, which surprised me.' In January 1741 the collector confirmed to the solicitor that he had 'lost several of my most material evidences, who are gone out of the country. Yet I can prove these suspicious circumstances'.

On 13 June 1740 two customs officers at Perth received information about 'a great number of horse loads of goods going from the coast of Fife westward'. They set off along the road and were told 'by the herds of eighteen horse load being before them. But ... they found only one horse load of tobacco, which they seized and brought to the warehouse. The carrier showed a letter to the surveyor directed to Mrs Beny at Alloa for two horse load of tobacco from Dundee'. However, 'Thomson says that he is positively informed that this tobacco is part of the cargo of tobacco run lately in Anstruther collection where the officers were deforced'. At the same time 'there was no offer made to prove the credit far less the identity [of the tobacco] but only a protest taken against the collector and surveyor for costs and damages because the collector refused to deliver up the tobacco without your orders'.

On 27 February 1739 the collector at Montrose transmitted to the Board a return for four matts containing 607 lbs leaf tobacco seized by George Lockhart, tidesman, at the Red Ford about 11 miles to the south-west and nearly four miles from any part on the coast. On 6 March John Grant, merchant, made a protest against Lockhart for carrying off the tobacco, 'pretending it was a part of the tobaccos condemned in exchequer and delivered out of the warehouses of Dundee and this place by virtue of writs of delivery ... Mr Lockhart assures us that his informer told him the four matts tobacco were run out of a vessel at the West Haven and carried the night before to the place where he seized them'. The Board referred the case to their solicitor and replied 'As the condemnation of this tobacco depends wholly on the fact that it was run out of a vessel, Lockhart is the proper person to determine whether he can bring evidence to support it and when this evidence is stated we can then judge of the sufficiency of it'. This was not the only tobacco belonging to Grant that had been seized. In June 1740 the collector reported 'Yesterday David Buchanan, for John Grant merchant, came here and demanded from us a permit to ship thirty matts containing 4,500 lbs leaf tobacco on board the *Katharine* of Ethiehaven, John Thorn master, for Leith which the collector refusing to grant (seeing your Honours was pleased to direct by your letter of the 16 March 1739 that we should grant no coast dispatches for the tobacco seized at Carmylie ...). Mr Buchanan, in [the] name of Mr Grant, took a protest against the collector that he should be liable in damages etc. We hope your Honours will be pleased to give directions there anent in case Mr Grant shall insist in a pursuit against the collector for any damages. We humbly beg you will be pleased to give us orders in case any more coast dispatches shall be required from us for the Carmylie tobacco'.

In November 1770 Dundee received an express from the collector at Anstruther, enclosing one from the Board 'directing from several suspicious circumstances attending the *Catherine* of Dundee, Robert Hutchison master, loaded with tobacco at Greenock and in the harbour of Elie said to be bound for Rotterdam, that the uppermost hogsheads of the cargo should be landed and weighed and that the weight compared with the weights mentioned in the cocket and to report the result'. In the meantime the vessel had sailed for Dundee, where the top ten hogsheads were weighed. Eight agreed with the cocket but 'one was 10 lbs less and another 7 lbs for which reason we lodged these two in the king's warehouse and detained the vessel'. On 8 December the collector reported 'We have interrogated the master as to the reason for his coming up the Firth to Burntisland then putting into Elie and afterwards Dundee who alleges it was owing to bad weather ... we have placed two additional officers on the ship so as she is now guarded by two tidewaiters and two boatmen and we have communicated your Honours order to Captain John Read of the *Princess Caroline* sloop for detaining the vessel in case any attempt should be made for carrying her to sea'.

The tailpiece describes the deforcement of officers attempting to make a seizure at Stirling Bridge. There are further details about Stirling in Chapter Nine.

The Story of Stirling Bridge

On Monday 7 May 1764 William Robertson and James Reid, landcarriage waiters stationed at Stirling Bridge, seized a load of tobacco from the carts of John Peters, Perth carrier, on his way from Glasgow. But a crowd of people attacked them and carried away the tobacco.

Henry Stewart, John Peters's servant, was believed to have 'carried some of the tobacco and snuff through a yard belonging to James Sherrar at the Bridge of Stirling and the witnesses who will prove the same are John Jaffray carrier, William Bachop servant to Peter Johnston flasher, John Donaldson tanner, servant to Mr Morrison, tanner, John Shedden, vintner, and Agnes Lawrie, servant to William Lawrie, carrier, all in Stirling, besides many others they did not know'.

In February 1765 attempts were made to arrest Stewart. 'Notwithstanding all the precaution we have been able to use Henry Stewart ... has yet avoided us ... unluckily [he] passed at Stirling Bridge on the night betwixt Saturday and Sunday, which was not usual. John Jaffray and William Bachop we can lay our hands on at any time but we are willing to have Stewart first secured, in case the apprehending of others should give him the alarm and so escape us. He was arrested on 26 February and imprisoned at Stirling.

'The agent employed to carry on the prosecution is of opinion that the two officers deforced will be the most material evidences, as the prosecution is at the instance of the collector on behalf of the crown [which meant that the Board's solicitor did not believe there was sufficient evidence]. It will therefore be necessary that James Reid be ordered to attend when the trial comes on. He at present resides at Glasgow, having been placed upon the superannuation fund since the deforcement happened [see Chapter One]'.

On 1 March 1765 Alloa wrote to the collector at Glasgow explaining that Reid should be at Stirling the night before the trial, which was due to take place on Tuesday, 5 March. Reid's expenses would be paid 'whatever they are'.

Reid was not in a fit condition to attend the court and was the only witness still to be examined. 'The justices refused to grant commission to take

contd.

The Story of Stirling Bridge contd.

Reid's oath at Glasgow, although it was strenuously insisted on in court in regard to his valetudinary state, but they adjourned their sessions till Tuesday next ... that James Reid might be examined by them at Stirling. From this you will see the necessity of Reid's being at that town ... and therefore we earnestly entreat you will give directions for his conveyance, either on a carriage or such other manner as shall be most eligible'.

On 15 March 1765 the justices found 'the information not proven, assoilised the defendants and dismissed them from the bar ... The reasons he (William McKillop) thinks are owing to William Robertson's evidence falling short ... and the other evidence, James Reid, not coming from Glasgow to depone but who sent a certificate of his old age and infirmity, which the justices would not accept of, nor grant a commissioner to take his oath in Glasgow'.

The collector reported to the Board on Robertson's behaviour. 'He, being the evidence on which we had most reason to depend, was first examined. From his strong assertions before the trail we made not the least doubt but that his deposition as to the identity of the deforcers would have been quite clear. But to our utter astonishment he declared before the justices that he could not particularise a single person concerned in the deforcement. This palpable deviation from what he not only said but gave under his hand leaves the strongest reason to suspect that the defender's influence, which appeared manifest over the other evidences, had extended to Mr Robertson. Also upon the whole the proof turned out so lame that we have no reason to expect a favourable sentence, owing as we humbly apprehend to our being misled by Robertson'.

Asked to explain himself, Robertson replied that other witnesses who were present had told him that Stewart was the principal deforcer. 'To excuse himself he says that the hurry and confusion he was in he could not exactly notice who were the persons most active, and alleges that the distance of time betwixt the deforcement and prosecution might have been the reason why the witnesses had forgot the circumstances of the deforcement and the persons concerned therein. As the deforcement happened in the daytime we think it very singular that William Robertson could not particularise any of the offenders when he was examined before the justices, although in his letter to us of the 7th May last he says some of them he knew'.

CHAPTER SEVEN: THE SMUGGLERS AND THEIR FRIENDS

'I am afraid, sir, this martyr [Andrew Wilson] to this new heretical sect of smuggling was too much favoured by the misled and unwary multitude; too many of them thought as he himself did, sir, that he was unjustly condemned, and every one who firmly believed this would, no doubt, think it his duty to save and to rescue this innocent person (as they thought) from the rigour of law'. [From the speech of Patrick Lindsay, member of Parliament for Edinburgh, on 16 May 1737, as quoted in the Gentleman's Magazine]

It is one of the dreams of the researcher into smuggling history that intimate details about individual smugglers will appear in the custom house letter-books. In this context, the area between Montrose and Dunbar has proved exceptionally fruitful.

The Smuggling Companies

The clearest description of a smuggling organisation actually comes from the Aberdeen letter-books. The story starts on 3 February 1800 when Mr Sim, the collector's clerk, and William Corbet, junior officer of excise, seized the *Anna*, George Mitchell master, which was stranded on the beach about 5 miles north of Aberdeen. They also seized the cargo, which included twenty-five boxes of manufactured tobacco, twenty ankers of brandy, five hundred and ninety-nine ankers of geneva from Alderney 'said to be bound for Bergen'. A subsequent enquiry showed that 'the state of the winds and weather was not such as to afford any grounds for the pretence they show [she] was forced in by stress of weather'. The cargo belonged to 'Henry Sharpy of Arbroath, partner of a house abroad (supposed Flushing) and agent in this country for said house, who send great quantities of contraband goods to this country'. Andrew Mitchell [possibly related to the master] was a farmer at Whiteness, near Slains, 'whose farm is situated hard by the Ward of Cruden, where a number of cargoes of contraband goods have within these few years been run ashore'. Finally Alexander Christie, spirit dealer in Aberdeen was part-owner in the cargo and 'employed to act as

Figure 10: John Metcalf, Blind Jack of Knaresborough

There follows an extract from the Life of John Metcalf [see Chapter One and Figure 3]:

'Once having disposed of a string of horses, he bought, with the produce, a quantity of rum, brandy, and tea, to the amount of £200, put them on board a vessel for Leith, and travelled overland on foot, to meet the vessel there. He had about 30 miles to walk, and carried near five stone weight of goods which he did not choose to put on shipboard. At Leith he had the mortification to wait six weeks, without receiving any tidings of the vessel, which many supposed to have been lost, there having been a storm in the interval. The distress of mind resulting from this, induced him once to say, 'If she is lost, I wish I had been in her; for she had all my property on board.' Soon after, however, the ship got into Leith harbour. He there went on board, and set sail for Newcastle; but another storm arising, the mate was washed overboard, the mainsail carried away, and the ship driven near the coast of Norway. Despair now became general; the prospect of going to the bottom seeming almost certain. He now reflected on the impiety of his wish with respecting the former storm; and so effectually was his way of thinking changed, that had he had all the current coin of the universe, he would have given it to have been on shore. It now appeared to him a dreadful thing to leave the world in the midst of health and vigour; but the wind changing, hope began to return, and the captain put about for the Scottish coast, intending to make Arbroath. A signal of distress was put up, but the sea ran so high, that no boat could venture out with a pilot. He then stood in for the harbour, but struck against the pier end, owing to the unmanageable state of the vessel, from the loss of her mainsail; she narrowly escaped being bulged; but having got to the back of the pier, was towed round into the harbour, with near five feet of water in her hold. Her escape from the merciless elements, however, did not seem to terminate her dangers, the country people showing a disposition to seize her as a wreck, and plunder her; but fortunately there was at hand a party consisting of an officer and twenty men, of Pulteney's regiment, who had been in pursuit of some smugglers; and Metcalf knowing them well, (Colonel Thornton's company being attached to that regiment) the officer sent three files of men to protect the vessel, while the crew were removing the goods to a warehouse'.

agent in the business'. No reference has been found to Sharpy in the Montrose letter-books. However in March 1800 Peter Caw, shipmaster in Perth, and Charles Archer & Co, merchants there 'owners of the ship *Mary & Ann* of Perth, now called the *Anna* of Emden' were claiming the vessel from Mitchell. Again nothing further has been found about this, which is disappointing as one wonders how Sharpy/Mitchell obtained the vessel. There is some information about the vessel, however. In July 1790 John Ogilvie, commander of the *Royal George* excise yacht, seized the *Mary & Ann* of Perth, Peter Caw master, with cards, china and nankeen on board. The ship was set free on a payment of £7 11s 6d to Ogilvie. In 1795 French wine was seized on her when she arrived from Gothenburg. Charles Archer is referred to as shipmaster and owner of the *Hope* and in 1795 there were problems over her cargo of wood from Easterizer.

While a man living in Arbroath was organising smuggling into the Aberdeen district, a man in Folkestone, Kent, was one of the major suppliers of smuggled goods to the Auchmithie-Havens area. In a long report about smuggling dated 1807 the collector at Anstruther states that one of the main reasons for the decline of smuggling in the area was 'from the total loss of James Butcher, the principal smuggler to this coast and (whose residence was at Folkestone) together with a large cutter-rigged sloop deeply laden for the coast and valued at £4 or £5,000. This man was a constant trader'. The Folkestone letter-books do not exist for this period but according to the Dunbar records a Folkestone vessel, which had sailed out of Berwick Bay at daybreak in September 1801, was described as 60 tons burthen, all black from the gunwales to the water edge, having an English jack at her mizzen mast head but no guns. According to the story told in Chapter Five, William Butcher was on shore north of Arbroath making signals to a smuggling lugger in 1790 while John Braid, who is discussed at length later in this chapter, purchased his geneva from 'the Butchers and the smugglers at Arbroath, who were the actual importers'. Butchard 'a well known smuggler' residing at Arbroath was the spokesman for Baird and Middleton at Braid's creditors' meetings described in the tailpiece to this chapter. In 1805 a lugger owned by Bouchier was expected off the coast with a cargo of 1,200 ankers of gin. Research to identify the exact individuals involved and the structure of any 'company' continues.

Lord Elphinstone

In June 1737 the collector at Alloa reported to the Board 'having upon Monday last received information ... that a quantity of soap, brandy, wine and other goods were lately brought to this port by Buckhaven boats and that part thereof, belonging to Mr Dundas, were lodged either at his cellars at Elphinstonepans or in his father's cellars at Letham house and the remainder at the Throsk and Cuckspow, the former about two and the latter about one mile this side of Stirling on the opposite side of the water to this ... when we came to Letham house we found the father [Thomas Dundas - one of the members of the jury at the Porteous trial described in Chapter One] but not the son at home, who upon acquainting him with our business told us that if his son dealt that way it was without his knowledge or allowance and that he should meet with no encouragement from him and accordingly gave us immediate access to all the corners of the house ...

'Upon our return to Elphinstonepans we were refused access to the cellars there by a servant of Lord Elphinstone, who kept the keys, as Mr Dundas's father informed us ... after this we proceeded by water with the party to Throsk and Cuckspow ... we returned to Elphinstonepans with the party to put them so far in their way to Airth, where they are quartered. But upon coming there we were extremely surprised to be informed that Lord Elphinstone had been there threatening the officers and abusing, them as well as us, in the most shameful manner for daring, as he said, to break open any doors about his works. That for the constable he would instantly have him set aside for daring to go along to assist us without his orders, and Mr Ritchie, reputed a most inveterate immobile, who my Lord has lately taken into his service and who daily abuses the officers, threatened that if he had been present when the doors were broken open and we were looking through his house, which is immediately above Mr Dundas's cellars, he would have thrown one of us over the stairs. However we did not think proper on this occasion to resent such usage further than laying the same before your Honours.

'The sergeant and party in returning to Airth, finding a cask of soap amongst the corns, carried it along with them and lodged it in the house of one Mr Stevens, merchant in Airth, who keeps a public house there. Mr Miln, the tidewaiter at that place, getting notice of this, went to the house where it was and seized it and acquainted the collector therewith. He sent the boat to bring it up to the custom house and enclosed we send your Honours the return ... together with the copy of the order, which my Lord sent to the landlord of the house where the soap was lodged, upon his being informed of the directions the collector had given for bringing the same to the warehouse ...

'We think it our duty to further acquaint your Honours that we are credibly informed that the day before yesterday my Lord Elphinstone held a justices of the peace court at Airth and had the constable discharged, at least suspended from exercising that office for six months, on account of his going along to assist us that day, as he before had threatened ...

'PS Since writing the above we have certain information that ... the justices present were my Lord Elphinstone, his son and James Bruce of Powfoulis'.

The customs did not retain the seizure for long. On 23 August they were directed to deliver to Mr Dundas the wines seized from him at Letham 'upon his signing a release of damages'.

This was not the first occasion when Lord Elphinstone had behaved in a high-handed fashion. Between midnight and one o'clock in the morning on 11 May 1734 Robert Ellis, landcarriage waiter, seized six firkins of soap and six casks of brandy 'as they were coming on horseback' into Stirling. These were returned to the Board as a seizure and as the goods were not claimed they were condemned in the court of exchequer. 'Since which time one John Mitchell, a noted smuggler in this place, had brought an action before the justices of the peace for the recovery of the value of the soap from the officer who seized the same, pretending to have bought it in the lawful way of trade'. The collector instructed Ellis to explain to the justices that 'the soap being condemned they had no power of judging in that affair. Besides had the person who here claims the property of the goods desired to have made oath before them within ten days after they were stopped that he had bought them ... even in that case the justices had no power to meddle in it further than taking the affidavit'. [See Chapter Eight] Despite this the justices fined

Ellis £5 10s, as the value of the soap and the charge of prosecuting him before them. He was then imprisoned in the tolbooth, where he was held for several weeks 'till liberate by order of the lords of justiciary'.

Those present at the meeting of the justices included Lord Elphinstone, Sir James Campbell of Arkiness, Sir George Dunbar, Messrs Grames elder and younger of Borklivy and the provost. 'I understand that Sir James Campbell was very much against the justices proceeding in this court and that upon being over-ruled he protested he might not be liable for their procedure. But as to this I cannot give your Honours so particular an account as I could wish, the clerk to the justices being out of town and therefore I cannot have the copy of the process'.

In 1732 John Schaw, tidewaiter, acting on information provided by the excise officers, had seized a quantity of soap. 'Some of the justices present at this [1734] court were upon that occasion called together by the proprietor [of the soap]' and Shaw was imprisoned.

John Braid, smuggler of St Andrews

The seizure by Robert Boyack of three boats from the Havens was described in Chapter Seven. Thirty-seven casks of spirits were seized after this smuggle. Ten of these were hidden in the house of Andrew Cochrane, weaver at Rabbit Hall, Links of St Andrews.

On 31 January 1805 the collector at Anstruther wrote '[We] humbly pray leave to state to your Honours that as the most effectual way to prevent and suppress illicit trade that Andrew Cochrane ... should be immediately prosecuted for the penalties ... We do not believe that Cochrane is a man of property or a smuggler himself. But ... he might be induced to tell the truth and be the means of getting hold of John Wilson, John Braid and Thomas Mitchell the three persons who are well known to be the smugglers in St Andrews'. He then referred to a similar case in 1800 when Bell was prosecuted and 'although he did not discover the name of the smuggler, yet it was well known it was Mr Adamson of Kingsbarns, who paid the penalties for him. It had the effect (as we have most undoubted authority for stating) of this Adamson's never being engaged in smuggling since and his capital, for he is a man of property, being now entirely invested in farming'.

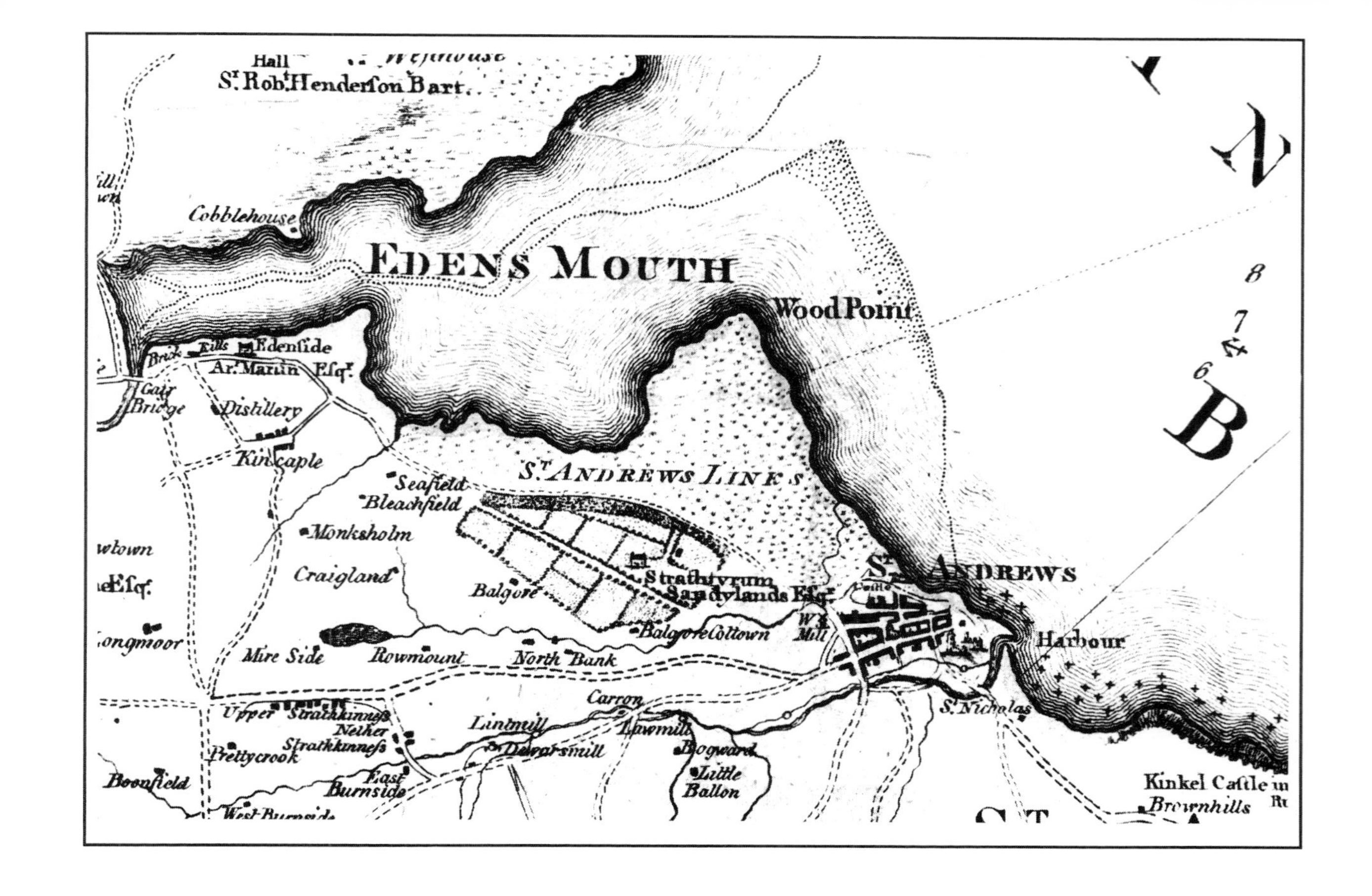

Hall
St. Robt. Henderson Bart.
Cobblehouse
EDENS MOUTH
Wood Point
Brick Kills
Edenside
Ar. Martin Esqr.
Guard Bridge
Distillery
Kincaple
Seafield
Bleachfield
Monksholm
Craigland
Balgove
St. ANDREWS LINKS
Strathtyrum
Sandylands Esqr.
Balgove Cottown
W. Mill
St. ANDREWS
Harbour
St. Nicholas
Mire Side
Rowmount
North Bank
Longmoor
Upper Strathkinness
Nether Strathkinness
Prettycrook
Boonfield
East Burnside
West Burnside
Linnmill
Carron
Lawmill
Denbraesmill
Bogward
Little Ballon
Kinkel Castle in Ru.
Brownhills
8
7
6
B

Figure 11: The St Andrews District in the Eighteenth Century

This map indicates the section of St Andrews bay including Kinkel castle, the town and harbour, the Links (where Rabbit Hall was located) and the Eden's mouth as far upstream as Guard [Gair] Bridge.

There follows the story of a deaf and dumb fisherman. According to the collector at Anstruther, John Hay, carter, was 'willing to depone ... that on Sunday morning, 30th January 1803, he was taking a walk along the shore on the West Sands of St Andrews where he met with a fisherman of his acquaintance, who had just found several ankers that appeared to have been buried in the sands but washed up by the tide. He and the fisherman carried them up to the bents when immediately Andrew Cochrane and some other men started up from behind a bush and claimed these ankers, informing them they were smuggled gin belonging to John Braid, that they had been hid by them in the sands for fear of the revenue officers and that they were watching them till it was dark, when they might be brought into St Andrews. One of the persons pierced a cask and gave them both a draw of it. This was not far from Cochrane's house at Rabbit Hall and Cochrane and those that were with him appeared to be going and coming between it and the place where the gin was. By [the] desire of Cochrane he took his acquaintance the fisherman, who is both deaf and dumb, away in John Braid's house in St Andrews and kept him there all the day, lest he should have made signs to some of the revenue officers informing them of the smuggle. When it was dark he (John Hay) assisted them in digging up and bringing into Braid's house the smuggled gin. He saw both Braid and his wife, who promised him a great deal for his assistance and for concealing the smuggle. But he never got a shilling for Braid became bankrupt shortly after that. He supposed there was not less than one hundred ankers [in the smuggle] ...

'From the above narrative I humbly conceive that John Hay would be a useful witness in case this matter should come to a trial, as it would go fully to establish the connection which subsisted between Braid and Cochrane in their smuggling transactions. The fisherman who accompanied him being both deaf and dumb I do not know how far he would be held a competent witness'.

As a result the Board agreed that Cochrane should be prosecuted for receiving and harbouring run geneva. The collector went to St Andrews, where he inspected Cochrane's premises. 'The door of the hogsty, where three of the ankers of gin was found, is close to and within three feet of the door of the dwelling house. The sty itself is built to and upon the wall of the house, opposite to the apartment where the family sits and sleeps, and the door of it is so small that the ankers must have been over-ended in putting them in. Of course it is impossible to suppose they could be lodged there at any hour without the family's knowledge. The barn, where seven ankers was found, having a byre between it and the dwelling house, they might ... be lodged there without Cochrane's knowledge, provided the door of the barn had been left open. But this could not be the case. There is a good lock and key upon the door and at the time of the seizure there was corn in bags standing in the barn. And being within a short mile of St Andrews it is not likely he would under such circumstances leave the door open with the key in it. The road which the carts passed that conveyed the gin is within eight short paces of the door of the house ... the petitioner was not in bed at the time of the seizure, as stated in his petition, but up and at his work. We from these circumstances are firmly of opinion that the petitioner was in the full knowledge of the whole transaction notwithstanding he still persists in denying the smallest knowledge of any part of it'.

Cochrane was formerly a servant to John Braid, a merchant in St Andrews, who was supposed to be the owner of the smuggled gin. 'It was with a view to aid and assist Braid that Cochrane (who is a weaver) left the town of St Andrews to reside at Rabbit Hall, which is a distance from any neighbouring and that in putting in his work etc. he is often obliged to send to some distance for persons to assist him, which would not be necessary if he had continued to reside in St Andrews, and that he is habit and repute the confidential agent of Braid'. As a result of his time with Braid 'he seems to have acquired the habits of a hardened smuggler. Yet there is no saying but he or his wife [Euphemina Fortune] may alter their tone'.

It has been possible to build up a detailed picture of the witnesses against Cochrane from the letters between the collector and/or comptroller at Anstruther and Alexander Osborn, the Board's solicitor.

Alexander Fairnie, rabbit catcher at Rabbit Hall, Links of St Andrews

Fairnie had helped the officers carry the geneva out of Cochrane's offices. The collector believed that he would 'speak out the truth on oath before the court. But on this I may be mistaken and therefore much reliance cannot be put upon it'. A subpoena was served on him to appear as a witness but the collector reported on 26 November 'I am informed that [he] ... is not in good health and intends to apply to a medical man for a certificate of his inability to attend the trial'. By December the collector was doubtful if Fairnie would be a proper witness, 'even if his health permitted him to attend the trial, because I am informed he has liberty from Mr Dempster (whose servant he is) to go into Cochrane's barn for straw for his cow at any time, though it is not likely that Cochrane would leave his barn door open merely to accommodate him'.

Robert Paton, weaver in St Andrews

The collector had an alternative suggestion - Robert Paton, now foreman to Mr Charles Dempster. 'This man is represented to me as having formerly been the confidential servant of Braid but now his great enemy'. Paton would be able to link Cochrane with concealing smuggled goods for Braid on 'many circumstances'. But 'then I could not depend on him speaking the truth' for although he was currently against Braid 'yet as he is a servant to Mr Dempster (one of the witnesses and friendly to Braid), [also] ... very little dependence can be had on the evidence of a man who has been formerly a smuggler, as Paton was while servant to Braid ... I know that the subpoenaing Paton would alarm Braid very much and induce him to step forward in support of Cochrane [he paid for his horse hire to go to Edinburgh and report to the court]. Paton, however, could be no proof that Braid was the smuggler and proprietor of the goods found in Cochrane's custody, because he had left his services before that transaction took place'. The collector's instinct was right. Paton was 'much alarmed' when the subpoena was served and had previously declared to John Ramsay, tidesman, 'that if he (Paton) was in Cochrane's place he would soon clear himself by giving up Braid'.

John Hay, carrier between Anstruther and St Andrews

Possibly the most bizarre of the witnesses was John Hay, who gave the collector a statement about a smuggle that had taken place in 1803 [see Figure 11]. This evidence prompted the collector to attempt an actual prosecution against Braid - see later.

Charles Dempster, merchant in St Andrews

The collector first contacted Dempster over the creditors meeting described in the tailpiece to this chapter. Subsequently Dempster told Mr Brodie, supervisor of excise in St Andrews, that there had been another ten ankers of geneva actually concealed in Cochrane's house. 'Upon enquiring at the officers, they admit that they did not search the dwelling house at all, not having any suspicion of goods being concealed there. I examined the inside of the house myself and am convinced there is room enough to conceal ten ankers of gin and John Ramsay and Robert Boyack ... declares that Mr Brodie informed them of this circumstance and that Mr Dempster was his authority ... I further pray leave to observe that Mr Dempster owns the house and land at Rabbit Hall, where Cochrane resides, and he likewise employs him as a weaver in his sailcloth manufactory. It is therefore most likely Mr Dempster knows the person to whom the geneva belonged as well as the particulars of the whole transaction'. The collector's suggestion that both Dempster and Brodie should be called as witnesses was accepted by the solicitor.

The collector added on 9 December 'from all I have been able to search and find it [is] generally reported that John Braid himself mentioned the circumstance of the ten ankers being in Cochrane's dwelling house at a public meeting at a mason lodge in St Andrews. As Mr Dempster generally attends these meetings, it is very likely he was there. I do not however find that it was ever stated that these ankers were the property of Braid, though there is not a man in St Andrews who does not believe them to have been so ... I should have mentioned in the first part of my letter that John Wilson, merchant in St Andrews, is reputed to have been one of the persons present at the mason lodge when Braid made the declaration about the ten ankers ... But as Wilson is one of the greatest smugglers in St Andrews it would answer no good purpose to subpoena him'.

On 13 December the collector had the first hint that the trial might not go ahead. Fairnie had told someone that 'Cochrane informed him yesterday that he would not need to go to Edinburgh as the affair was made up. Yet I have my doubts as to the truth of this. For although Braid has still a great deal of money and property among his hands, yet he is not in that flourishing situation he once was, besides having lately lost his best friend, to whom he applied in all cases of difficulty and who got him out of many scrape, I mean the late Dr John Hill, whose natural son was Braid'.

The collector was wrong, as is seen from his PS to this very letter 'since writing this ... have received yours of 12th ordering the subpoenas to be withdrawn'.

In early January 1806 the collector was amassing the evidence for the prosecution against Braid for the smuggle in January 1803 [see Figure 11]. His witnesses would be: John Hay, carrier from Anstruther to St Andrews; Robert Paton, weaver in St Andrews formerly a steward to Braid; Alexander Simpson, labourer in St Andrews and also formerly servant to Braid; Andrew Cochrane, weaver at Rabbit Hall; Alexander Greig, formerly and still steward to Braid; Robert Gray, William Gray, William Ramsay, George Kirk and Richard Cooper all carters in St Andrews and Robert Mitchell, weaver in St Andrews.

Almost as a footnote, on 4 February 1806 the collector makes one of the more interesting comments about Braid. 'As it may appear extraordinary why Braid should apparently take so little charge of his own affairs and that it may not be imputed to more prudential motives it is necessary to mention that he is lame and walks with crutches and they are very unfit to aid or assist personally in smuggling transactions'.

A week later the solicitor had explained that as the smuggle had happened three years ago there could be no prosecution. But the collector remained optimistic. 'I am fully of opinion he [Braid] never was concerned in the actual importation of the geneva, that is to say the actual bringing it ashore from on board the smuggling vessels that conveyed it from foreign parts. His mode of dealing was to purchase from the Butchers and the smugglers at Arbroath, who were the actual importers. There are two persons in St Andrews, Robert Paton and Alexander Simpson, formerly Braid's servants and who he was in habit of sending to opposite coast of Angus for that purpose. They sometimes returned in two days at other times they stayed longer. They might perhaps receive the geneva at a particular time direct from on board the smuggling vessels but in general I apprehend it would be loaded into the boats from the numerous concealments belonging to the smugglers on the coast of Angus. Both these people has left Braid service three years ago, though if their evidence against him was necessary it could be easily obtained as they are both in very bad habits with him ... In the meantime I hope you will be satisfied with my conduct and that, although I may not be successful in my endeavours to convict Braid and thus prove a great mean of preventing smuggling, I have done my duty to the utmost of my abilities in endeavouring so to do'.

The collector's perseverance was certainly impressive. In the tailpiece to this chapter is the evidence that he collected about a meeting of Braid's creditors.

The Story of a Bankrupt's Affairs

'With respect to that part of the [anonymous] letter which relates to the creditors of John Braid of St Andrews, a bankrupt, we in the first place applied to Mr Robert Meldrum, agent for the Bank of Scotland at St Andrews and trustee for the creditors of Braid. He informed us that Messrs Butchard, Baird and Middleton, well known smugglers residing at Arbroath and the neighbourhood thereof, were creditors of Braid to the amount of £1,200, avowedly for smuggled gin sold and delivered to him. Butchard had for himself and as proxy for the other two attended several meetings of the creditors and insisted upon being ranked and drawing a dividend along with the other creditors. But which measure has not been acceded to by them. But that it was most likely it would be so, as it appeared that great part of the funds to be divided among the creditors had arisen from the smuggled goods. But that it was to be settled finally at a meeting to be held for that purpose on the 5th inst.

'We then requested him to show us the bankrupt's books and papers. Those he said had gone out of his hands into those of the bankrupt some time ago but that neither from them or from the bills granted for the smuggled gin could any information be gathered, as there was nothing mentioned in either but such as 'for goods' or 'value received' or value on jarn etc. He however assured us he would in the meantime gather all the information he could and report to us accordingly.

'Having obtained a list of the names of the creditors, we next applied to Mr Haig, the distiller at Kincaple, and Mr Dempster, merchant in St Andrews, two of the principal of them. The first of these gentlemen entered warmly into our views for the suppression of smuggling and we pray leave to transmit to your Honours his letter to us ... on that subject and which will explain to your Honours the transactions of the meeting of the 5th. It appeared from this gentleman's account that Mr Butchard, the smuggler, appeared there and produced a memorial and opinion signed by Mr Adam Gilles, advocate, in which he gave his decided opinion that the smugglers from their not being, as they alleged, the first importers of the gin but only the purchasers of it from those that were, that of course they are by law entitled to bring actions and recover debts for such gin. Although that at the same time they purchased, sold and delivered the same they knew that it had not paid any of His Majesty's duties and was liable to be seized by any of His Majesty's officers of customs

contd.

The Story of a Bankrupt's Affairs contd.

or excise. And therefore Butchard claimed a right to be ranked with the other creditors. Accordingly Mr Meldrum, the trustee, was requested to read this opinion to the meeting but was not allowed by Butchard to keep the original or take a copy.

'Your Honours will see from Mr Haig's letter that this claim was resisted by him in particular and so effectually that the smugglers withdrew their claims on condition of the fair traders accepting 12s a pound, it appearing that the funds would pay 12s 8d, and discharging Braid, which last measure they made a principal stipulation, their motives for which may be easily guessed at.

'We have therefore thought it our duty to lay the account of this transaction and our proceedings thereon before your Honours, as it appears to us a most extraordinary circumstance that a set of men like these smugglers should have the effrontery to come forward and publicly own their dealings in contraband goods and claim an equal participation of a bankrupt's effects with the fair trader. And this founded on the opinion of an eminent counsel. And that, if there is not already, a law should be enacted implicitly declaring void all such claims. For had it not been for our application to Messrs Meldrum, Haig and Dempster we have no doubt but the smugglers would have been permitted to have ranked with the other creditors and drawn their full dividend. And should such proceedings be allowed to go on the greatest encouragement to illicit trade could be given.

'How far these men may be liable in penalty we do not pretend to know. But if they should [be] there is no want of evidence, as they made at these meetings a public avowal of their contraband trade. And although these smugglers pretend that they were not importers, there can be no doubt but that they were. For independent of the Butchards owning a lugger, which has been running all winter, the practice of these people are that as soon as the lugger makes her appearance they send boats from the shore and bring off the gin from on board the vessel and of course they become the importers. We were at the same time informed by Mr Meldrum, the trustee, that although Braid the bankrupt is a notorious smuggler and much the friend of Butchard and the people of Arbroath, yet were he put on oath he is of opinion he would tell the truth'.

CHAPTER EIGHT: SEIZURES OF UNCUSTOMED AND PROHIBITED GOODS

'We have used all the endeavours we possibly can to get an account of the ship's name out of which the brandy ... was run but can get neither proof nor intelligence what she was. All that the surveyor and tidesman knows is that they saw a vessel with one mast, like a sloop, hovering off and on the Red Head two days, which gave them suspicion that she designed to commit some fraud. Likewise the night before they seized the brandy they saw two boats on board of her with which she stood off to sea and night coming on they lost sight of her and them. This made them watch along the coast that night and next day searching about found the tracks of some carts coming from the sea shore, which they judged had been carrying of the goods. They traced them to the place where they found the goods. The boatmen along the coast and country people favour and assist the smugglers in carrying on their smuggling trade so much that it's almost impracticable for an officer to get any intelligence from them. When any poor man happens to bring an information to an officer he is afraid (if discovered) of his life, or at least of being obliged to leave this part of the country'. [Letter from the Collector at Montrose to the Board dated 21 October 1725]

Information on seizures can be obtained from the Class 1 and Class 2 letter-books, from the Registers of Seizures sometimes found in the Class 4 records and from other sources, including the Condemnation Accounts and Seizure Vouchers (for the Justices of the Peace) or from the Seizure Lists for individual ports, both held at the Scottish Record Office.

The amount of information available from the letter-books varies. Sometimes returns of seizure are accompanied by covering letters. Completing the story is a matter of chance, depending on whether or not the Board required further details within the next few days or whether subsequent writs of appraisement and burning/sale of condemned goods can be traced back to a particular seizure with confidence. By the latter half of the century each return was numbered. Here the Montrose letter-books are particularly valuable. For example, 1785 includes a virtually complete record [see Table III]. One of the more interesting features in this table is that it gives a picture of several branches of the revenue service all working together to combat smuggling. By 1790 the picture had changed. The returns start in January at No 162 [suggesting that during the previous four years there were a further 119 seizures i.e. an average of 30 per year] and continue in a complete numerical series to No 179 in December. Eleven of the seizures, including 2,738 gallons of geneva, brandy, rum and cordial waters, 2,854 lbs tobacco and 108 lbs coffee beans together with five open boats and the sloop *Margaret* of Arbroath were made by the revenue cruisers *Princess Royal* and *Osnaburgh* or row boats connected with them. In comparison the five seizures by tidesmen totalled 172 gallons geneva and 8½ gallons brandy. Two of the seizures that year did not relate to smuggled goods. There had been a dramatic drop in seizures by 1800 with only five recorded throughout the whole year: 26 lbs soft soap, 26 gallons geneva, 103 lbs feathers for beds, 365 gallons geneva and 576 packs playing cards and 8½ gallons geneva. Other letter-books are not so explicit, often simply commenting 'Enclosed five returns of seizure'.

The Class 4 records for Alloa include a register of seizures. Between 1 April 1846 and 22 October 1859 there were twenty-seven seizures registered at Alloa [the returns for Michaelmas Quarter 1845, Christmas Quarter 1845 and Lady Day Quarter 1846 had been nil]. Twenty-five of these were found on vessels, all named, one illegally landed from some vessel or vessels unknown 'without payment of duty' and one goods unshipped by Andrew Bain, pilot of Clackmannan, who had received these in part payment of pilotage. The seizures tended to be small, for example 2 lbs of tobacco found concealed in the longboat on the deck of the *Carlitian Maid* in September 1849. This was claimed by William Taylor, one of the seamen. He was taken before a justice of the peace, convicted of smuggling and fined 'in the mitigated penalty of 10s'. The tobacco was burned. The mate, steward and a seaman on board the *Elizabeth* were offenders in April 1852 and October 1857. But the seizures only totalled 6 lbs 9 ozs tobacco and 1 lb tea. The tobacco was burned and the tea was 'so very inferior and much damaged that it would not fetch the duty. It was therefore destroyed'.

Rosemary Goring attempted to correlate the Justices of the Peace condemnation accounts with the letter-books and concluded 'Unfortunately, these sources have certain drawbacks, not least that they do not always correlate closely with the letter-book material'. Although the St Andrews seizures between 1723 and 1728 were abstracted from the Anstruther list, these were not thought to be worthy of further study by this author.

How were the Seizures made?

Seizures were made either by information or by chance. The information came from sources as varied as government 'spies' in foreign ports, anonymous letters written to the Boards of Customs in Edinburgh or London or the collector, the collectors of other ports, an officer with local knowledge or someone wanting to earn money/seek revenge on a rival. The warnings relating to vessels are discussed in Chapter Two. On 1 July 1735 wine was seized by David Mitchelson, tidesman, 'by an information from the excise officers at Arbroath' and on 19 July 1735 a box of syrup of maiden hair was seized by William Herdman, landwaiter, 'called upon by the officer of excise at Arbroath to go along with him in pursuit of some run goods'. There were also obvious pointers like the ones quoted at the head of this chapter and in Figure 12.

Half the Montrose seizures in 1735 and 1740 were 'by information' but it is the other half which produce the picture of how the goods were found. 'They were watching about the town and seeing some people about the watermouth they went there and found the hogshead of wine lying in the brae' and 'by chance' a box of sugar candy seized by George Lockhart [tidesman], which he found on the fish shore when he was out watching'. Finally there were the cases of 'some starch seized by David Mitchelson tidesman which he tells us he got by chance on the links when out looking for goods running upon the coast' and soap seized by John Campbell comptroller 'which he found when walking in the links'. In April 1780 William Blues [see Figure 9] seized in the house of David Cargill, vintner in Auchmithie, two bags of tea and two ankers of brandy. The tea had been concealed in Alexander Child's [the servant's] bed amongst the clothes, one anker of brandy was in the same room covered with an empty corn sack and the other anker in a closet in which the entered stock was kept. Cargill is mentioned again in Chapter Eleven.

TABLE III: Summary of Seizures made at the Port of Montrose in 1785

Date of return	No	Goods	Seized by
5 May	18	26 ankers geneva 2 ankers brandy 8 horses & 4 carts	William Blues tidesman
8 June	19	5 ankers geneva 4 ankers brandy 2 horses & cart	4 of the boatmen & Thomas Mills tidesman
21 June	21	small sloop rum, brandy, tobacco stalks	William McGregor tidesman
	22	201 gallons geneva 17 gallons brandy fishing boat	John Ferrier *Princess Royal* cutter
25 June	23	13½ gallons brandy 2½ lbs coarse bohea tea ¾ lbs coarse green tea 223 lbs tobacco stalks	boatmen
	24	41 gallons geneva small boat	John Blair commander of the king's boat
	25	30 gallons geneva 4 horses	John Blair
26 July	26 27	349 lbs tobacco stalks 1172 lbs leaf tobacco horse & cart	John Mitchell supervisor of excise
2 August	28	29 matts tobacco stalks	William Blues John Watt boatman
4 August	29	2 hhds Portugal wine	John Mitchell

20 August	30	foreign geneva	Thomas Mills tidesman John Watt & James Campbell boatmen
24 Sept	31	310 lbs leaf tobacco	John Mitchell
	32	2046½ gallons geneva 37 gallons Spanish wine small vessel Jonge Conelia of Flushing	John Forres commander of row boat belonging to *Princess Royal* cutter
3 Oct	33	766 lbs tobacco stalks	William McGregor tidesman
	34	71 gallons geneva	John Blair
	35	4 gallons geneva	
	36	637 lbs leaf tobacco horse & cart	
	37	2194 lbs leaf tobacco 995 lbs tobacco stalks 13 gallons foreign brandy	
	38	8 gallons aqua vitae a horse	
	39	16 gallons geneva	Thomas Mills tidesman
	40	699 lbs leaf tobacco	John Mitchell
22 Oct	41	8½ gallons geneva	David Fetter tidesman
	42	25 gallons geneva 9 gallons brandy	Thomas Mills
29 Nov	43	2244 lbs leaf tobacco 2 carts & horses	John Mitchell

What Happened to the Goods?

Once the goods had been seized and conveyed to the king's/queen's warehouse they were gauged by the excise officers and a return of seizure was sent to the Board - the basis of the information used earlier in this chapter. Then the goods had to be condemned in terms of confirming that they should be seized and destroyed or sold and possibly individuals charged with having been involved in the act of smuggling. There were two methods of condemning. Small amounts or perishable goods were considered before the justices of the peace while large cases were dealt with by the court of exchequer.

Since 1710 the justices were instructed in the treatment of 'more advanced matters of the revenue'. They were to meet once a month, or oftener, if occasion demanded 'to hear, determine and adjudge all matters and offences'. When they fined they were to make sure that the amount was not less than twice the sum which should have been paid as duty, in addition to the costs of the officers. To help in the operation of the law they were to place constables at the service of the revenue officers. The system did not operate easily. [See Chapter Seven for a view of the behaviour of the justices].

There were other problems, as indicated by the collector at Montrose in May 1785. The boatmen and one of the tidesmen belonging to his port had seized a cart and two horses 'found conveying nine ankers of foreign spirits not accompanied with an excise permit ... As there is just now a new commission of the peace issued for this county, in which the chief magistrates of the burghs are not nominated, and as we cannot learn of any of the gentlemen who have accepted or qualified themselves to act under the same, we are altogether at a loss how to proceed to the condemnation of the cart and horses'. The same collector complained that 'when seizures of carriages and horses for the illegal conveyance of spirits are made in the county of Kincardine and such carriages and horses brought to the custom house here no small difficulty occurs in getting the same condemned by justices of the peace for that county owing to the distance'.

On the morning of 26 July 1780 the commander of the king's boat stationed at Montrose was 'out in the country in quest of contraband goods [when he] fell in with a horse conveying two ankers of geneva ... of which they made seizure and brought the same to the king's warehouse'. But 'the horse upon examination proved to be so old and of so little value, having a gangrene on his back, that we did not judge it advisable to proceed to the condemnation of him, as the expense of same would have amounted to three times his worth. Neither did we choose to incur any expense in keeping so worthless an animal in a public stable and therefore delivered him to his former proprietor, on his depositing in our hands ten shillings, which is more than double his value, for the redelivery of him in case he should be called for'.

More information is given about the ownership of the horses than is found about individuals involved in other seizures. On 21 June 1785 John Blair seized two horses belonging to George Mill, farmer in Newbarns, and two horses belonging to David Smith, farmer in Newbigging both in the parish of Inverhiller (Forfar) and in September of that year one horse and cart belonging to Robert Napier, carter in Montrose and a second horse belonging to George Brebner in Brae of Fordun in the town of Montrose. On this occasion the Board wanted further information about why the horses were sold for so little. The answer was 'previous to their sale we found the horses old, worn out and miserably galled animals and the merest skeletons imaginable and the cart, which was composed of only a few spars nailed to two shafts, having no sides or ends, old and broken, and that to the best of our skill and judgement their real value did not exceed what they were sold for'.

If the goods were to be condemned in the exchequer court, this process included long correspondence with the Board's solicitor, confirming that the witnesses would be prepared under oath to give a true statement of the situation. [see Chapter Seven]. Once the case had been set up the offenders were arrested under a capias, issued by the local sheriff depute, and either imprisoned or released on bail to make appearance at the court. This was the theoretical situation. Several exchequer cases failed and were withdrawn almost at the last minute or the offenders were discharged [see Chapters Three and Seven]. In other words the revenue officers fought a losing battle - their authority could not be taken seriously because, as the whole population knew, the offenders would be treated lightly by the authorities.

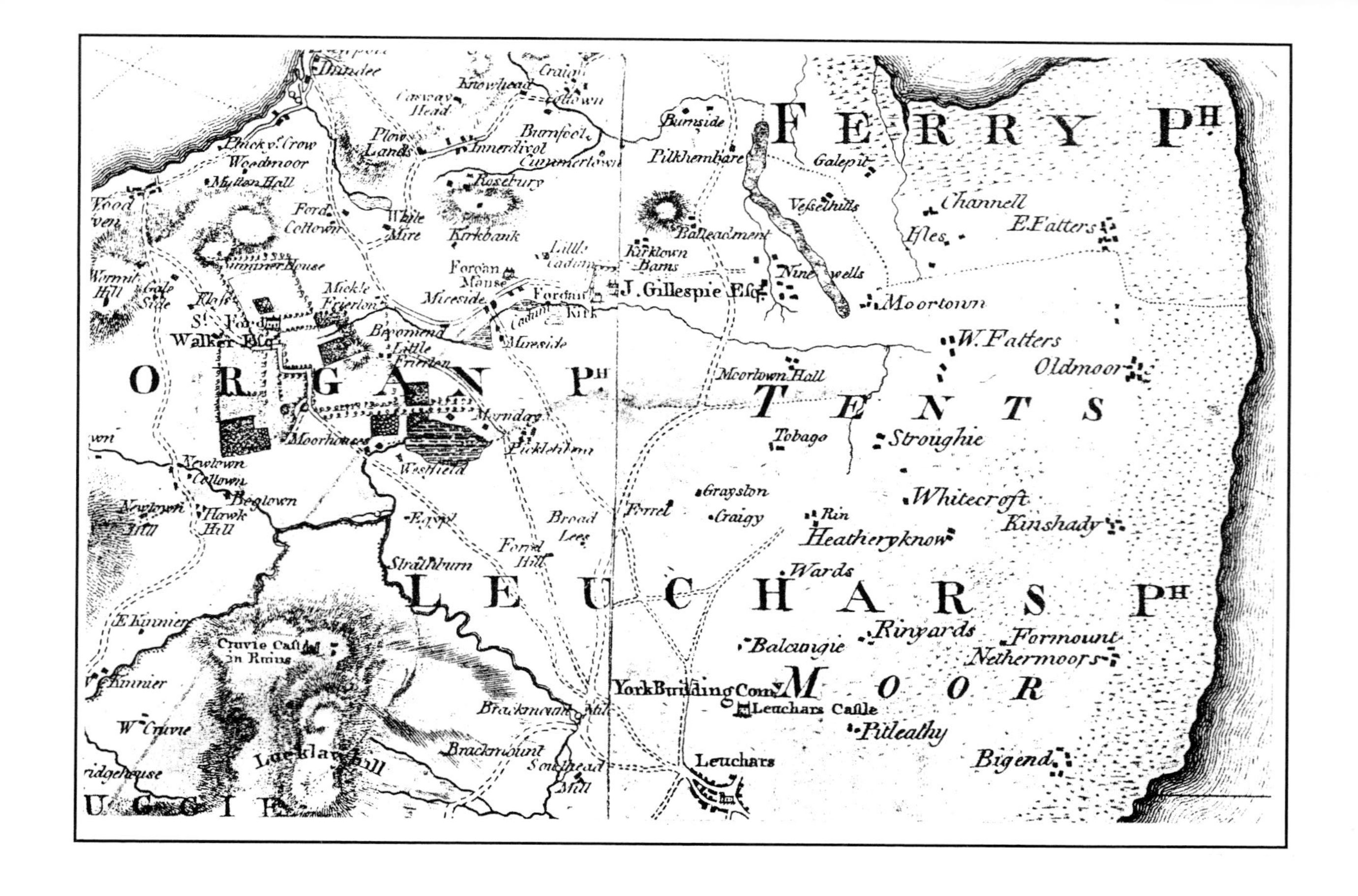
FERRY PH
ORGAN PH
TENTS
LEUCHARS PH
MOOR
Dundee
Knowhead
Cotttown
Burnfoot
Innerdivot
Cunmertown
Roseberry
Plow Lands
Woodmoor
Mylton Hall
White Mire
Kirkbank
Ford Cottown
Summer House
Mickle Frierton
Forgan Manse
Mireside
Forgan Kirk
Walker Esq.
Broomend
Little Frierton
Moorhouses
Westfield
Pickletillem
Newtown
Cottown
Beglown
Hawk Hill
Egypt
Broad Lees
Ford Hill
Strathburn
Burnside
Pilkhembare
Galepit
Vesselhills
Balleadment
Kirktown Barns
Ninewells
J. Gillespie Esq.
Moortown
Channell
Isles
E. Fatters
W. Fatters
Oldmoor
Moortown Hall
Tobago
Stroughie
Graystone
Craigy
Ferrel
Rin
Whitecroft
Kinshady
Heatheryknow
Wards
Rinyards
Formount
Nethermoors
Balcairgie
York Building Comp.
Leuchars Castle
Pitleathy
Leuchars
Bigend
Cruvie Castle in Ruins
E Kinnier
W Kinnier
W Cruvie
Brackmount
Southhead Mill

Figure 12: The Tentsmuir Area in the Eighteenth Century

This map illustrates the area between the river Eden to the south and the river Tay to the north.

In March 1790 the collector at Dundee reported that he had called upon Leslie Douglas, tidesurveyor, seizure-maker of the goods contained in return No 2, 'to say how he came by the information therein contained that the spirits mentioned were imported by a smuggling lugger, master's name unknown, but landed with the assistance and under the direction of Arthur Robertson, farmer at Old Muir, in Tentsmuir parish of Leuchars'. The answer was that his informer had seen it all 'from a place where he had screened himself and that he knew that Robertson was the active person in the smuggle'.

The second extract comes from the Coast Guard letter-book held at the University of St Andrews and is dated 18th January 1832.

'I have this morning received a letter from Lt Stark RN acquainting me of a suspicious brig seen in St Andrews Bay at daylight the other morning - and observed to make sail and stand out to sea - with reference therefore to this information as also to that of the brig *Hope* and to Marsh, a notorious smuggler, being at Leith, I have to desire you to proceed across the Eden after dusk with a man from St Andrews station and range the coast along to the northward, taking the Leuchars party with you, and see if there had been any traffic of carts etc. - I have further to direct that during the westerly winds you keep a most vigilant watch upon the coast under your charge and in order that nothing should interfere with your night duty you will not proceed to Leuchars in the day time but to make arrangements so as frequently to confer by night with the parties there. I have to direct further that you keep a strict watch on Boar Hills and communicate frequent with the parties at Kings Barns and with reference to quarantine matters you will instruct the pilots to be very cautious in approaching a vessel standing in for St Andrews, taking care before boarding they learn from whence she came and that she is in every respect free from quarantine restraint'.

Once goods had been condemned in the exchequer, before sale or burning they were appraised so that the seizure-makers share [and the king's moiety] could be calculated. In September 1725 Messrs Dent and Aikenhead were asked to appraise two seizures of wine and bone combs. But these had been greatly over-valued at £15 per hogshead and £27 for the lot whereas the purchase values were £12 in each case. The collector objected to having to pay their fees - which were assessed as a proportion of the appraisement value.

As there was a strong possibility that any seized boats might be reclaimed by the smugglers, they were disabled [see Chapter Five]. On 16 July 1769 Peter Carey, mariner on board the *Princess Caroline* sloop, commanded by Captain John Read, seized the *Peggy* of Montrose for importing spirits in small casks and delivered her over to Thomas Findlay shipbuilder, to prevent her being carried out of the river at Montrose when the tidesmen were all on duty. In September the collector received information that Findlay had 'abstracted six quarter deck beams and other particulars out of the vessel' and put these in the *Two Sisters* of Montrose, George Barclay master, which he was repairing at the same time. This could be proved by William Napier and George Barclay, both on board the *Two Sisters* at the time, and James Bunce, John Cowie, Francis Strachan and William Clerk, journeymen carpenters in Montrose, who worked for Findlay. The Board ordered that Findlay and any others involved in this should be prosecuted for theft before the sheriff. Findlay's servants were to be witnesses.

The first day of the hearing before the court was 21 November 1769. The defendant acknowledged that he had been given orders 'to take care of the ship and disable her effectually from going to sea' while the comptroller affirmed that he had taken away more than was necessary for this precaution. The collector had a poor view of Findlay who 'on all occasions ... is apt to snatch at every opportunity to take advantage and especially before this inferior court, where all the procurators of it seem to be in his interest. We are humbly of opinion it would tend to the advantage of the revenue that this matter were advocated to the court of session where everything is supposed to be conducted with impartiality'. Thwarted with one problem after another, the case continued, on and off, until November 1774, when Findlay was assoilised. In December 1775 he petitioned the sheriff depute of Forfar for his expenses 'as he has been brought to the defending this groundless and oppressive prosecution'. This time he was not successful.

Sale of Goods

The main problem over the sale of condemned goods was that the market was already fully supplied. On 11 January 1805 the collector at Dundee reported 'this day being a market day, after advertising the same at two different times, exposed to public sale the goods lying at this port under seizure and condemned last term in the court of exchequer'. The spirits actually sold for £21 above the appraised value but nobody bid for the silk handkerchiefs. The following August at Anstruther two ankers were 'after due advertisement through the town exposed to public sale. They were first exposed, agreeable to your Honours order, at the appraised value. When no purchasers appeared they were thereafter put up at £30, when no offer appeared. Then at £25, when they were sold for £28 10s'. If the goods did not reach either the appraised value or the calculated value of the duties then they would be withdrawn. At that stage they would be transferred to a supposedly better market - from Perth to Dundee, from Dundee and the other outports to Leith. In June 1786 the collector at Alloa had to explain the differences between the returns and what actually arrived at Leith after two trips by Captain Starks 'the cask of ashes was through the negligence of one of our porters and one of Captain Stark's men dropped into the sea'.

The long wait between seizure and sale might have resulted in leakage or disimprovement in quality. At Perth in 1760 two writs were put up for sale 'but though several people came and tasted the spirits nobody bid for them'. In December 1790 the collector at Montrose reported on these losses in the warehouse of 1 gallon geneva and 2 lbs roll tobacco. On 29 January 1795 he had to prove that 34 lbs sound tobacco stalks and 31 lbs damaged tobacco stalks had been lost through shrinkage and not embezzlement.

The tailpiece to this chapter returns to the problems, already described in Chapter Seven, of officers being arrested for doing their duty.

The Story of James Young

The arrests of Ellis and Schaw are described in Chapter Seven. These were not the only occasion on which customs officers were arrested and imprisoned. In January 1735 James Young, tidesman at Dundee, went to Arbroath 'upon an information' to seize a small parcel of French salt. 'But upon his getting horses and carts to carry it away, the provost thought fit ... to put him in prison'. Captain Starks and Graham, the local surveyor, went to Arbroath find out the facts. As a result the collector at Dundee was able to forward to the Board 'a journal kept by Young of his procedure in the country upon an information the 30th last month with a copy of a summons he received to appear before the Justices of the peace at Montrose the 10th inst for some riots alleged to be committed by him in his search, with a protest taken against John Grant, treasurer in Arbroath, for preventing him in the execution of his duty by ordering the doors to be shut against him ... if such procedures as these go unpunished and officers affronted and committed to prison for doing their duty, we are convinced that in a little time the government will have no occasion to station officers in this part of the country.

'We hope your Honours will fall upon some method for to bring James Young out of prison before he be carried prisoner in a sort of triumph to Montrose and be found guilty there of crimes of which were he at liberty he could easily prove himself innocent'. In the meantime Young had taken a protest against the provost of Arbroath for wrongous imprisonment.

Once a letter had been received from the Board 'I dispatched Mr Graham to that place that he might deliver it and observe the conduct of the magistrates carefully on that occasion. The provost after he had consulted the matter with some of his advisers thought convenient to condescend to liberate James Young without demanding the fine. As always there were expenses, totalling £3 14s and including £1 5s advanced by Graham to Young 'to defray his expenses while in prison' and Graham's own expenses including horse hire, 12s.

CHAPTER NINE: THE CUSTOMS AND THE EXCISE

'It seems to me that there is no good will between this officer of excise [Thomas Wedderburn at Anstruther] and those of the customs, which may be the reason that foul language passed betwixt him and the comptroller unbecoming officers of the revenue to give one another. But the spring of it all seems to come from the seizing that small parcel of green tea [this 1/2 lb of tea belonged to Wedderburn himself and 'was taken carrying down to a boat going to Dunbar', as admitted by the excise officer]. Upon the whole the complaint seems to be so frivolous that in my opinion it does not merit the attention of either of the Honourable Boards'. [Collector at Dundee to the Board 27 September 1735]

The main role of customs and excise was not the prevention of smuggling, although this occupied a high proportion of their time. By its very nature, the suppression of the illegal trade meant that the revenue officers clashed not only with the local population but also amongst themselves.

The Trials of a Collector

In August 1738 the collector at Alloa was asked by James Watson, a merchant in Edinburgh, to deliver to Bailie Marshall in Stirling all the customable goods that Watson had purchased following condemnation in the exchequer court and which were lodged in the castle. The collector went immediately to Stirling, where he contacted Dalmahoy, surveyor of the landcarriage, David Rummage, landcarriage waiter and Mr Jaffray, storehousekeeper at the castle. However, as Mr Montgomery, excise officer, held one of the keys to the store, they had to wait until he arrived before they could gain access to the goods. 'About eleven in the forenoon I sent Mr Rummage to let Mr Montgomery know that we were in the street waiting ... Mr Rummage found him at his home and his return was that he was not just at leisure to wait upon us but that he would be with us soon. We waited half an hour and there being no appearance of his coming [I] sent Mr Rummage a second time to him, who brought back the same answer. We waited half an hour longer and then sent Mr Rummage a third time to desire that if he could not come himself that he would send the key. His answer (which was delivered in a very uncivil manner) was that he would not send the key and if we would not wait till he took his breakfast we might do as we thought proper. By this time it was half an hour after twelve and we waited on the streets till after one. As Mr Montgomery neither came nor sent to us, we went to dinner. After dinner Mr Dalmahoy, the surveyor, told me that he had been for a fourth time with Mr Montgomery, who still refused to give the key but said he would either come or send it to the castle so soon as he had seen the supervisor. Upon this we went up to the castle and I waited there till about six at night and as during that time Mr Montgomery neither came nor sent the key, I was obliged to return to this place, without being able to deliver the goods'.

The collector wrote to Watson explaining 'what I had done for his service. But he was so far from thinking himself in the least obliged to me for the dispatch I had endeavoured to procure for him that in return thereto he wrote me a very impertinent letter'. Watson requested that the goods held in the warehouse at Alloa should be delivered to Mr Haig, who would forward them to Leith by water. The collector's clerk offered to weigh the goods before they were handed over but Haig 'made choice to take them as they lay'. Watson wrote a second time to the collector, complaining that the liquorice was 17 lbs short and 'if I did not order immediate payment of the value he would sue for it. This I thought so ridiculous a demand that it required no answer'. A third letter was written by Watson on 25 October 'ordering me upon receipt thereof to send a permit to his agent in Stirling for the goods he had lying there. Otherwise he would make me know my duty'. This letter was received on the king's birthday, when the collector 'did not (considering his [Watson's] former usage) think myself in duty obliged to do business myself in the custom house that day besides going in quest of the other officers and prevailing them to do their part thereof'. Inevitably Watson complained to the Board about the collector's behaviour.

The collector at Alloa and the excise at Stirling

The collector at Alloa seemed to be plagued with difficulties over the behaviour of the excise officers at Stirling. In particular there was a problem with Robert Ogilvie, supervisor of excise. In January 1740 Ogilvie explained a discrepancy between a return of seizure and the actual goods by accusing the collector of allowing 200 lbs of tobacco to be embezzled from the warehouse at Alloa. However, the collector was convinced that any loss could have occurred while it was under Ogilvie's care at the castle. 'Indeed the embezzlement of customable goods carried there by officers of excise had upon many occasions been most scandalous as well before as after making a return thereof'. He then cited the case of a cask of raisins. Ogilvie had returned thirty-nine firkins of soap as a seizure 'whereas in fact there was other goods seized by him at that time'. Eight days later, after constant pressure from the collector, Ogilvie went to Alloa where he made an oath that the cask of raisins seized at the same time had been embezzled by the soldiers who were out with him. 'How far this may be true I shall not take upon me to determine but I understand that since the 31st of December last, the day on which the raisins were seized, plum pudding has been in great plenty amongst the officers of excise at Stirling'. The Board directed that in future all the goods seized by the excise should be stored in the Alloa customs warehouse but by 10 February Ogilvie had not sent them there.

Another Story of James Young

The first James Young story is told in the tailpiece to Chapter Eight. In April 1740 the *Elizabeth & Ann*, John Westwater master, arrived in the Tay from Rotterdam [see Chapters Two and Five]. James Young, tidesman from Dundee, was the only officer on board when she passed Newburgh, near which place two boatloads of soap were run out of her. At a later stage he was joined by David Randie from Perth, two boatmen and a sergeant with a party of soldiers. When the ship arrived at the port and the collector and surveyor found the concealment described in Chapter Five, they examined both examined James Young and David Randie 'anent the goods we supposed had been run out of her. Young said if any goods were carried out it must have been in Randie's watch for he was in bed'. He did claim to have heard some noises on deck between one and two o'clock in the morning 'But he positively denied he knew of any goods being carried out'.

The collector and surveyor then examined the boatmen 'who told us that having been up for two nights before and fatigued they went to bed betwixt twelve and one, thinking everything secure, as the two tidesmen were up and a sergeant and six soldiers aboard. They had no sooner gone to bed but one of them fell asleep and the other was nailed fast, by whom he does not know, in his bed. The sailors having them thus secured fell to work and carried out the goods'. Donald McDonald, the boatman who had fallen asleep, was awakened by the noise and he called out to Randie to go and seize all the goods that went out of the ship 'for he did not want abundance of assistance'. Randie answered 'Take you your rest, you have nothing to say'. At this point McDonald jumped out of bed and went on deck, where he saw the goods being unloaded into a boat. 'But what they were he could not tell it being dark'. The other boatman could not get out of his bed but he looked through a small hole in the bed door and saw 'four or five boxes besides a great many casks carried out of the hold by the scuttle upon deck. But as it was an oblique view he had he could not tell what goods went out'.

Young remained adamant that he had not been involved in the smuggle. 'When placed face to face, Randie stated that he could swear to every particular in his earlier statement and that he was sorry he had followed his [Young's] pernicious advice. Young as positively denied every fact and said he was in bed the whole time the goods were run and knew nothing of the matter. The boatmen declared that Young came to McDonald and upbraided him for telling the truth and at that time confessed before him and William Thomson, tidewaiter, that he had been two or three times on deck whilst the goods 'were carrying out'. And that he, Young, had solicit Randie very earnestly to retract all that he had confessed and go with him to the master, mate and sailors to get them to sign a declaration of their innocence and of no goods being run out at the time mentioned, which would save them both, which he knew the sailors would do if Randie asked them. The boatmen asserted the same thing to Young's face. Young seemed drunk and confused and did not know what answer to make but still insisted on his innocency in evasive terms.

'We applied to the major ... to have the sergeant and party examined according to your directions, who was so good as to order them to attend this afternoon at the custom house and to desire Sir John Miln, the adjutant, to be present at the examination. When the sergeant was called he denied positively that he knew or saw any goods run out of the ship for when Young came out of bed about twelve o'clock at night he went into it and slept till four o'clock in the morning. But said that on the Sunday's evening, when he was walking upon the quarter deck, Randie told him he believed there was no prohibited goods aboard but only some jars of geneva belonging to the sailors and that they had had a hard winter. 'God forbid' that he should hurt them by hindering them to get them out. That he observed Randie, Young and the master speaking in the cabin and the master seemed very concerned and [he] heard the master say 'I'm afraid it will not do'. But what he meant he did not know. That he was asked by Randie if what he had spoke to him of [meaning letting the jars of geneva be smuggled] should be communicate to the men. The sergeant said he could do nothing secretly ... he owned that Young had been with him and got him to sign a paper, the contents of which he did not very well know, having many Latin phrases in it, and that he did only sign 'the above contents might be true for any thing he knew'.

'We called the soldiers, who all denied they knew any thing of goods being run out. One of them told that Young turned out upon deck at twelve o'clock at night and two of them that he had been with them and got them to sign a paper asserting that there were no goods run out. As the sergeant and two of them said they were abed asleep, we called McDonald the boatman who to their faces declared that there was none of them abed but drinking in the cabin'.

The collector finished the report of his enquiry with 'it appears plainly to us the fraud was committed. Young has been at abundance of pains to support his short answers. Randie's answers seem to carry an air of truth and concern'. They recommended that mercy should be shown to Randie 'upon account of his confession and being a young offender'. However, the collector gave Young a character of 'having been suspected to have been guilty of the like a great many years past'. He was dismissed.

As part of his revenge, Young made accusations the against other officers, including McDonald, the boatman. The collector admitted 'we have no very good opinion of McDonald or any bred at the ferry of Dundee, although he has been very serviceable in the discovery'.

The Story of Donald McDonald

In November 1740 the collector at Perth reported that Donald McDonald, boatman, had informed both him and the surveyor that in November 1739, when the *William & Mary*, William Graham master from Rotterdam lay between Balmerino and Dundee, William Thomson, one of the Perth tidesmen, and Thomas Brown, tidesmen at Dundee, the officers on board, the sailors of the vessel went to see one Clark, a boatman at Newburgh, and 'desired him to come with his boat and run goods out of the ship, which he positively refused to do. That night or the next the sailors took away his boat, run the goods and brought her back from whence they had carried her next morning and paid him for the use of his boat that he might hold his peace'.

Thomson was summoned to Perth from Newburgh and questioned. He justified himself 'very lamely saying let them prove it'. McDonald brought Clark to the custom house where he was examined 'in a bye-room' and said 'he durst not for his life or bread discover anything that might hurt the merchants or officers' but he would declare the truth on oath and 'McDonald spoke truth, Thomson was the liar'. As a result the collector stationed Clark at Perth 'that he might be more immediately under my eye'. However that night Clark went out of the district to Dundee 'without my knowledge to acquaint his associate Brown of what McDonald had acquainted me'.

When he got back to Newburgh, Clark 'vaunted that as McDonald was an unhappy man and was in debt before he was employed and diligence out against him in some people's hand at Dundee, which it seems Brown and he had interest enough to get put into the hands of one Lennox, a shop keeper in [Perth] ... that he would put him in prison ere long for daring to inform against him. Some few days after Thomson took the opportunity of coming up with a coasting vessel that he might spur Lennox to it, which he never used to do but on the contrary it has been his practice, as well as other officers, to certify the loading or unloading of goods without seeing either done, upon their receiving their fees. Upon McDonald being incarcerate he acquainted the surveyor with his misfortune, who went to Lennox to offer a bond ... if he would allow the poor man to go where his chest lay, where he said he had partial receipt would extinguish the debt to a trifle. He found Thomson waiting in Lennox's shop. Whether Thomson is fit after this to continue in this port is humbly submitted ...

'PS My servant acquaints me just now that some days ago Thomson desired him to give his service to me and tell me though I took McDonald by the hand yet he would fix his feet faster'.

At the end of November Thomson presented his replies to his charge. 'As to his being pointed out as a speckled bird, as he expresses himself, the collector ... has suspected him ever since he was removed from Alloa to that collection and therefore he removed him from station to station where he could do the least hurt'. Thomson denied attempting to get McDonald's creditors to incarcerate him, saying that he only knew Lennox. 'Truly Lennox is the person who incarcerate him upon a diligence obtained against McDonald at the instance of one Gowrie, who lives at Inverness, which diligence was in the hands of one Mr Dog at Dundee so that Lennox is the third hand ... Lennox said nothing would satisfy him but the money down for which he was imprisoned ...[the collector] applied to the magistrates for the benefit of Act of Grace for McDonald and sent off the petition to Inverness to be intimate to Mr Gowrie, the principal creditor, and took all proper steps for founding a process against Mr Lennox of wrongous imprisonment, as he was informed Lennox had no orders for doing what he had done but only borrowed the diligence to put a man out of the way, who by his informing would terrify the tidesmen from doing him favours for the future. Lennox being afraid of the consequence of this prosecution turned as anxious for his liberation as he had formerly been for his imprisonment and actually liberate him'.

Thomson 'begs pardon for it [the message to the collector by his servant] and says in a letter to the comptroller he was in a very great passion for McDonald calling him a rogue and villain to his master'. The tidesman gave two reasons for McDonald's resentment against him. The first was because he had informed the collector of McDonald's 'spoiling the king's boat by carrying coals. Thomson did not speak one word of it till the day the collector examined him anent the running of goods and after the examination was over told it. The second reason is an old one, that McDonald was afraid he should acquaint my Lady Lindors of his

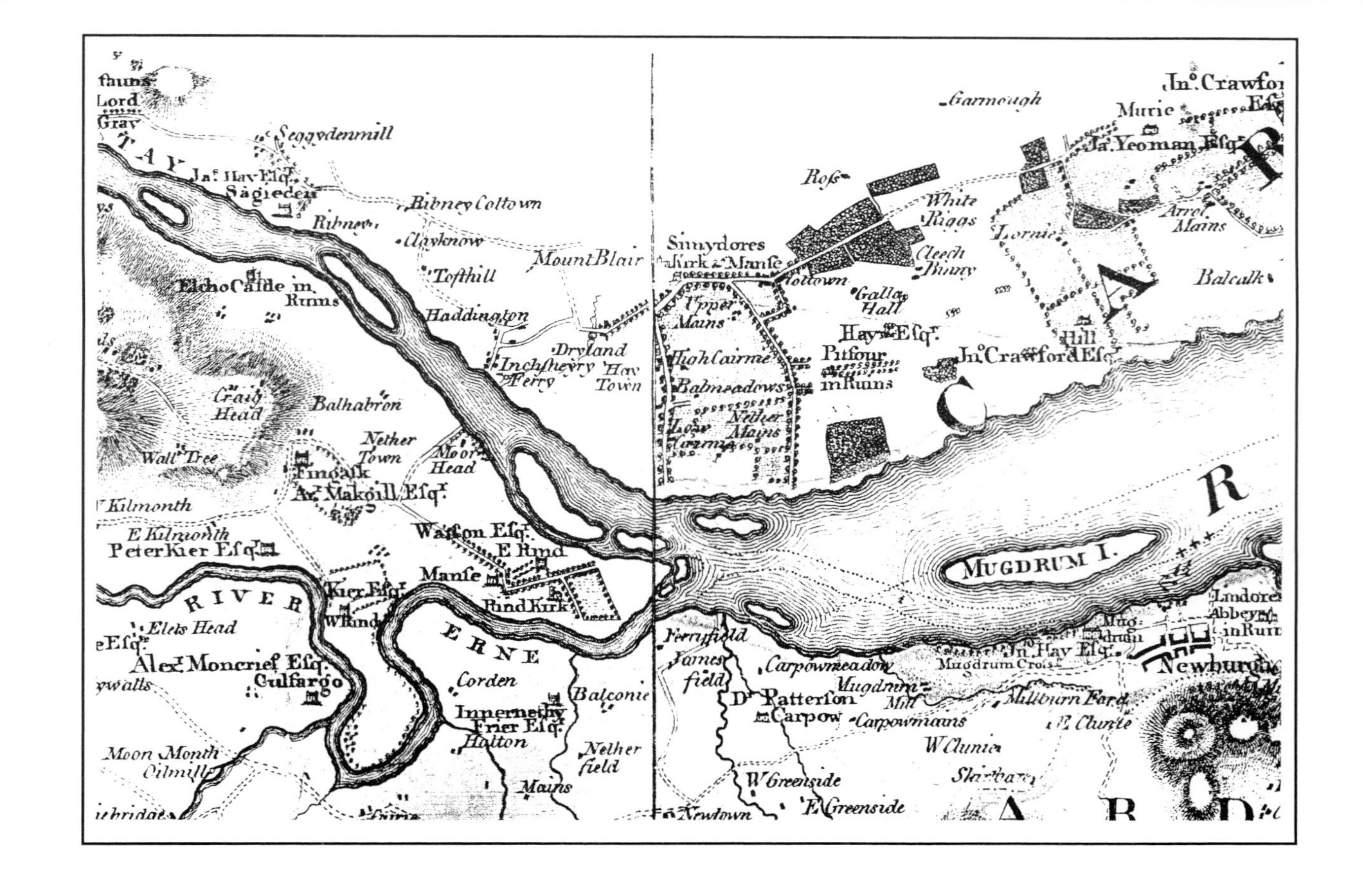
TAY
Seggydenmill
Jas. Hay Esq.
Sagieden
Ribney Coltown
Ribney
Clayknow
Mount Blair
Tofthill
Elcho Castle in Ruins
Haddington
Dryland
Inchsheyry Ferry
Hay Town
Craig Head
Balhabron
Nether Town
Moor Head
Wallr Tree
Fingask
Ar. Makoill Esq.
Kilmonth
E Kilmonth
Peter Kier Esq.
Watson Esq.
E Rind
Manse
Rind Kirk
Kier Esq.
W Rind
RIVER ERNE
Elets Head
Alex. Moncrief Esq.
Culfargo
Corden
Innernethy
Frier Esq.
Halton
Balconie
Nether field
Mains
Moon Month
Oilmill
Sinnydores
Kirk & Manse
Coltown
Upper Mains
High Cairnie
Balmeadows
Nether Mains
Ross
White Riggs
Cleech Binny
Galla Hall
Hay Esq.
Pitfour in Ruins
Jn. Crawford Esq.
Garnough
Murie
Jn. Crawford Esq.
Ja. Yeoman Esq.
Lornie
Arrel Mains
Balcalk
Hill
MUGDRUM I.
Ferryfield
James field
Carpowmeadow
Dr. Patterson
Carpow
Mugdrum Mill
Carpowmains
Mugdrum
Jn. Hay Esq.
Mugdrum Cross
Newburgh
Lindores Abbey in Ruin
Millburn Ford
E Clunie
W Clunie
W Greenside
E Greenside
Newtown

Figure 13: The Upper River Tay District in the Eighteenth Century

This map shows the river Tay above Newburgh. The area where the *Prime* ran aground [see Chapter Five] was below the mouth of the river Earn.

In August 1769 John Petrie was appointed as extraordinary tidesman at Perth. The following July the Board asked for a report on his progress. 'Petrie seems to be naturally vigilant and active. The field where he has the best opportunities of exerting his talents is in the lower part of the river in boarding and examining vessels. By this means he is pretty much removed from our inspection. To remedy this inconvenience we were desirous he should keep a journal but found he could not write. However, though we very seldom see him, we are informed he is almost perpetually on the cruise between Newburgh and Dundee. Yet what is very surprising, he has never made an effectual seizure, except only five hogsheads of soap at the shore of Perth on which several other officers had an information as well as he.

'There is one very singular part of Mr Petrie's conduct which is only come to our knowledge since we received your letter ... He never made the least complaint either to us or to the surveyor that the boatmen were disobedient to his orders or that the custom house boat was too heavy for the service. Nevertheless on some pretence of that sort we are assured he often steals away in a little skiff, which he keeps for that purpose, and boards vessels by himself. If Petrie was a man of unsuspected honesty this circumstance might have been overlooked or even interpreted to his advantage. But considering the infamous character he bore, long before he was taken into your Honours service, we own this behaviour has the appearance of a design to make private and corrupt bargains with the smugglers.

'But, as no particular crime has yet been fixed upon him since he has been honoured with your commission, we are humbly of opinion that it is expedient to continue him in employment till a further trial is made of him. His thorough acquaintance both with the men and vessels that are engaged in the smuggling business as well as the activity, diligence and cunning by which he is remarkably distinguished may certainly be turned to the benefit of the revenue, provided that care be taken that he always act before witnesses'.

having last winter shot some of her ladyship's pigeons'.

More of John Petrie [see Figure 13]

In August 1770 Alexander Martin, John Petrie and William Paton, tidesmen, were on board the *Thomas & Margaret*, David Robertson master, when 'about twilight in the evening' Petrie left his post and 'he tarried much longer than the purpose for which he pretends this was done required. This fault is indeed much slighter if it is true that William Paton was on deck when he went away and not asleep as Paton himself asserts. But unfortunately Petrie's character had long been such that almost any other persons averment will be believed in opposition to his ... There is one new circumstance ... which is extremely unfavourable to Petrie to wit that the very boat of which he pretended to be so jealous was lying alongside of Robertson's ship at the time that Petrie left it.

'It is needless to make any further observations on Petrie's defences. The long detail he gives of his subsequent conduct, supposing all he says to be true, is very little to the purpose and seems to be inserted with no other view than to draw your Honours attention from his behaviour on the 31st August, to which alone the charge is limited. The reflections thrown out by him against the other officers are mere assertions ... the circumstances set forth in the charge appear to us to be true. We own it does not necessarily follow that Petrie was bribed to connive at the running of goods out of Robertson's ship. Your honours will judge whether his conduct proceeded from knavery or an excess of folly'.

Petrie claimed to have seized the six chests containing 380 lbs of tea. 'It is true Petrie came to the collector and told him that two boxes were in view but as this happened near the time that the discharging officers resumed business after dinner and, as the collector on going to the quay not long after met Mr Wallace attending the tea to the warehouse, he could not but consider him as the principal seizure- maker though Petrie's station on board the ship had given him the opportunity of first seeing some of the boxes. Upon enquiry, however, we have since found that Mr Wallace was at work on another ship and was called together with Thomas Jameson to Petrie's assistance. We shall therefore order the return of the tea to be made in Petrie's name'.

Petrie also claimed the seizure of four hogsheads of wine and the ship, the *Thomas & Margaret*. The collector reported, 'Petrie showed us a letter from Gothenburg dated in July last informing him that ten boxes of tea and four hogsheads of wine were shipping at that time for Perth. Such informations, though ever so pointed, can be of little service. This of Petrie's was so defective as not to specify the name of the ship so that it was impossible for him to know whether these goods were on board Brown's or Robertson's vessels, which arrived from that place about the same time'. [See Chapter Two for a discussion of forewarnings] The Board instructed that Petrie should be allowed to return both the wine and the ship.

An Honest Officer

In January 1738 David Rummage, landcarriage waiter at Stirling, together with a party of the military, were deforced while making a seizure. The following May he was in a clash with the excise officers over a seizure at Gillespie's shop in Stirling, when another customs officer overheard Henry Corbet telling his supervisor, Ogilvie, that 'he had taken the key of the warehouse from Rummage by force, we suppose for some indirect end'. When Rummage reported that the other revenue officers at Stirling were in cahoots with the smugglers and requested to be returned to Glasgow, the collector did not take him seriously. Rummage was a good officer, although 'he is in a bad situation at Stirling in regard of his having detected the very magistrates more than once smuggling and were also all concerned in deforcing him, who no doubt encourage those of the inhabitants that are under their influence to insult and maltreat him, as they frequently do'. [See Lord Elphinstone in Chapter Seven] However, the collector could not explain why the officers of excise should abuse him or how they and Dalmahoy 'should have any fellowship with those of the magistrates and others who have been detected in smuggling and abusing the officers of the revenue'. [Dalmahoy was arrested and imprisoned for debt in 1742]

The Board suggested that the best solution would be to return Rummage to Glasgow, as he requested. 'But as we know him to be a faithful and diligent officer in his station [we] thought it would be of service to the revenue to continue at Stirling and therefore prevailed with him to stay for a time. But as we now find that he can be of little service there by reason of the ill-usage he meets with from the inhabitants of that place, who even threaten his life on account of his detecting their practices, which intimidates him from going about his duty, especially in the night' they agreed that he should return to Glasgow.

Another Porteous

In April 1745 John Anderson and Thomas Vernon, landcarriage waiters at the city gates of Edinburgh, acting as tidewaiters, and Francis Porteous, tidewaiter at Leith were stationed on the *Janet* of Leith, John Watt master, loaded with wine. At one stage Porteous left his duty and went on shore with the master and several of the sailors to drink with them 'and returned the worse for liquor', when 'he spirited up the sailors against Anderson and Vernon ... and threatened to throw them overboard'. According to the Leith collector, Porteous was 'a dangerous officer'. In the past he had been 'guilty of sundry misdemeanours in the execution of his duty, and excused upon promises to be exact and diligent in doing his duty in the future'. This gave them a sufficiently strong excuse for him to be dismissed. Apparently Porteous was not the first officer to be complained of by Anderson and Vernon - they had been 'repeatedly beaten and assaulted' by John Cunningham.

Robert Naismith and James Bruce, tidesmen at Ferry Pantoncraigs

In January 1765 when the Board ordered that James Bruce and Robert Naismith, tidesmen at Dundee, should be sent to Ferry Pantoncraigs 'they went with great reluctance. On that occasion [they] were somewhat indifferent to us but them having both wives and numerous families made us a little tender in reporting them to the Honourable Board'. However, a serious problem developed between the two men and according to Ambrose Starks, the tidesurveyor, 'so long as they are together the duty will never be well done, they refusing to do duty together ... there will never be peace till [they were separated at the port] ... they both being very troublesome'.

On 19 April two vessels from Rotterdam for Perth arrived off the lighthouse at the mouth of the Tay. Starks placed James Bruce and Robert Haliburton on the *Eagle* of Perth, George Shepherd master, and Robert Naismith and George Davidson on what was referred to as the Edward Leslie, possibly after the name of the master. The tidesmen had 'express orders that the two on board the ship first discharged should immediately join the other two and remain till all was discharged. They should assist one another in the discharge. Everything seized should be carried to the warehouse as it came to hand, without any exceptions'. Leslie's ship was discharged first but Naismith and Davidson returned to the Ferry instead of joining the others on the *Eagle*, because, as he claimed, Naismith was not well. Starks 'immediately commanded Naismith and John Mearns, in whom he could place more confidence than in Davidson, to go on board the *Eagle*, where they continued with the other two till discharge'.

According to Mearns, when Robert Naismith was coming down from the ship, James Bruce pushed the boat off and left him 'hanging by the hands. When he was called to take him (Robert Naismith) [Bruce] answered 'Damn him, let him go there''. The collector added 'we are well assured that ever since James Bruce and Robert Naismith were stationed at Ferry Pantoncraigs there has subsisted a great difference betwixt them' and the complaint from Bruce about Naismith's behaviour over a seizure on the *Eagle*, 'proceeds more from ill will to Robert Naismith than from any intention to serve the revenue'.

The Sale by Excise of a Customs Seizure

In January 1805 a seizure of thirty-seven ankers of geneva was taken to the excise warehouse at St Andrews. It was not until April that the collector at Anstruther discovered to his surprise that all these had been returned to the excise Board, condemned and sold, despite the fact that they had been seized by both revenues.

Brodie was the supervisor of excise at St Andrews and his justification for this action was that he had told the customs officers that 'there was to be a smuggle that night [so that] of consequence all the gin seized by these tidesmen the next day was from his information alone and that of course it by right was carried to the excise warehouse and sold there'. However, according to the tidesmen, although Brodie had showed them the marks of cart wheels on the shore it was no evidence that there had been a recent smuggle because 'the whole beach was covered with such marks occasioned by the farmers' carts in driving away the seaweed for manure. The only circumstance that lead to anything like a discovery of a smuggle was the anker hoop picked up by Boyack [tidesman], the place where he found it being marked by him and his brother officer'. After searching for some time and finding nothing they all went home, Brodie saying that he could do no more.

The search was continued by the tidesmen at daybreak 'when going their customary rounds along the shore with their spyglass they made the first seizure of one anker of gin by themselves. 'Had they acted by Mr Brodie as he did by them (having first gone out by himself and finding nothing he then called the assistance of the tidesmen) they would have made all the remaining seizures by themselves'. Instead they called on Brodie, who would not come out with them, and Crawford, with whom they made the remaining seizures of thirty-six ankers [ten of which were in Andrew Cochrane's house - see Chapter Seven].

The collector constantly exhorted the tidesmen to use their spyglass. As he wrote on to them individually on 1 February 1805 'The more we consider the particulars of the seizure you made on Saturday morning last the more we are convinced that all the information that either Messrs Brodie or Crawford had when they said there was to be a smuggle that morning arose from their either seeing themselves or being informed there was a lugger off the Head on Friday morning. Had Mr Ramsay made a proper use of his [spy]glass that way or on the Thursday, the day before, he ought certainly to have discovered the lugger which had he have done ... would have prevented in the first instance all pretensions of the excise to any part of your seizure'.

The Problems of Mr Cant, Customs Officer

In 1760 Mr Cant, the tidesurveyor at Perth, was in constant friction with the excise officers at that port. In May Clark, the collector of excise, claimed that Cant had no title to five hogsheads of geneva that he had seized. 'We directed [Cant] to give us in writing a detail of the circumstances ... These are set forth in so plain and artless a manner in the enclosed letter that it is almost unnecessary for us to add any remarks'.

The next accusation had more serious overtones because Cant was charged by Francis Young, supervisor of excise, with 'irregularity and omission'. Again Cant was questioned by the collector. 'He has assured us that the matter of fact is as follows. On Monday after the seizure was made he met with Mr Dick [tidesurveyor], who had likewise made a seizure of spirits the Saturday evening before. Mr Dick, having acquainted him that he was going in search of the port officer, Mr Cant requested the favour of him, as he himself was then obliged to attend his duty on the shore and as all the tidesmen were likewise employed, to desire Mr Boyle to take an account of his seizure. A little before dinner Mr Dick came to the shore and told him he had delivered his commission to the port gauger, who pretended he was not then at the seizure but said he would examine his spirits afterwards. ... No other notice was thought of or intended to be given him [Boyle] and indeed we believe it has never been the practice to serve the excise officers with formal or written intimations on these occasions. Mr Cant meeting this officer accidentally next day only enquired if he has yet taken the account of his seizure and this it seems Mr Boyle has thought fit to mark in his books as the first notice.

'Perhaps it may not be improper to remark that as the king's warehouse was at that time full the two hogsheads seized by Mr Dick as well as the five seized by Mr Cant were carried into the collector's house and happened to be placed in such manner that it was impossible to inspect the former without stepping over the latter, a circumstance that of itself gave a very sufficient intimation of the seizure, if Mr Boyle had not been disposed rather to cavil than execute the law with candour. But the truth is by the seizing of these spirits the officers of excise were disappointed of a very considerable perquisite, since which they have taken every opportunity of vending their spleen and rancour against your Honours officers'.

The story is continued in July, when Captain John Read of the *Princess Caroline* sloop wrote to the collector requesting a share of the seizure. The collector stated to the Board 'We have only to add that the marks which Captain Read's mate had chalked upon the packages did not distinguish the brandy, for which the duties were paid, from the geneva, which there was no warrant for discharging. To remedy this and to prevent the latter from being put ashore by mistake Mr Cant carried John Hally and George Scott, the two officers stationed on the ship, into the

Officers Names	Age	Family	Where Stationed	Where how long and in what Station employed	Capacity & Behaviour
Robert Hunter	58	Wife 3 Children	Montrose	From 1737 Collrs Clerk at Anstruther, Landwaiter at Kirkaldy & Surveyor at Anstruther to 1767 thence Collector here	Humbly Submitted
James Kennedy	32	Unmarried	Do	From 1753 to 1758 Comptrs Clerk here thence Comptr here	
Thomas Christie	37	Wife no Children	Do	Surveyor here since 1768	Very Capable & Sober
John Campbell	69	Wife 2 Children	Do	From 1723 to 1726 Tidesman at Leith & Bo'ness thence to 1729 Landwaiter at Anstruther, thence Landwaiter here	Do
Robert Maxwell	55	No Wife 2 Children	Do	Landwaiter here since 1751	Do
John Chalmers	66	Wife 1 Child	Do	Tidesman here since 1748	Capable & Sober
Joseph Davidson	62	Wife 6 Children	Do	Tidesman here since 1755	Do
John Cowie	47	Wife Children	Do	Tidesman here since 1757	Do
John Wilson	58	Wife 3 Children	Do	Tidesman here since 1762	Do
John Rodger	53	Wife 9 Children	Do	Tidesman here since 1754	Do
Robert Mitchell	53	Wife 2 Children	Do	From 1753 to 1765 Tidesman at Alloa thence Tidesman here	Do
Alexr Simpson	60	Wife 4 Children	Johnshaven	Tidesman here since 1755	Do
James Philip	50	Wife 2 Children	Gourdon	Tidesman here since 1764	Do
John Smith	31	Unmarried	Arbroath	Tidesman here since 1764	Do
Alexr Reid	58	Wife 2 Children	Do	Extry Tidr at Anstruther, Alloa & here since 1764	Do

Figure 14: The Staff List for Montrose dated July 1795

This staff list includes some of the names that appear elsewhere in the book. It is an example of the type of detailed information available in the letter-books about the careers of the customs officers.

When the Montrose custom house re-opened in 1746, the collector's first task was to undertake a review of what his staff had been doing during the last few months [see Chapter One]. His report to the Board was dated 26 February 1746.

'In obedience to your letter we have enquired into the conduct and behaviour of all the officers in this port during the unnatural rebellion carried on in the kingdom and we are informed that Robert Milne surveyor, who was most of the time in the country, has behaved himself dutifully and loyally.

'William Herdman landwaiter we are informed was in a public house with Patrick Beattie shipmaster (a disaffected person) and some of the French officers.

'John Campbell landwaiter has resided at Arbroath all the time of the rebellion and we are informed has behaved himself dutifully and loyally.

'David Mitchelson, John Scott, John Gray, Alexander Davidson, George Lockhart, Alexander Allan, William Hull and David Randie, tidewaiters, we are informed have all behaved themselves dutifully and loyally.

'The collector was obliged to go into the country most of the time of the rebellion and when in town lived privately, coming very seldom abroad.

'The comptroller went some time into the country and when in town lived very privately.

'This is a true and impartial account of the conduct and behaviour of all the officers belonging to this port to the best of our knowledge and information'.

hold and in their sight with his own hand marked (having first tasted) the hogsheads of geneva, succus liquorice and brandy with the letters G, SL and B respectively, charging the officers to suffer none of the first mentioned commodities to be landed. A precaution that would have effectually stifled all dispute and altercation on this subject if the marks had not been fraudulently defaced in order to make way for the smuggling of these goods. The above particulars are attested by John Hally. George Scott, whose station is at Newburgh, we had no opportunity of examining'.

Finally the collector commented 'We cannot dismiss this report without taking notice how particularly unfortunate Captain Cant is in having so many difficulties started and controversy moved with respect to his property in a seizure made on the justest and clearest grounds and ratified by your Honours express approbation. The officers of excise have claimed a moiety of this seizure and before it is known to them whether their pretensions are admitted or rejected the other half is attempted to be carried off by Captain Read'.

The Problems of Mr Mitchell, Excise Officer

On the morning of 8 May 1770, John Mitchell, excise officer at Montrose, told Alexander Maxwell, excise officer at Ferryden that he had an information that some hogsheads were lodged in George Watson's cellar the night before. They went with a constable and Wright, another excise officer, to the cellar a little before two o'clock in the afternoon. But both the cellar and an adjacent loft were locked. A message was sent to Watson, who 'after a good deal of time spent' arrived with the key to the loft, where the officers found no goods. Mitchell explained that he wanted the key to the cellar, but Watson said that 'he had no other key and they might break open the door if they pleased and then went off'. Mitchell applied to the provost for a warrant to break open the door, 'which he declined to grant until he should receive the advice of a lawyer ... a considerable time was spent in searching for the lawyer, who could not be got'. At this stage Watson's wife called to Mitchell from the street that her husband had gone down with the key 'in order to open the cellar door and give him access and that he might follow him, which he accordingly did'. Mitchell, Wright and Maxwell found a hogshead in a dark corner of the cellar under some tow. A candle was brought and they drew off a glass of wine and carried it to the door to taste it. At this stage Thomas Christie, the customs surveyor, had arrived. He commented that the wine 'was quite thick and immediately turned round and seized it for His Majesty's use and his own. Mr Mitchell then said: 'Mr Christie the information was mine and I seize it for the king's use and my own'; at the same time Mr Christie gave a piece of chalk to Mr Mitchell to put his initials upon it and then the hogshead was brought to the king's warehouse accompanied by the surveyor, Mr Mitchell, Mr Wright and Mr Maxwell'.

Then Christie reasserted his claim to the seizure. It took a month for the collector to reply to the Board 'owing to Mr Christie's being confined to his bed by a fever, in which he was looked upon to be dying, since the time we received your Honours reference to the date of his letter'. On 13 June the Board ordered that Christie was to be reprimanded for interfering in the seizure which was to be returned as having been made by John Mitchell.

In 1785 Mitchell was still having problems over locked doors. 'Having received a very particular information of the two hogsheads of Portugal red wine lodged in an outhouse at Almericlose possessed by Stewart Lyell Esq he (Mitchell) went thither and applied to Mrs Lyell, Mr Lyell being then at Edinburgh, for leave to search the outhouses. She readily agreed thereto and gave him some keys. But none of those being the key of the house on which he had the information, he represented the same to her. She informed him that she had not that key in her custody but that she would send for it to a person who had it. Having waited for about an hour without the key being produced and having seen the two hogsheads through a crevice in the door, Mitchell, having a writ of assistance with him, although not accompanied by a constable, proceeded to break open the door, when he found the wine in question. Just about the time he had broke open the door the key was brought. The outhouse was detached from the dwelling house and contained nothing but some old timber, except the wine'.

During the subsequent enquiry, the Board wanted to know who had produced the key. 'Mrs Lyell upon repeated applications to her at last informed John Peddie, officer of excise, that it was in the possession of

George Lyell, merchant in Arbroath, her son'. Lyell had not been at the shop but his shopman, Frazer, had gone in search of the key. 'It was produced by Frazer about the time the officers proceeded to break open the door'.

The tailpiece describes the result of the excise laying claim to any goods on board either the *Love & Unity* or the *Hercules* when they arrived at Dundee in September 1770.

The Story of the *Love & Unity, September 1770*

'The ship *Hercules* [Alexander Miln master] from Riga arrived here on Sunday the 21st inst and was boarded in the offing by the tidesurveyor, who stationed on her two tidesmen. Next day the master made his report. When he came to the office upon the morning of Tuesday the 23rd we found that the officers of excise had (without saying one word to us about the matter, which we thought a little odd) taken possession of this vessel the evening before, that they had kept watch both below and upon deck the whole night, having the assistance of a military party. But we were still more surprised at receiving a message about eleven o'clock forenoon from the tidesurveyor beseeching us to come and interpose in his behalf as the excise officers were using him ill and threatening not only to turn him out of the hold but ashore from the vessel by military force. This obliged us to go down to the quay ...

'The only excise officer we saw upon the deck was Mr Scott. The rest were then in the hold. He told us they were obeying the orders of their supervisors. We considered that it would answer no good purpose for us to enter into altercation with inferior officers, especially as we were surrounded with a crowd of idle people, whom curiosity had drawn together to see what was passing. We therefore went directly to the house of Mr Campbell, the collector of excise, with whom we talked over the affair with great coolness and deliberation ... as it would certainly have been wrong in officers of the revenue among themselves to oppose force to force, we consented that what prohibited goods might be found on board should be lodged in the excise warehouse ...

'Upon the following day, which was the 24th October, the excise officers did in like manner take possession of the ship *Love & Unity*, David Myalls master, who arrived from Riga on the 22nd [with 200 dried cattle hides in her cargo]. Upon the afternoon of the 25th we received by express ... notice of His Majesty's Order in Council [dated 19 October 1770] extending the quarantine to all ships coming from ... and Livonia.

'In the morning of the 26th an express arrived here from your Honours with the solicitor's opinion relative to the two ships come in here from Riga ...

contd.

The Story of the *Love & Unity*, September 1770 contd.

This being sent for the Rule of our Conduct we gave immediate notice thereof to Mr Campbell ... observing that, as his officers had been on board these ships day and night, they would be called upon to perform quarantine and at same time ... every reasonable indulgence we could give should be granted them for settling their affairs in such manner that the revenue of excise should not suffer ...

'The landsurveyor and landwaiter were never on board the *Love & Unity* nor was the landsurveyor at all on board the *Hercules*. The landwaiter acknowledges he was on board the last mentioned ship but says he did not stay five minutes, as the business of rummaging the hold during the discharge ... was sufficiently done by the tidesurveyor and excise officers. The military, as we are informed, were never below but kept watch on the ship's deck, being relieved every two hours from the guardhouse. If they are obliged to perform quarantine the whole town, to the number of sixteen, must be put on board.

'We have in this whole affair respecting quarantine acted in concert with Captain John Read ... He gave it as his opinion that besides the masters and crews of the two ships, the tidesurveyor, three tidewaiters and two boatmen with the officers of excise to the number of six, being equally divided, should go on board the two ships ... Accordingly these officers ... belonging to the customs have been kept on board ever since Saturday last whereas the excise officers have lived entirely ashore. Nor have we used any force to compel them on board. We are therefore astonished to see in their petition that the officers of the customs have pointed out the petitioners and no others to go and perform quarantine ...

'We beg leave to assure your Honours that we have ever behaved towards the officers of the excise agreeable to the Rules of Decency and Good Manners. We were very much concerned at the last interference in point of duty and we leave it to your Honours to judge whether we have acted from pique or have been guilty of partiality in our conduct towards the officers of excise. Nay, rather if we have not upon this occasion shown as much lenity as possible and if the officers of customs now on board these ships in order to perform quarantine have not more ground to complain that the officers of excise'.

CHAPTER TEN: THE MILITARY AND THE ALLOA DEFORCEMENTS

'We beg lay before you the enclosed representation from John Campbell, landwaiter, and David Mitchelson, tidesman, of the treatment they received from a mob when they were bringing a seizure of some brandy to the king's warehouse. We are afraid though this affair were prosecute before the justices of the peace it would turn to nothing for want of sufficient evidence. The smugglers and country people hereabouts are turned so impudent and unruly that its in vain for the officers of the revenue to pretend to carry off a seizure in the country without being backed by the military'. [The collector at Montrose to the Board, 11 January 1735]

The need for military help is a constant theme throughout the letter-books. The problem was that the revenue officers needed protection when searching for goods, while seizing them, having made a seizure to carry it to the nearest warehouse and once at the warehouse to ensure that it was safe until the next stage in the proceedings.

On 11 January 1720 the collector at Alloa wrote to the Board 'I beg your Honours may apply to the General for a company of soldiers to quarter here. For without a military force we dare not offer to stir here. For I am now very well informed that there were about thirty able fellows concerned in that mob that deforced the officers aboard of the *Charles* of Elphinstone (7th January 1720, John Stone master, from Christiansands, unloading timber for the saw mills and tobacco (for some found floating in the harbour in the morning)) and that they were to be found lying lurking about the shore ready to have knocked us down if any of us had attempted to come to the relief of the officers aboard. Whereas if there had been any soldiers here we should have got a very good seizure of tobacco or if the silly fellows, the tidesmen, had told us on Monday what they did on Wednesday that the master had offered them some guineas that morning we should have had a party from Stirling, which is very expensive to us. We have sometimes occasion for soldiers that will not admit of so much time as to send to Stirling and we do not know but very soon that may be our case'.

Co-operation was not always forthcoming. According to the same collector writing in July 1741, 'to prevent the remainder of the cargo being carried off as well as the officers on board other vessels being in the like manner deforced the comptroller about eleven in the morning of the 22nd inst went to Stirling in order to have carried a part of the military lying there to Airth. But, when he came to apply to the major who commands at Stirling, he absolutely refused to let any of the officers or soldiers stir from Stirling without an order from the general at Edinburgh for that purpose. This refusal has been attended with very bad consequence to the revenue for by much the greater part of the victual or corns were run the night and day after the party was applied for and as there are other vessels here in the same situation we have no doubt of the officers being in like manner deforced and in that case the revenue cannot suffer less than £700 or £800 damage through the above refusal of the major'. He added 'at present there is no party of the military either at Airth or this place, which is what has not happened these many years past. There seems to be an absolute necessity for having a sergeant's command at least at each of these places. But, if only one can be afforded from Stirling, Alloa is by much the properest place'.

Montrose had similar problems. In May 1725 the collector wrote 'It is a considerable loss to the revenue that some soldiers are not appointed to quarter at Arbroath, there being more goods run in and about that place than on all this coast besides. Neither is it in our power to hinder the same. We can only spare one tidesman to stay there, who can do little service without the assistance of the troops for before he can run us an information and our officers get that length with a party the goods are carried up in the country and there dispersed out of their reach'.

One of the problems was that the military had other duties apart from helping customs. As the Montrose collector complained in May 1745, 'we are informed by the officer who commands the soldiers quartered in this place that he has received an order from General Guest to mount a guard at a small fort at the entry of this harbour on the south side of the river and to mount no guard within the town. Likewise to call in all his parties that are out against the smugglers. The order we understand proceeds from a letter wrote by the provost and bailies of this place to the General, acquainting him that they desired no guard might be kept within the town (being of no use to them) but that the soldiers' guard might be kept at their new fort for the ease of the inhabitants. This we humbly thought our duty to lay before your Honours as there is a large seizure of tea now lying in the custom house and the soldiers' guard where it is now kept of no service to the river but an encouragement to the smugglers to run goods into the town in the night time'. Yet by September 1745 Montrose was in the hands of the rebels [see Chapter One and Figure 13].

In January 1775 the collector at Dundee reported 'We lately applied to the commanding officer of a party of dragoons lying here for a sentry to the king's warehouse and custom house, as the streets are infested with a set of vagrants and disorderly persons, who have made many attempts upon private houses and broke into several. He begged to be excused from this duty as their whole number was but sixteen and they had their horses to take care of, so we did not insist upon it. We are informed that there are two companies of foot lying at Perth. If a detachment of them sufficient to keep a sentry could be spared to come down here it would keep the custom house in safety, which otherwise it can't be said to be'.

The collector firmly believed that the attack on the Perth warehouse, custom house and his own residence resulted from the lack of a military force in the town. In mid April 1723 the supervisor of excise seized at Lindors ten hogsheads of wine, three barrels of soap and four quarter casks of brandy. These were brought to the king's warehouse. Then on 24 April the customs seized three hogsheads of red wine 'in a barn without the gate of Perth so that we have now thirteen hogsheads [in the warehouse]. But to my great surprise the first division of Palms regiment that lay here in garrison marched to Inverness and the second and last division [went] out this morning the same way and none are come to supply the place. This afternoon [25 April] I waited on the provost and magistrates for a guard. But they told me they could give none but a constable so that I am under terror of the consequences, being apprehensive of being robbed. I have sent the surveyor to the collector of excise to get one or more of his gaugers ... and design to wait and watch the event'. He had been told that 'a detachment of forty men were on their march from Leith hither and that they would be here this day but none as yet appeared, though it be past seven of the clock at night'.

The inevitable happened. 'On the 25th about eleven at night we were attacked by about three hundred villains, our warehouse, custom house and dwelling house broke and plundered of all the goods, our persons barbarously treated, myself bruised and wounded that I have enough to do to write'. Two days later 'betwixt eight and nine o'clock came here to us a corporal and six men in a Kinghorn boat'. They carried a letter from the collector at Leith. Despite the fact that help had arrived too late, the collector thanked his colleague at Leith for his attempted assistance and closed 'I wish you prosperity'.

However, he took a long time to recover from the shock of the attack. On 23 May 1723 the collector wrote to the Board 'Enclosed is the monthly abstract from the 25th day of March 1723 to the 25th day of April following. It should have been sooner sent but for the confusion I have been in for above these fourteen days. I design tomorrow to remit some money to the receiver general by bill of exchange not daring to send it in cash or bank notes'. In 1725 he reported that there was still no information about those involved in 'the riot'.

In September 1770 James Hall and Alexander Robertson were on board 'Brown's' vessel at Perth. Convinced that there were some smuggled goods on board, Hall asked for help from some soldiers while he rummaged the hold. Shortly afterwards there was a riot and Hall complained to the collector that he had been 'deforced and abused in the execution of his duty'. The results of the enquiry were reported to the Board in October.

Hall's reason for asking the soldiers to help was supposed to be because he found by Alexander Robertson's behaviour the night before that he was not to be depended on - 'this distrust not only seemed to be groundless but cannot even be believed to be sincere'. Hall knew 'Robertson's care and vigilance had kept all things safe for several nights while himself had been sick and confined to bed. It is altogether incredible that an officer who wanted secretly to favour the smugglers should bully his partner to go to sleep for that purpose. But, if Hall's suspicions were unreasonable, his confidence was still more unaccountable. It was certainly the most extraordinary measure that ever entered into any man's head to commit a quantity of spirits in bottles to the keeping of soldiers, unknown to himself, assembled by no authority and subject to no discipline or command. It is no wonder that the clamour of the seamen, who found their ship and property thus delivered over to military execution, should quickly draw a mob together. Nor is it in the least surprising when the crowd became so numerous as to make it difficult to distinguish the actions of any particular person that Mr Hall's assistants should be the most forward to take their share of the booty. Accordingly, when a regular party was demanded by Mr Cant and sent from the guard, this party had more trouble in dispersing the soldiers than all the rest of the mob and it is remarkable that the only person engaged in the riot who could be discovered and convicted was a soldier of the 43rd regiment.

'The true motive that urged Hall to this impudent step we are persuaded was a desire to engross the property of the seizure. The soldiers, he supposed, would be satisfied with a few shillings whereas he apprehended his fellow officers might claim a share. For this reason he would not mention his design of rummaging to Mr Cant, though he saw him at work on the shore all that morning and knew he would return immediately after breakfast. With the same view he contrived to send Alexander Robertson away from the ship just when he was going to begin his search.

'Hall's conduct in the management of his seizure, as he certainly meant no harm to the revenue, may perhaps admit of some apology. But nothing can excuse the disingenuity he shows in his representation of this affair. For though the riot happened while he was yet on board, though he well knew all the consequences of it and even seemed to be sensible (when examined by us) that his own misconduct had produced so much mischief to himself, as well as to the revenue, yet is his narrative drawn in such a manner as to lead your Honours to believe that he had left all the goods found on board Brown's ship in the custody of Mr Cant.

'It is hardly necessary to take notice of the complaints in Hall's petition that are particularly levelled against ourselves. He charges us with giving him no more money than was due him and with refusing to send for a guard to escort him through a public street when we knew he was not in the least danger'.

In July 1735 Captain Nathaniel Tucker, commander of the *Prince William* sloop, brought into Montrose the *Margaret* of Dundee, which had been hovering off the Red Head. When the vessel was searched it was found that there were two hogsheads of red wine, one hogshead and two half hogsheads of white wine and a half hogshead of vinegar lying amongst the ballast. Under the hatch and behind the main mast there were over a hundred ankers of brandy, 'the one side of the vessel being most full-stowed with it and the other side quite empty. In a word to all manner of appearance she had been running her cargo and upon sight of the sloop she put to sea with the wine and brandy she has now on board'. The Board sent an express, telling the collector to keep the vessel in safe custody.

'There is placed on board her three of the trustiest tidesmen we have, two sentries all night and the guard at the end of the quay'. This military presence was maintained until the goods were delivered to Leith at the end of the month. Then the collector wrote 'The sergeant of the guard who has been upon the brigantine demands of us to be rewarded for his and the guard's trouble and as we don't know if that is customary we humbly crave your Honours directions in that case'.

The customs were also expected to supply some of the other expenses associated with the military presence. In June 1740 the collector at Montrose wrote to the Board 'As directed by your letter of the 13th December 1736 we have defrayed the expense of candles for the soldiers guard on the custom house from the 1st November last to the 29th ult, the charge of which amounts to £1 5s 10d sterling ... We furnished no coals to the guard this winter'.

At a later stage there were arguments at the same port about who should cover the costs of maintaining the military in the town. On 25 November 1780 the collector wrote 'Two days ago Lieutenant Gun of the

Sutherland fencibles quartered here informed the collector that he would be obliged to withdraw the sentinel from the custom house, as the man could no longer mount guard for the smallness of the allowance of coals made by the town to the military. In consequence of which the collector waited on the provost, who informed him that the allowance given to these soldiers was the same as had been always given to English regiments when quartered here and amounted nearly to £3 per week ... As there are at present goods lodged in the warehouse, it is not proper that it should remain without a sentinel'.

An enquiry showed that an allowance towards maintenance of the military had been paid by the customs until 20 August 1778, 'since which period the custom house has issued no money on that account except £4 7s 2d, which was expended by a military guard mounted by the custom house solely for the purpose of defending the warehouse, when there was a very large quantity of tea lodged in it, another guard being kept at the same time in the public guard house'. The reason for stopping the payment was because 'the provost of Montrose had notified to them [the collector] that in consequence of a letter from General Oughton, informing that four French privateers might soon be expected on the coast, the provost and commanding officer of the military at Montrose had ordered a proper guard to be kept in a house near the mouth of the river to prevent any landing from the privateers'. When the provost next applied to the collector for a contribution to coal and candle for the guard, this was referred to the Board. They had replied that as it appeared that the guard was appointed for the safety of the inhabitants in general they did not think themselves authorised to defray the expense for coal and candle out of the revenue under their management. 'The magistrates repeatedly afterwards applied to the late collector and comptroller for the usual allowance for coal and candle to the ordinary military guard which was constantly refused'. Now it was agreed that the payment could be justified again.

Other problems related to the facilities offered to the military. In September 1760 Alexander Law mate of the *Princess Caroline* sloop seized and brought into Montrose a boat with two hogsheads wine, three casks vinegar and twenty-four ankers spirits. 'We have therefore caused scuttle said boat and further to prevent her being carried off (as formerly seized boats, though scuttled, were from this harbour) have got a sentry to watch her all day and two sentinels to watch her all night since Monday last. But the commanding officer has told the comptroller that he will not allow sentries any longer without being furnished with a sentry box and has demanded from us two such boxes viz. one for the sentry at the custom house and the other for the sentry in the boat at the shore. We must therefore humbly beg to know if your Honours will be pleased to allow two boxes forthwith to be made'.

The Alloa Deforcements

Although deforcements were part of the way of life of a revenue officer, the Alloa letter-books from 1720 to 1750 are remarkably full of stories of the deforcements of officers on duty on board vessels. A few of these have been selected as examples for this chapter.

The Officers confined on Board

In December 1739 William Rule, tidewaiter, was on duty alone on the *Success* of Stirling, William Virtue master, from Bremen, when at two o'clock in the morning two boats arrived with Robert Hurrell and Thomas Kyd ferryman, the ship's boat with several of the crew, including Patrick Law one of the sailors, John Mackenzie master of the *Fortrose*, [see Figure 4 and Chapter Six] and George Haig. These all came on board and 'forced me down (being alone) where they confined me a considerable time till they did what they thought convenient in the hold. After their business was done I got access to come to the deck and found Patrick Law in the fore peak and told him he would not deny what he had seen. The boats were so far off the ship I did not see where they went'. It was significant that Patrick McFarlane, the other tidesman who was boarded with him, was ashore all night without leave.

On 22 July 1741 the tidesmen on board the *William* of Airth, John Stone master, loaded with corns and iron from Dantzick, were deforced. According to James Graham, surveyor, 'I no sooner got account ... [of this] but I went to the place and found a small quantity of rye had been taken out of the fore part of the ship and a good quantity of wheat out of the ship's stern. But the officers being confined could not see or know any of the people employed in the deforcement, as they came on board in the dark with blacked faces.

'I stayed there till one o'clock next morning, expecting a party of the military from Stirling to protect the officers [see the collector's letter quoted in the general military section of this chapter]. But finding none came and that there was no disturbance I left William Hay, tidesman, and William Sybett, boatman, to assist the officers on board and returned home, believing no further attempt would be made that day, as it was the preparation day before ninth sacrament, and the rather because the ship was now reported. I returned to Airth about eleven o'clock, where I found a great many people unloading the vessel but durst not attempt to hinder them. They continued to work all church time and till about seven at night, after which I went on board, where the officers told me they had been confined in the cabin from five in the morning.

'But it being then daylight, they knew six or eight of the persons employed, besides the ship's company ... I found also the mob had carried off the whole wheat and all the rye except about 40 quarters, as near as I could judge. Neither could I find any more than one bar of iron, though it's possible the remainder may be still on board under the matts betwixt the bottom of the hold and the rye remaining'.

On 29 December 1746 the *Primrose* of Elphinstone, John Dick master [see Figure 4], arrived at Airth from Rotterdam and Bergen. 'As soon as the tide could admit she was boarded from this by the collector's clerk, one tidesman, two boatmen, two extra boatmen about seven o'clock at night. When on their boarding her there was a multitude of people very busy running goods out of the ship into a boat lying alongside of her, who forcibly put all the people belonging into the custom house into the cabin, where they were kept for two hours, in which time the people in the hold continued working with the darkness of the night. They having themselves disguised, they could not be known, though they were seen by the officers putting goods into the boat in spite of all opposition that could be made'.

It was not always necessary for the mob to confine the officers on board. Sometimes they took shelter themselves, to save their lives.

In April 1750 the *Mary* of Airth, William Anderson master, from Rotterdam was boarded on her way up the Forth by Captain Hay of the

Port [illegible] } List of Officers Serving at this port in Midsummer Quar[ter]

Officers	Offices	time each Served	Sallary		
Walter Grosett	Collector	whole quarter	7	10	—
John Campbell	Comptroller	Ditto	5	2	—
Robert Haliday	Surveyor	Ditto	10	—	—
Robert Dunbar	Landwaiters	Ditto	6	5	—
Alexr Gordon		Ditto	6	5	—
William Thomsone		Ditto	5	—	—
William Hay		Ditto	5	—	—
John Shaw	Tydesmen	Ditto	5	—	—
William Mile		Ditto	5	—	—
James Corrie	to	Ditto to 23 aprile	1	13	4
James Loudon		from the 23 aprile	3	6	8
John Anderson		whole quarter	5	—	—
Duncan Cameron	Boatmen	Ditto	3	15	—
William Tibbetts		Ditto	3	15	—
			70	16	8

Figure 15: List of officers serving at Alloa in Midsummer Quarter 1737

This lists the staff at Alloa in 1737. They include William Grosett, the collector who wrote the letters to the Board about coal and tobacco smuggling [see Chapters Four and Six], John Campbell, Robert Haliday, Robert Dunbar, Alexander Gordon, William Thomson, William Hay, John Schaw, James Currie, James London, John Anderson, Duncan Cameron and William Sybett.

In July 1741 the *Providence* of Sunderland, Snaith Proctor master, arrived from Rotterdam with corn for George Robin, merchant of Stirling. William Freeman and Robert Neilson, boatmen at Queensferry, were on board and as the cargo consisted mostly of barley the surveyor added William Hay, tidesman, and Thomas Brown, tidesman extraordinary, to assist them.

Two days later, about half an hour after ten at night, the vessel went to Fallin Pow with John Arthur and John Hurrell acting as pilots, where she arrived about one or two o'clock next morning. The officers were immediately attacked by a mob of up to forty people, who came on board the ship, forced them into the ship's cabin and continued to unload the barley from two o'clock in the morning till about five at night. At this stage the officers 'were liberate and found the mob had carried off all the barley excepting 4 or 5 quarters, there being also about 100 quarters of oats on board none of which they meddled with. I judge both by my own observation and the report of the officers that there might be about 60 or 70 tons of corn on board the ship before the officers were deforced. The officers know none of the people who deforced them, only Robert Neilson saw a man measuring the barley in the hold, whose name he heard was James Chidslay ... in Stirling. Thomas Brown saw him also and knows him by sight but does not know him by name. Robert Eason, coal grieve at Fallin Pow, was also present but the officers did not see him assist the mob. They understood by the people's calling to one another that William Watt, Alexander Mackie, John Archibald, John Fairlie and John Finlayson were assisting but they knew not their designations nor places of residence. Robert Neilson boatman heard one of the people say the barley was carried to Polinais but does not know if it was so. Next day ... the ship returned to this Road to discharge the remainder of her cargo'.

Princess Ann sloop, 'who put three of his hands on board her and the surveyor, being suspicious of a fraud, placed three tidesmen and two boatmen along with them. Notwithstanding thereof they were attacked that evening about eleven o'clock from the shore by a mob, who with stones beat the two officers off the deck, who had the watch, so suddenly that they had not time to call up their partners to their assistance but were glad to take shelter in the cabin to save their lives. The mob immediately boarded the vessel, opened the hatches and were employed about three or four hours hoisting out goods out of the hold. All this time the officers did not attempt to go to the deck to interrupt them, there being two of the mob standing at the companion door with clubs to intercept them'.

Henry Corbet, excise officer at Airth, undertook to discover the offenders 'who accordingly has now found out seventeen of the grossest of them and a list whereof is here enclosed, as also a list of sixteen evidences for convicting them, [neither of these lists are transcribed] but the evidences were all concerned in the riot except the four last mentioned'.

Mob Violence on Board

The first deforcement in this section is only mentioned because of the surname of the shipmaster. At ten o'clock at night on 13 April 1742 the four tidesmen on board the *Mary* of Stirling, James Porteous master, [see Chapter Six] from Rotterdam, were deforced by a mob who came on board at Stirling quay.

In November of the same year, McCallum, tidesurveyor at South Queensferry, reported that he had been deforced on board a vessel, one Ross master, while lying off Elphinstone. The situation could have been worse. As soon as the surveyor received the information he 'went immediately to his assistance with the party of military, that lay here and found in his custody two of the persons he alleged to have been concerned in the deforcement and who he had secured by his boat's coming from Blackness Castle with three soldiers he had sent for from thence upon his first boarding the vessel. He told me that having made a search through the vessel, who was in ballast, long before the mob had come near him, he found seven ankers and a hogshead of brandy. The ankers were all carried off by the mob but Mr McCallum's boat returning before they had an opportunity of carrying off the hogshead prevented its likewise being run ashore ... nothing else was found'.

The master of the *Fortrose* of Leith was involved in the deforcement of William Rule, described in the previous section. When she arrived from Gothenburg in June 1743, the master was Andrew and not John Mackenzie. But Colin Skein, the boatman who had been boarded on her at Queensferry, had been deforced. The *Fortrose* also appears in Chapter Six.

Other Violence on Board

In December 1721 the *Charles* of Elphinstone, John Forsyth master, arrived at Airth from Norway. Mr Liddell, the landwaiter, boarded her and went down to inspect the hold with one of the boatmen. 'As they were coming up, Charles Logan, the carpenter of the ship, cursed them many times, asked them what was their business aboard, kicked the boatman's head and face with his foot and when he got up to the deck he beat him there again and endeavoured to throw him overboard. The boatman never struck at him for indeed he durst not and if he had the whole crew would have risen against him and for ought I know thrown all the custom house officers overboard. For I believe there is not such another set of people in Scotland for maltreating custom house officers as in that place and there is nowhere a constable in all that country'.

As can be seen from the tailpiece, the problem continued. In August 1723 the collector wrote 'I here must observe to your Honours that this ship [the *Elizabeth & Jean*] never comes up here but there are such abuses connected, particularly [on] the 2nd May last [when] Thomas Gill and James Leigh, tidesmen of Bo'ness, and James McDonald, tidesman, at this port were deforced aboard of the same ship .... I then acquainted the Board that Gill and Leigh, being strangers, did not know any of the deforcers, only by sight they knew Logan and Walker. This Logan is a constant deforcer of the officers'.

Despite the picture painted in this chapter, not every deforcement was successful. In February 1720 the *Primrose* of Elphinstone, Andrew Ross master, [see also the section on officers confined in the cabin] with a cargo of wine came to Higginsnook with Mark Starks, surveyor at Queensferry on board. 'And knowing before that her design was to run her whole cargo here ... we judged it proper immediately to put soldiers aboard of her. The tide not answering our boat to go down, Mr Douglas, the comptroller, went down at eleven o'clock at night with a party overland to Kincardine and there got a boat and boarded her. Mr Haliday, so soon as he could got the boat off, went down with some more soldiers and officers and likewise got aboard of her. They continued there all Thursday and Friday till night when she went down the water again and as I am told she is rowing to Leith. Mr Douglas and our landwaiter and what tidesmen we have here, with a sergeant and twelve soldiers, is along with her and will be sure to keep close with her till he deliver her to some other custom house officers to take care of her'.

The success of stopping this fraud was qualified. 'On Saturday night last our custom house boat was blown away from the side of the *Primrose* ... by the great storm that was that night, although she was fastened with two big ropes. She was found among the rocks near Limekilns. Mr Haliday has been down to see her and finds her very much bilged and damaged, her foresail and some other things lost. We are getting her repaired with all expedition imaginable, which I hope your Honours will approve of for we cannot want her'.

On 15 December 1749 the *Mary & Jean* of Airth, John Mackie master, arrived from Christiansands with a cargo of wood, which was reported. Three days later the collector received information that the vessel had been in Holland before she went to Norway and that a parcel of Dutch goods was hidden under the timber. As a result he warned the surveyor, who placed two additional tidesmen on board. 'But in the evening he observed a mob appear to threaten'. As a next move the collector placed a sergeant and four soldiers on the shore until 'we came at the goods', which included one hogshead, eight half hogsheads of wine, fifty-two firkins of soap, one box containing 83 lbs of tea and five ankers of spirits. The shipmaster and the merchant, John Watson, on finding 'their intended fraud was discovered' tried to make an additional report of the wine and soap, which the collector refused. The allowance paid to the soldiers who had been on duty totalled £2 7s.

It is hard to imagine the lifestyles of these revenue officers, constantly attacked when on duty and threatened when on their way home. Despite all this maltreatment many of them continued to serve in the revenue for long periods of their lives [see Figure 14]. Apart from the deforcements, the atmosphere of living in a hostile community must have proved stressful. The tailpiece to this chapter describes the action, or more accurately inaction, of one member of the community whom the collector believed should be in a position to exert sufficient influence for the situation to improve.

The Story of Support from Mr Graham, the Judge Admiral

In December 1721 the collector at Alloa wrote to the Board 'I once was telling Mr Graham of the barbarity of his town and he then assured me he would punish any of them that were guilty of such practices. He is now at Edinburgh and I hope your Honours will be pleased to take some method of getting some exemplary punishment inflicted upon this fellow [Logan], seeing there can be such good proof made of it. For many times the officers are severely treated, when we cannot get it proven. Last year this very Logan's brother had almost murdered the other boatman without any manner of provocation and I know that these two brethren have often threatened to murder the custom house officers. Indeed they never fail, when they see any, to abuse them with language and, where they dare, with hands'.

The collector was at Airth in May 1723, to attend the unloading of a wine ship. 'I do really think that the master has made a just report' or so he thought. While he was there he met Mr Graham 'who seems to have a strong inclination to discourage all those evil practices and declared that he should punish with the utmost severity those that were concerned in that deforcement [on board the *Elizabeth & Jean* of Airth - see quote in the section on Other Violence on Board], if it be proven against them.

'That very night ... about one o'clock there came above a dozen of fellows aboard of the wine ship, forced our officers into the cabin, there kept them prisoner the space of an hour. Some of the tidesmen came to me a little after two and told me what had happened ... which makes me think that the seamen has had some ankers aboard'. Clarkson, the merchant, cursed the officers and said 'if Mr Graham did not find out a way to put a stop to that way of doing that no honest man would continue to bring any more ships to Airth and he likewise said it to Mr Graham, who came down upon the hearing of it in full rage and was at great pains to find out the actors and will be at more ... none of our tidesmen [being strangers] could know them. I am this day to go to Airth again where I shall show Mr Graham the copy of these informations and then shall acquaint the commissioners of what he says'.

The collector must have been full of hope. But in August 1723 he reported 'since that time I have heard nothing about it and I humbly beg your Honours may be pleased to fall upon some method to put a stop to these wicked practices for the revenue both in customs and salt duties suffer very much in this collection by these [deforcements] and the like practices'.

CHAPTER ELEVEN: THE KING'S BOATS AND REVENUE CRUISERS

'There does not appear to us to be any 'creeks or places' within the precincts of this port where it will be necessary to station 'preventive boats' neither do we suppose there is any probability considering its local situation and limited extent of coast that any professed smuggling will be attempted within these limits; and provided boats of the above description stationed or to be stationed at the most eligible 'creeks and places' lower down the Firth are commanded and manned by steady, vigorous and thorough bred seamen (as to which the collector and comptroller of the respective ports will fall to report) we do not think it would be possible for any smuggling vessel or boat to pass so far up as this without interruption'. [Collector at Grangemouth to the Board 5 March 1816]

The revenue officers on the land were supported by king's boats, attached to the port and manned by the tidesurveyor and either four or six boatmen, and the revenue cruisers, which patrolled across several ports and reported directly to the Board. There were also excise yachts, with deputations to seize smuggling vessels, and from time to time, when not occupied elsewhere defending the realm, support would be given by naval ships. This chapter concentrates on the king's boats and revenue cruisers.

The King's Boats

Various references have been made throughout the book to the successes and failures of the king's boats to act as an effective deterrent to smuggling vessels running part or all of their cargoes.

As boats and their crews were established and withdrawn with regularity, depending on whether or not the Board thought that they were cost-effective, it is difficult to map their stations with any accuracy at a given period. However, normally along the Forth there were boats stationed at Queensferry and Alloa while in the Tay they were based at

South Ferry, Dundee and Newburgh or Perth. There were also boats established at Dunbar, Crail, St Andrews and Montrose.

In August 1765 the Board directed the collector at Perth to send two boatmen to Ferry Pantoncraigs to bring the boat which had been used by Ambrose Starks to Perth 'to be employed in the service of the revenue here. We immediately dispatched Alexander Robertson and Alexander Martin for this purpose with a letter to Mr Starks acquainting him with your order and desiring him to send us an inventory of the furniture which he should deliver with the boat'. The inventory was depressing. 'The boat wants much to be dressed, being quite foul. Mainmast, foremast, boltsprit, mainsprit, foresprit, boat-hook with rudder, tiller and four oars all good. Mainsail and foresail almost unfit for service and not sufficient in a gale of wind. Gib half worn. Two grapnels, painter and grapnel rope unfit for service - the boat not to be trusted to them. A boat's dish and ensign staff'. The collector then listed the utensils belonging to the boat not sent by Mr Starks: a trackline; a chain and padlock; a hammer and hatchet; a spyglass; three cutlasses and two muskets; a jerque spit; an iron jack staff; a marline spike; a padlock for the lockers; a blackboard and an ensign jack and pendant.

'The boat can be of little use till it shall have undergone considerable repairs and be provided with several new articles'. The carpenter's estimate was £1 5s 2d. 'But neither sails nor cordage of the proper sort, we are informed, can be purchased in this place'.

'We flatter ourselves that your Honours will ratify the choice we have made of boatmen. Robertson has served honestly for several years as a custom house boatman and since Mr Starks left this district [he was appointed to Arbroath], has acted occasionally as a supernumerary. Martin is a very slightly young fellow and has been in use to be employed by the shipmasters as a pilot in this river. In case you shall be pleased to confirm these men in their office we apprehend it will be necessary to grant them deputations, empowering them to make seizures, as their duty will often require them to board and search vessels without the presence or assistance of any established officer. They are both under security [they had taken bonds, with securities, to be of good behaviour and not to become indebted to the revenue]'.

In 1805 the collector at Anstruther wrote a detailed report to the Board on smuggling. They were clearly impressed by this because on 15 April he wrote that he had received their letter 'in which your Honours are pleased to express your approbation of the collector's conduct in respect to the manner he has used towards detection and suppression of smuggling, which is highly gratifying to him. We hope it will be an additional spur to him in a zealous discharge of the performance of his duty'. The collector added 'This letter being wrote after hours the comptroller is not in the office to sign it'. One wonders whether all this report writing was done without the assistance/knowledge of the comptroller.

A further report detailing the smuggling problems north of the Tay was requested and submitted on 27 April [sadly not transcribed in the letter-book - clearly the information contained in it was of too sensitive a nature]. It is possible to assess the amount of effort that the collector put into producing this from his list of expenses: 'I was under the necessity of going seven times to St Andrews, distance 10 miles, once to Cupar, 16 miles and once to the parish of Leuchars in the district of the port of Dundee, which occasioned me to an expense of £4 1s 6d, which I have noted down in my memorandum book as the journeys to each place. [There is] a further sum of 16s 5d for postage of letters from and to the several persons I received my information from, which I could not charge in the postage account of this port for various reasons. May I therefore pray your Honours will be pleased to reimburse me for the sums'.

Part of his April report included recommendations about how to combat the smuggling and one suggestion was to establish a king's boat at Auchmithie. On 22 June he replied to a request from the Board 'to give my opinion in what manner lodgings may be procured at Auchmithie' for a boat's crew. The answer is transcribed here in full, as it gives a vivid picture of the problems faced by the crews of the king's boats. 'Auchmithie is a fishing village in the Parish of St Vigians, the property of Lord Northick, and in which no person but fishermen and their families reside, houses being built for them upon wanted and of a small size suitable to persons of their description by Lord Northick. The houses being all of a small size and the families of fishermen in general very numerous, there is less chance of strangers meeting with accommodation of the kind in a fishing town than a place of any other kind of same size. There is only one public house in the town, kept by a David Cargill, [see Chapter Eight] who is also a brewer and a small farmer. This man is deeply connected with the smugglers and his son comes over to the Fifeside with the smuggling boats, acting as a kind of supercargo [the merchant actually on board a ship to arrange sale of the cargo].

'For these reasons ... I conceive it will not be an easy matter to obtain lodgings for seven or eight men. The only way of doing it in my humble opinion is by application to Lord Northick (and he being at present abroad) his agent or factor. By his influence it might be accomplished, when any other method failed (at same time I pray leave to represent that in the course of my enquiries I'm afraid that his lordship's servants who are left in charge of his lordship's house in his absence make a very bad use of their power in secreting run goods). I have no doubt but David Cargill, who keeps the public house, would give them victuals but not lodgings.

'I further pray leave to report that a great sea breaks in upon Auchmithie. The fishing boats belonging thereto are obliged to be hauled up on the rocks out of the way of the surge in the winter time, in which women and children assist. If a revenue boat was stationed there, it is not likely the boat's crew would receive much assistance from the inhabitants. It would therefore be necessary to erect a small cable to assist in hauling up the boat, which would be erected at a small expense. A skiff would be absolutely necessary in addition to the large boat. Having pointed out the difficulties that would attend the stationing the boat at Auchmithie, I pray leave to observe that I am still of the same opinion as to the great advantages that would result to this, the revenue, were a boat put there - the place where the smuggling vessels in general come to when they lie off that [part of the coast]. [From there] they can see not only all the vessels that are approaching them from the sea but they have a view of the Firth of Forth and can discover the cruisers that may be coming down upon them from the Leith Roads, which they cannot do either at the Havens or Arbroath or in Lunan Bay. At same time I pray leave to observe that, if fixing a boat at Auchmithie could not be accomplished, Arbroath is certainly the next best place, being about three miles west of Auchmithie and as many more east of the Havens.

Further no difficulties would be met with in getting accommodation for the men and if this measure were gone into two of the crew, when not employed on other duty, should be constantly at Auchmithie shore and patrol between that and Arbroath and the Havens'.

A Story of the King's Boat at Dundee

A story about the Dundee tidesurveyor, Finlayson, was included in Chapter Five. This material comes from a similar source - not the standard transcribed letters in the book but some original documents slipped in at the back. As a result the story is incomplete - no other references have been found to the event or the subsequent enquiry.

On Saturday morning, 2 May 1730, as the boatmen were rowing up to Dundee in the custom house boat, a boy running along bank waved at them to come to the south shore, where he delivered a letter to Mr Finlayson. Having read this, Finlayson set off again, first for Dundee and then back to Ferry Pantoncraigs. 'The boatmen take notice that that night Mr Finlayson neither went off himself nor desired the boatmen to go upon the river, notwithstanding they all knew there were ships upon the coast and that they had for several nights before gone always off to prevent boats from landing any goods'. The insinuation is that the letter had told Finlayson to 'look the other way'.

Between eight and nine the next morning the custom house boat went up the river again so that they could all go to church. On the way, Alexander Nicol saw a boat lying at anchor by Balmerino, where the boatmen knew that boats frequently unloaded brandy. The boatmen proposed to the tidesurveyor that they should go there immediately 'which he refused that time but desired them to go over (after he had landed [on the north shore, at Dundee]) and in case they found anything ... to come back and call him. They immediately proceeded in quest of said boat and were so very near that they saw casks in her'. According to the evidence of one of the boatmen 'upon our approach she immediately weighed anchor and stood over to the northside'. There were not enough hands in the boat to catch up with her. Instead they landed at Dundee and David Frazer went in search of Finlayson whom he found at the house of Thomas Ogilvie. They then went to Magdalen Ford, half a mile west of

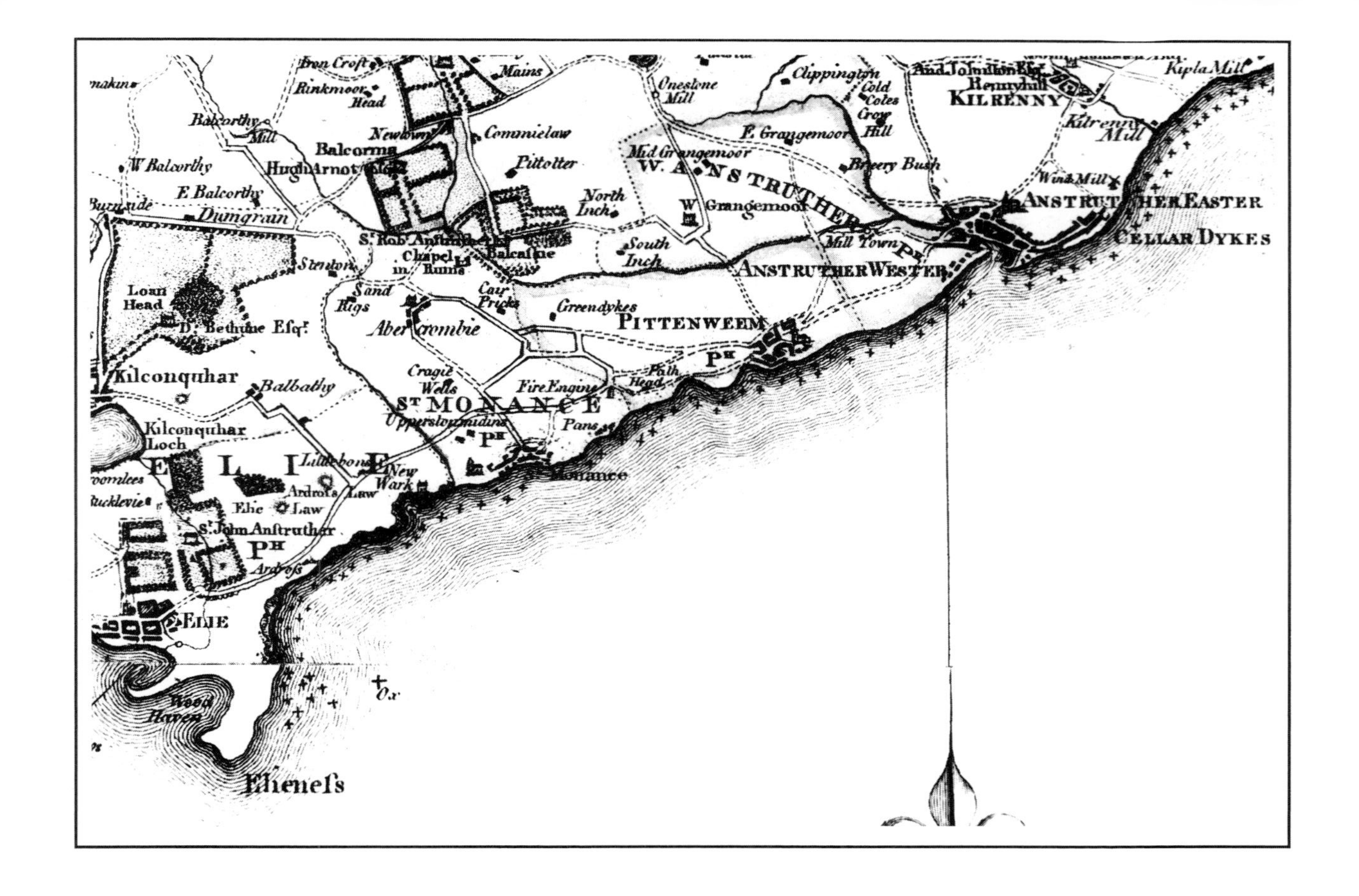
Iron Croft
Rinkmoor Head
Mains
Balcorthy Mill
Newtown
Commielaw
Balcormo
W Balcorthy
Hugh Arnot
Pittotter
E Balcorthy
Burnside
Dungrain
North Inch
South Inch
Chapel in Ruins
Balcaskie
Loan Head
Sand Rigs
Car Pricks
Greendykes
D. Bethune Esq.
Abercrombie
PITTENWEEM
Kilconquhar
Balbathy
Cragie Wells
Fire Engine
Path Head
ST MONANCE
Pans
Kilconquhar Loch
E L I E
New Wark
Ardross Law
Elie Law
St. John Anstruther
Ardross
ELIE
Wood Haven
Elieness
Ox
Onestone Mill
Clippington
Cold Coles
Crow Hill
Kipla Mill
KILRENNY
Kilrenny Mill
E. Grangemoor
Mid Grangemoor
W. ANSTRUTHER
Breery Bush
Wind Mill
W Grangemoor
ANSTRUTHER EASTER
Mill Town
CELLAR DYKES
ANSTRUTHER WESTER

Figure 16: The Anstruther District in the Eighteenth Century

This map indicates the area from Anstruther to Elie. On 1 January 1808 the collector at Anstruther reporting on the value of Elie as a harbour, commented that the following excise vessels went in there regularly to have their bottoms cleaned: the *Prince of Wales,* Captain Henderson; *Royal George*, Captain Currie; *Charlotte*, Captain Robertson and the *Henry Dundas* also Captain Robertson.

There follows a list of the revenue cruisers mentioned most often in the custom house letter-books together with their commanders, as identified during the research for this book.

***Princess Caroline* sloop**
1730 Captain Middleton
1735 Captain Arthur Starks
1755 Captain John Read
1775 Captain Laurence Brown

***Prince William* sloop**
1735 Captain Nathaniel Tucker
1755 Captain Charles Hay
1770 Captain Alexander Read

***Princess Ann* sloop**
1740 Captain Hay (and 1750)
1765 Captain James Kyd (and 1786)

***Princess Royal* sloop**
1786 Laurence Brown

***Osnaburgh* sloop**
1787 Captain Kyd

The comments from the commanders of the *Princess Royal* and *Osnaburgh* sloops were used to produce the spirits smuggling section in Chapter Four.

Dundee. At this stage Finlayson sent Frazer to inform the collector of what had happened and to see if he could get a boat. The tidesurveyor then planned to 'go off with a party to stop the [smuggling] boat getting out of the river'.

In the meantime, when the collector came out of church, he was told by a couple of people that instead of chasing an obvious smuggling boat Finlayson was at Magdalen Ford. The collector set off with two tidesmen and found a boat, but could not persuade any of the local boatmen to take them out into the river. They met Frazer, whom the collector ordered to go to Finlayson at Magdalen Ford and 'desire him to come along with the boat. The party was now able to cross to the south side of the river, where they seized 14 1/2 hogsheads of sherry'.

The Revenue Cruisers

The collector at Anstruther wrote to the Board once more on the subject of smuggling in a letter dated 26 October 1807. In this he listed the main reasons for the recent decline in smuggling. The first of these, as already seen in Chapter Seven, was the death of James Butcher. 'Secondly from the adoption of more vigorous measures for the suppression of smuggling by both the Board of Customs and of Excise, particularly the keeping the cruisers constantly at sea, as far as circumstances permitted, which has certainly had a great effect in the prevention of smuggling. For within these two years we have heard of several instances when the smuggling vessels have been obliged to leave the coast without being able to land a single anker of geneva, a circumstance which was formerly unknown in the smuggling trade and proves that if the cruisers cannot detect they will at least prevent the smuggler from landing the goods on that part of the coast where they are stationed ...

'In obedience to the latter part of your Honours order wherein it is directed that we give our opinion what are the most effectual means to suppress such illicit trade, we humbly beg leave to report that in order to point out the best mode of suppressing this trade it is necessary we take a short view of the different circumstances and situations in which the smuggled goods are placed previous to their coming into the hands of the consumer ...

'The first situation therefore in which the smuggled goods (say geneva) are placed is on board the smuggling vessel that brings it from the place of growth and that generally in quantities of from 300 to 1,500 ankers of spirits; secondly on board of the boats which convey it from these vessels to the shore and then it is generally in quantities from twenty to a hundred ankers and lastly in carts and on the backs of men, women and horses, who convey it either to the houses of the consumer or to concealments at no great distance from the shore. It will readily appear that, if seizures of smuggled goods could be made whilst in the two first of the above-mentioned situations, it would tend more effectually to suppress smuggling than if allowed to be laid on land, when it can be seized only in smaller quantities.

'We have already taken leave to state to your Honours that effectual means have been employed, we understand, to keep the cruisers at their duty and thus to facilitate the seizure of the smuggling vessels with their cargoes. The next thing is to lay hold of the boats that convey the smuggled goods from the luggers to the shore or, which would be next to the same thing effectually, to prevent our fishing boats from engaging in this illicit traffic. For if the smuggler is obliged to land his goods by his own boats, the operation is so tedious that he must be detected by our cruisers before half his cargo is landed. This can only be done, we humbly conceive, by stationing revenue boats on the coast in the very places where these smuggling boats belong to. The revenue boats being commanded by active vigilant and enterprising officers appointed either by your Honours or from your recommendation of them to the Lords of the Treasury from a knowledge of their possessing the above-mentioned qualities. For without the commanding officer in particular be a man of this description, it will not answer the end in view and with such a salary as independent of seizures will put him above the temptation of a bribe, a thing not unknown as we have been informed to the smugglers on the coast of Angus'.

There are frequent references to the revenue cruisers in the letter-books because the collector had to report each time one of them arrived at or sailed from his port. Based on this information an attempt has been made to recreate the log book for the *Prince William* sloop, commanded by Captain Alexander Read, for the year 1770, to give a flavour of the type of activity involved. From this analysis it appears that the cruiser went into Dundee at regular intervals. For example, she 'arrived from a cruise' on 5 March, 2 May, 19 June, 16 July, 28 July, 6 August, 24 August, 8 October, 29 October, 30 November and 26 December. She would then leave after two or three days in port, again 'on a cruise'. On at least two occasions during the year she went into Montrose.

The revenue cruisers had various reasons for going into a port. They wanted to be aware of any 'intelligence' available about smuggling vessels known to be or expected in the area. On 2 February 1775 the collector at Dundee wrote to the Board's secretary that 'immediately upon receipt of your letter of the 27th ult containing intelligence of the ships *Minerva* and *Dispatch* we transmitted the same first to Captain Brown of the *Princess Caroline* sloop and after that by express to Mr Dick, who commands the king's boat stationed at Broughty Castle. The same method we also took with your letter of the 31st ult advising a lug-sailed smuggling vessel being on the coast'.

It was also an opportunity to pass on any information that they might have obtained. On 29 December 1755 the collector at Dundee wrote to Captain John Read of the *Princess Caroline* at Montrose 'The two ships mentioned in yours of the 28th inst are not yet arrived in this river nor have we any accounts of them'.

They were expected to escort any suspicious vessels. As the collector at Dundee reported in June 1765 the *Princess Caroline* sloop had come into the Tay 'on orders to attend the two ships load with wine and salt mentioned in our letter of the 10th inst. But the morning before the receipt of your order of the 11th both ships sailed directly out of the river, [as] no reason appeared for detaining them'. On other occasions the cruiser was on time. In 1775 the *Princess Caroline* sailed from the river Tay, attending the *Fame*, William Thornton master, for Madeira with four pieces of brandy on board.

The cruisers needed to bring any seizures into port so that they could be returned to the Board and so that they were free to sail off again. There are details of the *Prince William* being involved in at least three seizures of vessels in 1770. On 6 January twenty-four half and one whole hogsheads of brandy, six hogsheads of wine, two casks of tea, two kits of china, one chest of bottled wine and three kegs of herrings were found on board the *Surprise* of St Andrews, John Frazer master, from Gothenburg. She was taken into port by the revenue cruiser. Six hogsheads of wine were brought into the king's warehouse. The remainder of her cargo, consisting of iron and deals, was lodged in the town warehouse, upon the warehousekeeper's receipt, until the duties were paid, because 'there being no room for these in the king's warehouse at present'. The *Prince William* then sailed on a cruise. As the military could not help, James Dick, the tidesurveyor, had been requested to bring up the boat's crew from the Ferry to 'strengthen our guard' on the vessel. On 9 February the revenue cruiser took the goods to Leith.

The *Prince William* brought other seizures into port but often there were no further details about how they had been seized - on 15 March six ankers of geneva and eight boxes of tea and on 28 May tea, spirits and tobacco stalks.

In April the collector at Dundee reported that on receiving information from the Board about the sloop *Janet & Barbara*, James Liddell master, 'we communicated the particulars thereof to Mr Gordon, mate of the *Prince William* sloop, whose boats were then employed to cruise in St Andrews Bay waiting the arrival of some ships expected from Holland. She was brought into the Tay on 18 April. James Dick boarded the vessel and 'found on examining the hold twelve pipes, ten hogsheads, nineteen quarter casks full and one quarter cask of wine almost empty'. The merchant made a double entry and on 14 May she sailed on her pretended voyage to Bergen. The *Prince William* was requested to escort her off the coast and other outports were forewarned.

On another occasion two of the *Prince William's* men were boarded on the *Mansfield* of Crail, James Stephen master, from Moss in Norway. She arrived at Dundee from Anstruther and then sailed on up the river to Perth.

Other reasons for going into port included for a supply of provisions, 'for want of some books and paper' or put in by a hard gale of wind. In May 1765 the collector at Dundee reported that Captain Kyd, commander of the *Princess Ann* yacht 'came up to the Ferry Road yesterday but not having seen nor heard from him we can assign no reason for his coming up this river'.

The *Prince Augustus Frederick* cutter, Peterhead.

Captain Dorvie was commander of the *Prince Augustus Frederick* cutter, which was stationed at Peterhead but appears to have been driven southwards frequently by bad weather, as he was in constant contact with the collector at Anstruther. In April 1807 Dorvie seized 16 1/2 gallons of foreign geneva and 6 gallons of foreign brandy on board the Danish galliot *Harbet*, Jacob Tonneson master, from Christiansands. The Anstruther collector wrote to him, at Peterhead, on 28 April 'I was favoured with yours of the 8th inst and would have answered it sooner but waited till I got the Board's directions about your seizure. They have ordered 5 gallons of the spirits to be returned and the master to pay a fine of £8 to you and crew so that there now remains 17 1/2 gallons gin and brandy and in my hands £8, which I shall keep till you come this way or remit to you as you desire ... Below is a copy of the Board's order about the spirits. Though there were many other orders besides tis the last, which only came last night. The master wanted to get back more spirits etc. etc. and the Board would only allow 3 gallons of both wine and spirits the allowance permitted by the order of 15 October 1793 not being applicable as the master did not produce his stores openly to you'. The problem with this seizure was that masters could claim certain quantities of spirits, tea and tobacco as 'stores' for their journey. But they were supposed to show these to anyone who boarded the vessel.

The more significant comment from the collector is 'As to the other part of your letter I have long thought of it but the peoples in Edinburgh [the Board] dont seem inclined, though a circumstance has occurred just now which may perhaps have some effect and of which I will inform you at our meeting, which I hope you will make as early as possible ... In your way to this place I would recommend you to call at Montrose, see the officers of customs and endeavour to pick up what intelligence you can. For although I believe they know a good deal, yet they dont give themselves much or indeed any trouble so that something may be gathered from them. With Best Wishes, I am dear Sir'.

Then on 7 June 1807 the collector applied to the Board and was granted ten days leave of absence for his 'private affairs'. As a result he was not in post when the *Prince Augustus Frederick* arrived at Anstruther on 24 June 'to get her bottom cleaned'. Nor was he there when she sailed on the 24th of that month. The cutter was back, in Elie, twice in October and in November. But the records do not show the result of any meeting between the collector and Captain Dorvie to discuss the more effective suppression of smuggling.

The Story of the *Prince William Henry* cutter, Leith

In November Captain Hamilton was in urgent need of seamen and so he applied to the collector at Anstruther for help in finding a crew. There followed a long correspondence, the letters from George Forrester, collector at Anstruther, are all addressed to Captain Hamilton the *Prince William Henry* Customs Cutter, Leith.

The first was dated 4 November 1807. 'There are no doubt a great many seamen to be got in this part of the country, especially at this season of the year, when the Baltic trade is at an end for some months to come. But unfortunately the encouragement given by excise is too superior to what is allowed by the customs. Until all the cutters on the former establishment are fully manned none will enter with the customs. This is the uniform answer I have received from all the seamen in this neighbourhood. Two young men, whose names are Alexander Bruce and James Swinton, inform me that they have sent to Leith Roads to enquire if they can get berths in some of the excise cutters now lying there. Should they be already full manned they have promised to proceed immediately to your ship. I shall continue to be on the look out.

'PS Since writing the above a young man has applied to enter. His name is John Finlay, at present weaver but was 6½ years on board the *Princess Charlotte* excise cutter, Captain Elder Robinson. He left the cutter last April [and] is a smart young man of 30 years age. If you approve of him send me a protection [so that he would not be impressed into the navy] for him immediately, when he will join you.'

The next letter is dated 14 November 1807. 'In return to your letter of 13th I have to inform you that Finlay, whom I engaged, not hearing from you nor I having received a letter on the subject, has engaged himself somewhere else. But I sent two others to you yesterday, who informed me they were to join you immediately ... They are both discharged from the *Prince of Wales* excise cutter, Captain Henderson. Their cause of dismissal was staying ashore one night. Henderson, who resides here, had other men in his offer, which

contd.

The Story of the *Prince William Henry* cutter, Leith contd.

made him reject them the more easily. These men you can take or not as you please. Their names are William Strachan and Robert Mackie. The first served his time to the sea. The last was bred a weaver but had been on board Captain Henderson upwards of two years.

'As to their moral character I can say very little having made no inquiry, not supposing it necessary. Indeed between you and I it is the first time I ever heard of the morals of a seaman being inquired into. But I believe measuring them by the general standard of cutter men they will not be found inferior to their neighbours. You are quite correct in your conjunctions as to the Baltic trade men are and will be plentier from the circumstance of its being at an end for the present. But until your wages are on a par with the excise you must be content with accepting the refuse of their crew, the disadvantage of which to the service you are no doubt a better judge of than I can be. In the meantime I shall continue my inquiries and endeavours to supply you with men until you order me to the contrary. Only be pleased to reply to my letters (when any answer is required) as early as possible and give me what directions you think proper.

Five days later Forrester reported that since his previous letter 'I have had an application from two seamen belonging to Crail in the neighbourhood of this place to enter to your cutter viz. Paten Hunter, who has been 18 years at sea and George Wemyss, who has likewise been some years at sea. They are both young men of good character, having made enquiries to that effect. The last mentioned person is a carpenter and were you not provided with a person of that description he would gladly enter with you on that footing. In the meantime I have wrote you to know if you are inclined to take them because it would be needless for them to proceed to Leith unless you were so inclined and you may perhaps have by this time obtained your compliment. I will therefore thank you to write me in course.'

The final letter in this series is dated 14 December 1807. 'I have received your letter of the 12th inst. It is quite needless to speak to seamen

contd.

The Story of the *Prince William Henry* cutter, Leith contd.

about the rise of wages until it is actually in course of payment. When that is the case and if you are to come into the Elie I have no doubt but you would soon get men. Indeed as the wages now stand you would get men much better than at Leith. In my letter to you of the 13th November. I mentioned a good seaman of the name of Hunter, who wishes to be engaged, but you gave me no direct answer about him whither you would have him or not. Men in their station cannot remain unemployed. By referring to my letter you will see him described and you should through me give him a direct answer. I also mentioned in the same letter another seaman of the name of Wemyss but he has since gone in a coasting vessel. I have made the meaning of your letter as public as possible'.

CHAPTER TWELVE: AND THEN ...

'The first thing to be remembered is, that an officer who only rummages a portion of a vessel thoroughly is worth a hundred fold more to the crown than one who scampers all over her, and, failing to discover any contraband goods, arrives at the conclusion that there are none to be found. When, during the search of a vessel, an officer finds himself anxiously watched by any member of the crew, he must draw his own conclusions from the circumstance. Probably the man is in fear that the officer will discover his hiding place ... Successful officers are keen observers of human nature ... Smugglers are also keen observers of the tactics and qualifications of the officers and take mental notes of their proceedings and from these notes they make their calculations as to the risk they would run by engaging in illicit traffic. The wood linings of a vessel are answerable for the majority of concealments to be found on board ship ... Indeed without the wooden portion of a ship smugglers would be reduced to the necessity of hiding their tobacco etc. in the multifarious holes and corners which always abound in sailing vessels as well as steamers'. [From a Confidential Report on Modern Smuggling and its Detection. London 1888]

This is not the place to enter into a detailed discussion of the various reasons why there was a marked decline in smuggling throughout the nineteenth century, as already mentioned in Chapter Eight.

In October and November 1823 Arbroath received two forewarning of major smuggles to be attempted in their area. These started with a letter dated 17 October. 'I have it in command to acquaint you for your own information and government and that of the officers under your survey that the Board have received intelligence (which may be depended upon) that a cargo of contraband goods is hourly expected between Arbroath and the Tay and to direct you to use your best endeavours to detect any fraud which may be attempted'. A month later there were two possible candidates. The cutter *Mary* had sailed from Jersey with fruit for Scotland but she was reputed to have on board 'many passengers, noted smugglers, and to be load with silks'. A couple of days later a large smuggling lugger was on her way with spirits and tobacco and, significantly, 'a person who is understood to be agent for the vessel' had just passed through Edinburgh on his way north.

By the 1830s the majority of monthly reports on the state of smuggling in the area were 'nil'. For example on 29 October 1834 Leith reported that 'we have made every enquiry in our power respecting the present state of smuggling and the result is we have reason to believe there has not been any attempt to carry on illicit practices within this port during the last quarter, other than a few instances in which small quantities of tobacco have been found concealed on board regular trading vessels from foreign ports, which the crews of such vessels evidently intended to have run had they not been detected'.

There were exceptions. But as suggested by the Leith letter, the smuggling was of a somewhat different nature to that discussed at length throughout the other chapters. Two seizures made at Grangemouth in 1874 and 1877 are described here. In November 1874 the steamer *Snowdoun* of Leith, William Staig master, arrived at Grangemouth from Hamburg. When she was rummaged three bags of tobacco were found concealed in the forehold. 'On mustering the crew three men came forward and admitted that they were the owners of the respective bags viz. William Flett, boatswain, one bag containing 33 lbs 8 oz manufactured tobacco; William Gowans, able seaman, one bag containing 20 lb 8 oz tobacco and Maxwell Nelson, able seamen, one bag containing 15 lb 3 oz manufactured tobacco, being in all 69 lb 3 oz.

'The tobacco is deposited in the queen's warehouse as a seizure and the three men have been arrested and were this day taken before a magistrate in Falkirk and remanded to Stirling gaol until Tuesday next the 10th inst. I submit my proceedings in this case for your Honours approval and request instructions for such further proceedings against the prisoners as your Honours may see fit to direct.

'The ship has been placed under detention. There is no reason to suppose that the master or any of the superior officers were privy to the concealment of the tobacco but it is probable that your Honours may be of opinion that so large a quantity could not have been brought on board without their knowledge, if they had exercised proper vigilance. I shall exact a deposit of £100 in the event of the owners applying to have her released. This ship is owned by the same parties [James Currie & Co] as the steamer *Dresden* recently released on a deposit'.

A few days later the *Snowdoun* was released on the deposit 'to meet any fine your Honours may see fit to inflict for the breach of the revenue laws for which she was detained'. In the case of the *Dresden*, £5 was retained as a fine and the steward, Franklin Jones, was proceeded against and convicted in a penalty of £2 14s 6d, including 7s 6d costs, which he paid.

Three years later the steamer *Grangemouth*, Wallace master, defined as 'a regular trader between this port and Rotterdam' was rummaged. The following goods were found concealed in the steward's cabin: thirty-five paper packages containing: 38½ lbs manufactured tobacco; one paper package containing ¾ lb cigars and three bottles containing 6¾ gills eau de cologne. These were seized and the vessel was placed under detention. 'There is no doubt that the goods belonged to the steward Frank Meyers, a Dutchman, who has the sole use of the cabin in which they were concealed. He was present when the officers commenced rummaging the cabin but had gone ashore unobserved before the goods were discovered and effected his escape and has not since been found, although the officers have used their best endeavours to trace him. There is no reason to suspect that the master was in any way privy to the concealment of the goods or that he connived at the escape of the steward and I have felt justified in releasing the vessel taking a deposit of £50 from Mr W H Durie, the agent for the owners, to meet any fine your Honours may see fit to impose'.

Several of the Leith Class 4 records provide insights into the involvement of the revenue officers in small smuggles and other infringements. James Borthwick, born September 1836, was appointed as clerk at Leith in January 1858. In 1872 he was charged with a false plea of illness to account for absence from duty. This did not sound too serious an offence. But then he was dismissed in July 1875 for having been charged with and found guilty of 'having falsified official documents and retained public monies in his possession'.

Michael Egan, appointed as an outdoor officer at Leith from November 1877, did not appear to have been knowingly involved with smuggling so much as having been lax in his duty. In 1878 he was charged with having absented himself from the watch house without leave; having left the steamer *Dwana* of Hamburg, of which he was in charge, and when told to return having used 'insubordinate conduct' to his superior and with continued insubordination the next day, when rummaging the steamer *Maria Stuart*, under supervision. In June 1881, when allowed to be absent for dinner from the steamer *Berlin*, he failed to return and left a note at the watch house stating that 'suffering from diarrhea and a slight attack of piles he felt unable to resume his duty' whereas there was proof that instead of going straight home and staying there he had been absent from his lodgings from four o'clock to a late hour the same night. In October he was fined £3 for having been 'found asleep during his watch on board the steamer *North Star* from Hamburg'. In January 1882 he was dismissed, final charge not evident.

Born in January 1846, John Cairns had a somewhat varied customs career serving at Grangemouth, London and Leith before being sent to Goole 'at his own expense to fill the office of preventive officer, lower section'. The problem was that he had felt sorry for a smuggler called Kerman Grass. When he found Grass involved in a smuggling transaction [unspecified but one can guess that it might have been a small quantity of tobacco] instead of arresting him and keeping him in custody, Cairns allowed him to 'go into town in order to obtain money and get a confederate'. Finally he had failed to appear in court on time to hear the case against Grass. The Board considered that he had acted throughout these proceedings 'with a want of intelligence and absence of knowledge of the duties of his office and a lack of zeal which ... constitutes danger to the revenue'.

This was in 1901. Have things changed since then? It would appear not. Two recent incidents along the Forth suggest that nothing is new. The master of a vessel 'made it known' that he had cigarettes, tobacco and liquor for sale on board. It would have concerned the anonymous letter writer from Eyemouth in 1800 to know that the profits from these sales were still not going into Scottish hands. On the second occasion the goods were seized once they were on shore because the 'runner' could not carry the weight of contraband involved. One is reminded of the problems of dispersing the horseloads of tobacco at speed. The rest of the smuggling story, as it appears in current documents, will not be available to the researcher for another fifity years or more. For once the author wishes that the cliffs along the coast from Montrose to Dunbar could speak!

The Story of the End of Smuggling

This is the response from Perth to a circular from the Board asking for comments on changes now that the Isle of Man was vested in the crown. The letter is dated 3 September 1766.

'We received your letter of the 26th ult requiring us to transmit to your Honours as accurate a state as we can make or procure of the illicit trade carried on at present to and from the Isle of Man and to report what consequence the Act of Parliament for vesting the ports in the Island in His Majesty has had in checking or preventing the smuggling on the coasts of this part of the kingdom.

'We have reason to think that the merchants in this precinct have never had any commercial correspondence with the Isle of Man. The long, perplexed and dangerous navigation between that Island and this country has placed an almost insuperable bar in the way of such a trade and the expense of landcarriage from any of the ports that lie conveniently for that commerce would be so exorbitant (not to mention the hazard to which prohibited goods must be exposed) that we may safely affirm with respect to this town that it has at no time driven any trade directly or indirectly with the Isle of Man.

'There is one consequence that might have been apprehended from the Act of Parliament above mentioned which your Honours have a right to expect we should take notice of. It might naturally be thought that smuggling, excluded by the regulations of this statute from the western coast, should break in with more violence upon this side of the island. What may have happened in those ports that lie nearer the ocean we cannot say but we never knew of any period when the trade of this place was so little tainted with irregular and contraband importations as it has been during these last twelve or fourteen months. This happy circumstance must be ascribed to that seasonable and well judged law by virtue of which even a small quantity of spirituous liquor subjects vessels under 100 tons burthen to forfeiture. A law which took place nearly about the same time with that for vesting the sea ports of the Isle of Man in His Majesty'.

APPENDIX

Extract from: The Report by Thomas Tucker upon the Settlement of the Revenues of Excise and Customs in Scotland 1656 as presented to Sir Walter Scott, President, and the other members of the Bannatyne Club in 1885

Note: Where appropriate, the modern spellings of the placenames have been used throughout this extract.

'The town of Dunbar, or village rather, (for all the towns of Scotland unless the burgh towns deserve no other appellation, did not use and custom of speech give them a bigger title,) is a fisher town, famous for the herring fishing, who are caught thereabouts, and brought thither and afterward made, cured, and barrelled up either for merchandise, or sold and vended to the country people, who come thither far and near at that season, which is from about the middle of August to the latter end of September, and buy great quantities of fish, which they carry away, and either spend them presently or else salt and lay up for the winter provision of their families. The trade here is little else except salt, which is brought hither and laid up, and are sold for the fishing; the people of these parts which are not fishermen, employing themselves in tillage, and in affairs of husbandry. But yet the conveniency of an indifferent good harbour and landing-place, hath occasioned the placing of a waiter here, not only for preventing any goods from being brought privately on shore, but also to look backward as far as Eyemouth, and forward as Prestonpans and Newhaven, two small places adjoining one another, and both lying on a flat shore where there are many saltpans, which is the trade of the place and employment of the people. Hither many small vessels come to fetch salt, and oftentimes bring goods with them, which would be stole ashore were there not a waiter in these places who takes care of them, and upon all occasions looks back as far as Dunbar and forward to Musselborough; a small, or rather three or four small towns joining together, the inhabitants fishermen and husbandmen, having an open harbour on the outside of their town for small boats or vessels, and a very opportune place for carrying out and bringing in of goods unto or from any ship that shall be lying in the road if not looked after. From this to Leith the shore being open upon a flat sand with some rocks before it, nothing can either safely or commodiously be landed; besides that it lies all in sight. As for the tract of ground beyond Leith, and yet in the district thereof, there are only a few fishermen with some two or three empty houses, the ruins of some saltworks, and the little country village of Cramond, not worth the placing any officer there, and for that cause left to the care of all the officers in general, who may easily in the day-time from the town of Leith discover any vessels (or boats from them) going to the shore, and be as soon as themselves at their place of landing. And yet, if anything do, or should happen to slip in at night, the same being for account of the Leith or Edinburgh merchants, must afterward be brought to some of those two places, and if so, or to any other burgh town where there are officers attending, they can hardly escape the being seized upon. There are belonging to the port of Leith and members, some twelve or fourteen vessels, two or three whereof are of some two or three hundred tons a piece, the rest small vessels for lading and carrying out salt, and to and from the coast of England, the chief part of the trade of these parts being driven thence, the rest being from Norway, the Eastland, Low Countries, or France, immediately from the places themselves.

'The next port is Bo'ness, lying on an even low shore on the south side of the Firth, about mid way betwixt Leith and Stirling. The town is a mercat town, but subservient and belonging to (as the port) to the town of Linlithgow, two miles distant thence. The district of this port reaches from Cramond exclusive, on the south side of the Firth to Stirling inclusive, and thence all along the north side of the same Firth as far as a little town called Limekilns. This port, next to Leith, hath of late been the chief port one of them in Scotland, as well because it is not far from Edinburgh, as because of the great quantity of coal and salt that is made and digged here, and afterward carried hence by the Dutch and others, and the commodities some time brought in by those Dutch who, avoiding and passing by Leith, do run up the Firth, and did usually obtain opportunity of landing their goods on each side in their passage, the Firth a little above Burntisland contracting and running along in a more narrow channel. There are constantly resident at this port a collector, a check, and some four waiters to attend the coast and Inchgarvie.

'The member ports on this side of the head port, and on the south side, are

'Queensferry, a small town, where formerly goods have been landed, but not of late, because of Inchgarvie lying over against it in the middle of the river, and that being furnished with soldiers, and an officer or two, to examine and search all ships in their passage, have kept them from that practice thereabouts.

'Blackness, Cuff-abowt, and Grange, the former of them sometimes reported to have been a town, and at that time the port of Linlithgow, but not now nothing more than three or four pitiful houses, and a piece of an old castle. The other two are likewise some few houses standing on two places of the shore nigh some saltpans and coal-haughs.

'On the other side of the port (but of the same side of the Firth) is Elphinstone, a small town, where there is a pretty store of great coal shipped for beyond the seas. And although there be never a vessel belong to this place, yet the Dutch mostly, and some others, choose to lade there because of the goodness of the coal and its measure. The river here being narrow, the waiter on the opposite side takes care as well as account of what is shipped here.

'The next place beyond and furthest of the district this way, is Stirling, a pretty burgh, famous for the strength of the castle and bridge, which is laid over the Firth at that place, this being the head of it, and the tide not flowing not a mile above it. Here live some merchants, but the shallowness of the river, with the windings thereof, making the way long, and not permitting a boat of burthen to pass up so high all goods are entered first, and cleared below at Bo'ness, and thence afterward carried up in small boats as the merchant hath occasion for them.

'On the north side of the Firth, there is a pretty fine burgh called Alloa, having a fine harbour, and an excellent coal, which is for the most part shipped and carried away by the Dutch, there being no vessel belonging to the place. Nevertheless, there hath usually been a pretty trade for that commodity, but interrupted of late by some difference happening among some of the proprietors of the coal haughs. Here is a waiter constantly resident, to take care of this and the town of Kennett, where likewise is a very good great coal, but chiefly sent from port to port, and never or seldom outwards.

'The next are Kincardine and Culross, the first a small, and the other a burgh town. From these two places salt only goes out. There is indeed a coal at Valleyfield adjoining to Culross, and at Kincardine also, but brought up and spent by the country, and not sent out. There were lately some five vessels belonging to Culross, but lost and taken all except two of the best, which still remain. These two places have a waiter constantly to attend them, with the adjoining town of Torryburn, the chief place for shipping out small coals, where he is mostly resident. There are three vessels, belonging to this town, one of some an hundred and twenty, another of an hundred, and the third of sixty tons.

'The last place in this district is Limekilns, a town whence some small coals hath some time been sent out, but very little of late, and, for this reason, it hath been commenced to the waiter of the next place, to have an eye and take account when any coal shall be shipped out, but not esteemed worth the placing of an officer purposely.

'The next head port is Burntisland, lying opposite to Leith, on the north side of the Firth, whose districts reach from Inverkeithing all along the shore to the county of Fife, unto the banks of the river Tay. The trade of these parts inwards, is from Norway, the East Country, and sometimes from France with wines, and outwards with coal and salt, at all times very small, and worth little; for, although this be the bounds of one of the best and richest counties of Scotland, yet the goodness and riches of the country arising more from the goodness and fertility of the soil and lands than any traffic, hath made it the residence and seat of many of the gentry of that nation, who have wholly driven out all but their tenants and peasants even to the shore side. There is one collector and five officers constantly attending in this port, and members thereof, which are on the west of Burntisland, Inverkeithing; on the east Aberdare, Kinghorn,

Kirkcaldy, Dysart, Wemyss, Leven, Elie, St Monance, Pittenweem, Anstruther, Crail, St Andrews and Southferry; all pitiful small towns on the coast, inhabited by seamen, colliers, salt makers, and such like people, except St Andrews, which (if I mistake not) is a burgh town, but if not, a pretty neat thing - which hath formerly been bigger, and although sufficiently humbled in the time of the intestine troubles, continues still proud in the ruins of her former magnificence, and in being yet a seat for the Muses.

'To this port and members thereof, there are very many vessels belonging, which are employed for the carrying coal and salt outwards and to the coast, and generally everywhere in Scotland rather than the ports to which they do belong, but have received their names and denominations from the places of abode and habitation of their respective masters, owners, or mariners, who live plentifully hereabouts, because of the Road lying before them, and are in number, and of the tunnage each, as follows: viz. - Burntisland, seven whereof one 40 tons, two 30 tons, one 24 tons and three 20 tons; Kinghorn one of 50 tons; Kirkcaldy twelve two 100 tons, one 70 tons, three 40 tons, three 36 tons, one 24 tons and two 30 tons; Dysart four, one 50 tons, two 20 tons and one 14 tons; Wemyss six, three 20 tons, one 18 tons, one 14 tons and one 12 tons; Leven two, one 20 tons and one 18 tons; Elie two, one 50 tons and one 40 tons; St Monance one of 36 tons; Pittenweem two, one 100 tons and one 80 tons; Anstruther ten, one 50 tons, one 40 tons, one 30 tons, one 25 tons, one 20 tons, two 15 tons, one 14 tons and two 13 tons; Crail one of 90 tons; St Andrews one of 20 tons and Southferry one of 18 tons.

'The port of Dundee comes next in view, which is a pretty considerable place, lying at the mouth of the river Tay which, springing out of the mountains of Albany, and running through the fields, at length spreads itself into a lough full of islands, and afterward contracting itself, takes in Almond (a river of Athol,) passes on to Dunkeld, and thence by Scoone maketh its way into the German ocean. The town of Dundee was sometime a town of riches and trade, but the many recontres it has met with all in the time of domestic commotions, and her obstinacy and pride of late years rendering her a prey to the soldier, have much shaken and abated her former grandeur; and notwithstanding all, she remains still, though not glorious, yet not contemptible.

'The trade of this place inwards is, from Norway, the East Country, Holland, and France; and outwards, the salmon and pladding. Here is a collector, a check, and five waiters established, three of which waiters constantly reside here, and the rest are bestowed in the member ports, which are,

'1. St Johnstons [Perth], an handsome walled town, with a citadel added thereunto of late years, lying a good way up the river Tay, where there is a waiter always attending, not so much because of any great trading there, as to prevent the carrying out of wools, skins and hide, of which commodities great plenty is brought thither out of the Highlands, and there brought up and engrossed by the Lowlandmen.

'2. Arbroath, a small town without any trade, but for their own expense, which is but little.

'3. Montrose, seated betwixt the North and South Esks. A pretty town, with a safe harbour, risen by the fall and ruin of another town of the same name, not far off. Here, likewise, is a waiter, because there hath usually been salt brought in, and salmon, pladding and corn usually sent forth. The vessels belonging to this port and members are -

'Dundee, ten viz. two 120 tons; one 90 tons, one 60 tons, one 55 tons, one 50 tons, one 40 ton, one 30 tons and two 25 tons and Montrose, twelve viz one 26 lasts, two 18 tons, two 16 tons, two 12 tons, one 7 tons, three 6 tons and one 5 tons'.

BIBLIOGRAPHY

Custom House letter-books (CEs)

In this section of the Bibliography the material studied has been listed in terms of letter-book numbers. Each archive or record office consulted possesses a 'keyed' copy of this book with the exact references quoted written in the margin. Any further query should be referred to the author direct c/o the Publishers. For more information on Customs records see *Scottish Customs & Excise Records* by Frances Wilkins

CE52 Perth (Perth and Kinross District Archive)
Class 1: CE52 1/1, 1/3, 1/4, 1/5, 1/6, 1/7, 1/8, 1/9, 1/10 and 1/11
Class 2: CE52 2/1, 2/2, 2/3, 2/4, 2/6 and 2/8

CE53 Montrose (the Archive and Record Centre, City of Dundee District Council)
Class 1: CE53 1/1, 1/2, 1/3, 1/4, 1/5, 1/7, 1/9, 1/10, 1/11, 1/12, 1/14, 1/15, 1/16 and 1/17
Class 2: CE53 2/1, 2/2, 2/5 and 2/6

CE56 Dunbar (West Search Room, Scottish Record Office, Edinburgh)
Class 2: CE56 2/1, 2/2, 2/3, 2/4, 2/5, 2/6, 2/7, 2/8 and 2/9

CE57 Leith (West Search Room, Scottish Record Office, Edinburgh)
Class 1: CE57 1/1
Class 2: CE57 2/1, 2/2, 2/3, 2/4, 2/5, 2/6 and 2/251
Class 4: CE57 4/31, 4/43, 4/63, 4/71, 4/72 and 4/82

CE58 Bo'ness (Central Regional Council Archives, Stirling)
Class 1: CE58 1/1
Class 2: CE58 2/1a

CE63 Kirkcaldy (West Search Room, Scottish Record Office, Edinburgh)
Note: These include letters from the collector and comptroller Anstruther.
Class 1: CE63 1/1, 1/2 and 1/3
Class 2: CE63 2/1

CE67 Alloa (Central Regional Council Archives, Stirling)
Class 1: CE67 1/1, 1/2, 1/3, 1/4, 1/5, 1/6, 1/7, 1/8, 1/9, 1/10, 1/21, 1/22, 1/23, 1/25, 1/26, 1/27, 1/28, 1/29, 1/30 and 1/31
Class 2: CE67 2/1, 2/2, 2/3, 2/90, 2/91, 2/93, 2/95 and 2/96
Class 4: CE67 4/6
Class 11: CE67 11/2, 11/3 and 11/6

CE68 Grangemouth (Central Regional Council Archives, Stirling)
Class 1: CE68 1/1, 1/2, 1/3, 1/4, 1/5 and 1/15

CE70 Dundee (Archive and Record Centre, City of Dundee District Council)
Class 1: CE70 1/1, 1/2, 1/3, 1/4, 1/5, 1/6, 1/7, 1/8, 1/9 and 1/10
Class 2: CE70 2/1, 2/4 and 2/7
Class 4: CE70 4/4

CE80 Arbroath (Archive and Record Centre, City of Dundee District Council)
Class 2: CE80 2/1

From outside the area (West Search Room, Scottish Record Office, Edinburgh)
CE51 Dumfries: Class 1: 1/1
CE87 Aberdeen: Class 1: 1/2 and 1/12

Note: The following custom house letter-books held at PRO, Kew were also consulted. CUST55 Folkestone, CUST82 Whitehaven, CUST84 Newcastle, CUST85 Sunderland, CUST90 Whitby, CUST91 Scarborough and CUST96 King's Lynn

Other Primary Sources

The *Benefactor* of Bo'ness Charter Party and Bond. Edinburgh City Archive Moses Bundle 140, No 5482

University of St Andrews Minutes 1728. St Andrews University Muniments UY 452

Notes on Seizures: Anstruther 1723-1728. Scottish Record Office E369/10

George Moore letter-book 1750-1760. Manx National Heritage Library BH501C MIC68
Letter-book of Alexander Oliphant & Co Wine Merchants of Ayr. Scottish Record Office
The *Nancy*. Livres d'Amiraute 1765. States of Guernsey Archive Service
Entitled Established and Incidental Salaries now paid in the Department of Customs Scotland and Prospective reductions 1821 National Library of Scotland Melville Papers MS1058 ff 148-152
St Andrews Coast Guards General Order Book 1831-1833. St Andrews Univeristy Muniments ms DA890 SICG8

Secondary Sources

Anderson, M S *Europe in the Eighteenth Century 1713-1783* 2nd Ed Longman 1976 ISBN 0 582 48671 8
Atton, Henry & Holland, Henry Hurst *The King's Customs Vols 1 & 11* London John Murray 1908 & 1910
Davidson, John & Gray, Alexander *The Scottish Staple at Veere. A study in the Economic History of Scotland* Longmans, Green & Co 1909
Defoe, Daniel *A Tour through the whole Island of Great Britain Vol II* London 1727
Donnachie, Ian and Hewitt, George *A Companion to Scottish History* BT Batsford Ltd 1989 ISBN 0 7134 5739 2
Fischer, T A edited by Kirkpatrick, John *The Scots in Sweden being a contribution towards the history of the Scot abroad* Otto Schulze & Co Edinburgh 1907
Fraser, Duncan *The Smugglers* Standard Press Montrose 1978
Hay, George *History of Arbroath* Arbroath 1876
Hewison, W S *Smuggling in Eighteenth Century Orkney* Orkney Miscellany No 3
Hogg, Garry *Blind Jack of Knaresborough Road Builder Extraordinary* Phoenix 1967
Goring, Rosemary *Eighteenth-Century Scottish Smugglers: The Evidence from Montrose and Dumfries* ROSC (Review of Scottish Culture) Issue 3 1987
The Life of John Metcalf, commonly called Blind Jack of Knaresborough York 1795

The Ordnance Survey Gazetteer of Great Britain 2nd Ed *All Names from the 1:50,000 Landranger Map Series* Macmillan Reference Books 1989 ISBN 0 333 49999 9
Platt, Richard *Smugglers' Britain* Cassell Publishers Ltd 1991 ISBN 0304 340650
Scottish History Society. *Narrative of Mr James Nimmo, a Covenanter 1654-1709* Ed W G Scott-Moncrieff First Series No 6 Edinburgh 1889
Scottish History Society. *Letter-book of Bailie John Steuart of Inverness 1715-1752* Ed William Mackay Second Series No 9 Edinburgh 1915
Scottish History Society. *The Minutes of the Justices of the Peace for Lanarkshire 1707-1723* Transcribed and edited by Charles A Malcolm. Third Series Vol XVII Edinburgh 1931
Smout, T C *Customhouse Letters to the Officers at Dunbar, 1765* Transactions of the East Lothian Antiquarian and Field Naturalists Society Vol XI 1968
Stevenson, Stephanie *Anstruther A History* John Donald Publishers Ltd 1989 0 85976 243 3
The Gentleman's Magazine 1732, 1736, 1737
The Listener 1939 Nansen
Report by Thomas Tucker upon the settlement of the revenues of Excise and Customs in Scotland A D MDCLVI. The Bannatyne Club Vol 7 1825
Wood, *The East Neuk of Fife*

Recommended Reading

Dobson, David The Mariners of Kirkcaldy and West Fife, 1600-1700 St Andrews 1992
Dobson, David The Mariners of Angus, 1600-1700 St Andrews
Dobson, David The Mariners of St Andrews and the East Neuk of Fife 1600-1700 St Andrews 1992
Dobson, David The Mariners of the Lothians, 1600-1700 (2 vols) St Andrews 1993
Jackson, Gordon with Kinnear, Kate The Trade and Shipping of Dundee 1780-1850 Abertay Historical Society Publication No 31 Dundee 1991 ISBN 0 900019 27 1
Mowat, Sue The Port of Leith John Donald 1994
Mui, Hon-cheung and Mui, Lorna H ed *William Melrose in China 1845-1855* Letters of a Scottish Tea Merchant Edinburgh printed for the

Scottish History Society by T & A Constable Ltd 1973 ISBN 9500260 6 9
Pellew, Ada The Maltmen, Customs and Excisemen of Dundee 1700 to 1850 Tay Valley Family History Society 1991 1 873032 06 4
Roughead, William Ed. *The Trial of Captain Porteous*. Hodge Glasgow/Edinburgh 1909
Whatley, C A 'That Important and Necessary Article' The Salt Industry and its Trade in Fife and Tayside c 1570-1850 Abertay Historical Society Publication No 22 Dundee 1984 ISBN 0 900019 18 2

INDEX OF NAMES

WYRE FOREST PRESS

Wyre Forest Press was established in 1992 to publish books on smuggling history and related contemporary documents. *The Isle of Man in Smuggling History* was followed by a series on Scotland's Smuggling Story. Two further titles in this series will be published in 1994 and 1995. A description of this aspect of Scotland's maritime history will continue with a series of Smuggling Trail booklets, covering smaller areas. Aimed at the local historian, schools and tourists, these will include maps and plans of locations where major smuggling events took place. The first booklets in this series, covering Galloway and Cowal, will appear soon.